SMALL ACTS OF KINDNESS

STRIVING FOR *DERECH ERETZ* IN EVERYDAY LIFE

SHALOM FREEDMAN

URIM PUBLICATIONS
Jerusalem • New York

Small Acts of Kindness: Striving for *Derech Eretz* in Everyday Life
by Shalom Freedman
Copyright © 2004 by Shalom Freedman

All rights reserved. No part of this book may be used or reproduced in any manner whatsoever without written permission from the copyright owner, except in the case of brief quotations embodied in reviews and articles.
Printed at Hemed Press, Israel. First Edition.
ISBN 965-7108-59-4

Urim Publications, P.O. Box 52287, Jerusalem 91521 Israel

Lambda Publishers Inc.
3709 13th Avenue Brooklyn, New York 11218 U.S.A.
Tel: 718-972-5449 Fax: 718-972-6307
Email: mh@ejudaica.com

www.UrimPublications.com

For

The Holy Teacher,

Mayim Chayim David Hillel

ben Shraga Faivel and Rivkah Herzberg

The week after I had finished making what I thought would be the final corrections on this manuscript, I heard the heartbreaking news that the holy teacher had passed from this world. I cannot, in a few lines, begin to express the depth of my appreciation of, and love for, this man, the best friend I have ever had, and will ever have.

My teacher in Torah, and everything connected with it, always greeted others with love and joy. He was born on the seventh of *Av*, fifty-one years before he passed from this world on *erev Tu B'Av*, 5762. He left behind his loving wife, Sarah Eiger, his brother, Walter Herzberg, four daughters and two stepchildren. He was a pupil of his beloved Rebbe, Reb Shlomo Carlebach and, like his teacher, taught Torah with song and story, as well as with traditional learning from a *sefer*, usually one written by one of his beloved chasidic masters.

For close to ten years, it has been my great privilege to meet with the holy teacher each week, usually on Tuesdays (*pa'amayim ki tov*). During these sessions, I did not so much learn with him as from him. I know that I am not the best of students, and I regret now that I did not sufficiently learn from the wealth of Torah teachings that he shared with me.

One of the things I did learn, however, is that *sichat chaverim*, the conversation of friends, is a true form of Torah. Each time we met, the holy teacher also taught me the first principle given by the *Ba'al Shem Tov*: to relate to other human beings with *varmkeit*, a kind of acceptance that enables people to feel that they are of value. Another one of the holy teacher's many good friends, Chaim Dovid Sarachik, spoke of the holy teacher's remarkable capacity to lift the spirits of each and every person he met. It might have been a word, a gesture, or just a small joke (of which he was a master too), but he always had that ability to make the person feel better about themselves, to make him or her feel that they were living in a meaningful world, and were of meaning themselves. He was able to achieve all this despite the fact that he felt the pain of this world in the deepest way and would always teach that we live in a broken generation. His capacity to cheer others is especially remarkable in light of the fact that he was struggling inside of himself for wholeness, acceptance, recognition and love, and felt broken in spirit.

Although it is difficult for me to understand and accept how God could take the holy teacher away so young when it is obviously Jews like him who are so badly needed now, I do feel (and I know I can speak for almost all who met him) a deep gratitude that I was able to spend some time in his holy presence in my time on this earth. The holy teacher would continually teach Torah and would engender a love of God and Israel and, indeed, a love for each and every Jew and human being. I have never had a friend who was such a constant pleasure and joy to be with, and from whom I so perpetually derived Torah wisdom.

May God, who gave and then took back such a holy Jew, raise his soul to the highest of the high levels in the world-to-come.

May God give those of us who are left in this world the ability to derive some consolation from the stories, songs, writings and personal memories he has given us.

CONTENTS

PREFACE 11

THE JOURNAL 15

DERECH ERETZ IN ISRAEL:
A FEW THOUGHTS ON IMPROVING THE SITUATION 261

A YEAR LATER: THE CHANGES IN THE SITUATIONS OF, AND MY
RELATIONSHIPS WITH, THE CENTRAL CHARACTERS IN THIS WORK 266

MY PERSONAL DEVELOPMENT IN THE AREA OF *DERECH ERETZ* 272

WORKS THAT CAN HELP ONE ACHIEVE GREATER LEVELS OF
DERECH ERETZ 275

COLLECTIVE *DERECH ERETZ* – TWO YEARS LATER 276

GLOSSARY 278

ACKNOWLEDGMENTS

All the characters in this work have been, in one way or another, my teachers in *derech eretz*. This book is dedicated to them.

I would like to express a special debt of gratitude to the family of the late Melvin Fenson. Throughout his long illness, Mel and his family showed courage and kindness that have been a real source of inspiration to me. Mel was a person of great intelligence and humor whose company I feel privileged to have shared. He and his wife Ruth have not only been good friends to me, but were an example of the kind of partnership between husband and wife which is the true realization of the Jewish ideal in marriage. Another loving and kind couple, whom I have known for many years, are Menahem and Naomi Kaiser. They too have been an inspiration and help to me. Unfortunately, Naomi *z"l* passed away shortly before the publication of this book.

Finally, I would like to express my warm appreciation to my publisher Tzvi Mauer, and editor, Sorelle Weinstein, for their belief in this work and for the considerable effort they have invested into reshaping and improving it. I owe a special word of thanks to my friend Dr. Lewis Rosen who read this work in its early stages, and made valuable suggestions for its improvement.

PREFACE

Ideally, Jews in Israel are meant to be a kingdom of priests and a holy nation – a light unto the nations – whose everyday actions should serve as an example to others. Paradoxically, however, what I have found over the last thirty years is that many fellow Israelis admit that we have less to teach than we have to learn in the area of *derech eretz*. Several of my friends who immigrated to Israel from Anglo-Saxon countries complain that public behavior is markedly worse in Israel than in the countries from which they emigrated. Time and again, they bemoan the rudeness and incivility of their fellow Israeli citizens that surfaces in both everyday encounters and in professional contexts.

Derech eretz is, in its broadest sense, demonstrating love and honor to our fellow human beings and, in so doing, fulfilling the will of God. In Jewish religious terms, everyday life presents us with constant struggles to act in the correct way. We are continuously battling between good and evil. It is a never-ending ethical drama in which an individual should always be striving to serve God in the best possible way.

This work consists largely of a journal spanning a year, covering the period from Shavuot 5759 (1999) to Shavuot 5760 (2000). In it, I endeavor to record my pursuit of living a life of *derech eretz*, attempting to discover how best to serve God in everyday life. In one sense, I am gathering evidence, trying to observe what happens in society and see where there is room for improvement in our consideration and caring for others. I am trying to understand if I can, even if it is in the smallest way, contribute to the advancement of our goal of living as "a light unto the nations." I am striving to test myself and make my own way in *derech eretz*. I am searching to serve God, guided by the adage of *Pirkei Avot* that "he who is pleasant to mankind is pleasant in the eyes of God."

As this work is a journal, it consists of many everyday encounters with friends and acquaintances. Some of these people we will come across frequently and are, in effect, the central characters of the journal. This work would not have been possible without them, and in a sense I owe a debt of gratitude to them all. In order to spare them any embarrassment or insult, I have substituted pseudonyms for almost all of them; I only use the authentic names of public figures, usually those of rabbis.

I have also chosen to refer to various concepts and expressions in the original Hebrew in order to retain authenticity. A short glossary at the end of the work provides brief definitions for these terms and expressions. The journal is followed by a few concluding remarks in which I try to encapsulate the lessons that I have derived from my experiences.

THE JOURNAL

Tuesday, May 4, 1999
18 *Iyar, Lag B'Omer,* 5759

Today, I will begin to record my everyday encounters in which I try to live a life of *derech eretz,* in service of God.

I just met my elderly neighbor, Israel R., who is worried about his sick sister. He thanked me for bringing money to the *gabbai* for him, and having a blessing made for her recovery. He is about to have a cataract operation. I told him that I would try to locate the name of the doctor who had operated on me. A truly saintly person would have become more deeply involved, but I am a person whose righteousness does not extend that far.

I am running an errand to deliver two of Professor Zeigelman's books to my friend Yaakov Fogelman. This is an act of kindness as Professor Zeigelman is not well.

I overcame my awkwardness and said some words of consolation to the daughter and wife of Dr. Veschler this morning.

Last night I went to the F. family's house. Mel F. was in great discomfort. *Hashem yirachem.*

Today I went to an *azkarah* for a former member of the congregation.

Yesterday, I did my best to help Israel R., whose sister, his closest relative, died the day before. The problem is that we have no common language because my conversational Yiddish is not good enough. Fortunately, there are others who help him. At the same time that I am assisting my neighbor, I am troubled at having to give my time to another person.

There is a long list of people I know who are unfortunately sick. Perhaps there is an explanation for this: maybe I only really get to know people when I visit them during their sicknesses.

Monday, May 10
24 Iyar

I have not been much of a *tzaddik* today. I did not help my neighbor who lost his sister. Leiberman, a quiet holy Jew, helped him.

I called Mel last night. I pray for his recovery.

I will now call Menahem K. Both he and his wife are seriously ill and although I am reluctant to become involved, I feel I must help if I can.

Tuesday, May 11
25 Iyar

I called Menahem last night. Thank God, he and his wife are better.

I am writing now at home as a *shiur* is about to commence at the *shul*, where I could have helped to complete a *minyan*. I am putting my own selfish concerns before the good of others, which is the antithesis of *derech eretz*.

I just finished picking up some boxes that were lying in the middle of the road and throwing them into the garbage bin. I also picked up litter two other times today, fulfilling the *mitzvah* of beautifying the land of Israel.

I went out of my way to buy goods at the local grocery store instead of at the supermarket, following my father's long-time rule of giving the small-time businessman a break.

I did not respond to a raving, anti-state, waiting-for-the-messiah person I saw in the street. A few minutes later I saw him shaking his hands violently. *Hashem yirachem.* There seem to be so many disturbed people on the streets nowadays.

I am a largely ineffectual, yet well-intentioned person, a Don Quixote with Torah guidance.

Motzei Shabbat, May 15
Rosh Chodesh Sivan

I walked Israel R. home from *shul* today. He is close to ninety years old. The sister who died last week was his last surviving sibling. He was born in Czernovitz, survived the concentration camps, lived in Bucharest after the war and came to Israel nine years ago. I will have to work on my Yiddish so that I can talk to him more and try to understand him.

Sunday, May 16
Rosh Chodesh Sivan

I spent a couple of hours with Mel this morning. His wife does not want him to spend time alone, as he may have heart palpitations. Spending time with him is a pleasure; he is a master conversationalist, rich in life experience.

Wednesday, May 19
4 Sivan

I have not felt particularly generous since hearing the election results. There is an atmosphere here of rejection and competitiveness, leading to a lack of super-consideration. What do I mean by super-consideration? Not buying an extra roll of bread so as to consider the person who might come into the store after me and will therefore be unable to purchase one as a result. Not buying a newspaper in the belief that someone else might enjoy it more. Here I do not know where to draw the line.

I was a good person this morning. I walked Israel R., the old mourner, home, and learned that he had been an accountant. I notice his small, slow steps and his deep grief.

While I was out walking last night, I saw Dr. Veschler's widow. What is there to say, but a few words to make her feel part of the human world?

Dov E. has also suffered a new grief; he has just come from his sister's husband's funeral. There is the question of whether or not to tell his mother about the loss. I shared with him my own personal experience with Ma when Jakie died, how I sensed that she knew despite the fact that she was never told.

I am not made for all this pain. I want to run away to a world of youth and joy but do not know how to get there.

It is Dad's *yahrtzeit* today. I brought *kibbud* to *shul*, which both morning *minyanim* benefited from.

Yesterday, I went to my holy teacher. I listened to him. I love learning from him. Whatever chassidic text we learn, he always finds in it a way of speaking to the needs of my heart at that moment. It is as he taught me many times: whenever the *Ba'al Shem Tov* would have a problem, he would open up the Tanach and find an answer to it on that page. For so many years now, week after week, the holy teacher has been opening up that page of Tanach for me.

I think that it is important not to abandon him in his hour of great need. I make the effort every week to come to his *shiur*, even when it is inconvenient for me to do so. Despite his tremendous knowledge of *chassidut*, there are times when there are very few people at his *shiurim*. He is now undergoing a tremendous struggle against a life-threatening disease and yet he continually raises the spirits of those who come to see him and, in some way, try to strengthen him.

I have not spoken with the F. family in a week and a half. This is not right. I know that I should do this, so why am I so reluctant?

Sunday, May 23
8 *Sivan*

I walked Israel R. home last night. I was so grateful for the opportunity to do this. The old man took my arm and I felt that it was not me who was giving him strength, but he who was giving it to me.

Last night, I went to Ramot to pay a *shivah* visit to Chaim M. I spoke to his uncle, who knew my childhood Hebrew schoolteacher, Mr. Friend. The old world, the old people. I felt I behaved correctly in helping people talk about that lost world.

Yesterday, I met someone with whom I had been in the army, a modest person, who is now out of work. I spoke to him but he was reluctant to talk about his situation; he is a person with a sense of dignity. He is yet another individual who I have met in the past couple of weeks who is very eager to work, is honest and trustworthy, and yet is unemployed.

My visit last night to the F. family was difficult and heartbreaking. Mel now speaks with difficulty and is in constant discomfort. I could not help him get up from his chair – I was simply unable to lift him. They have a doctor's appointment today. I told them that they could call me at anytime to come over and sit with him.

Last night, I decided to go and see Mel instead of going to a conference I did not really care to go to. This raises the dilemma of sacrificing one's own pleasure for the sake of helping others. I am only involved in such sacrifice in very minor ways. For example, the previous night, I chose to show concern for individuals (the *shivah* visit) above attending public events in which I did, in fact, wish to participate.

Wednesday, June 2
19 *Sivan*

Yesterday, I went to the *azkarah* ceremony for Dr. Veschler, a holy man who accomplished so much in the most important tasks of all – saving lives and relieving the suffering of many. He was an embodiment of true *derech eretz*.

How impatient I was yesterday at the start of the ceremony! Mrs. Z. asked me to look after her husband, who is in mental decline, to make sure he did not stray. I did so, of course, but with a reluctant heart. Fortunately, there were others who also helped. As it turned out, the son of Mr. Z. came to the *azkarah*. I was moved by how happy the son was to see his father. This son is now one of his father's caretakers. The family has another, older son who is retarded – a good-natured boy. I often think of the two healthy children in this family and the responsibility that has been placed upon their shoulders. Even though I know it has made them into especially kind people, I wonder if they have been treated fairly in all this.

My inadequate behavior really struck me yesterday during the *azkarah*. My previous two evenings had been devoted, respectively, to a *shivah* visit and a *bikkur cholim* visit to a friend, and earlier tonight was the memorial. The first two cases were ones in which my presence clearly made a difference, but tonight I was just one of the crowd. Resentment began to churn inside me. When do I dedicate time to myself, to building a new life? At times I feel that in being kind to others, I am not really being kind to myself. As I immerse myself in caring for others, I conveniently avoid facing my own problems.

Another source of my resentment (which is probably unjustified) is the feeling that I have of being overly imposed upon. People know that I can be asked to do things, and so they ask. I have especially resented the good Rav A. For some years now, I have given him *tzedakah* for families on Pesach. I have also assisted his own family: when he married off two of his children last year and asked for my help, I gave him a generous gift. He recently told me that he now has another child to marry off, mentioning that he is in huge debt. I will help him. What bothered me was his heavy hint at the cemetery, that giving *tzedakah* saves the donor from death. Perhaps he did not intend for it to come out in this way at all, but what I inferred from his comment was, "If you don't want to arrive *there* [death] sooner than you think, then come up with the money." But I was, in any event, intending to give! And his comment had nothing to do with my "arriving" at the cemetery later rather than sooner, as I am certain I will ultimately arrive there one day. In fact, if anything, the recent death of a relatively young, true *tzaddik* like Dr. Veschler, who helped people in ways I could never imagine, adds to the skepticism I have regarding simplistic formulas connecting virtuous actions to the number of one's days on this earth.

My inner frustration, as usual, relates to my annoyance at not having invested any time in "real growth" – both in my private life and as a part of the Jewish people. I feel it is the world of the young that is most important, yet I am not close to that world, except as it relates to my children. Perhaps my general sense of dissatisfaction also relates to my son's having gone traveling around the world rather than remaining here this year to study.

On the way to Rabbi Breitowitz's *shiur* yesterday, I was stopped by a man in a wheelchair to whom I often give *tzedakah* and from whom I once bought a book of poetry. He asked me to help him with two phone calls. I came into his house, helped him find his bag, found the phone number, and solved some additional problem. I noticed he kept asking for one small thing after another – I was going to be late. Then he requested yet another thing from me: to cut his nails. I surprised myself and refused, experiencing a momentary pang of regret. And then, as I was leaving, he enlisted the help of the next passerby to come in and do it. This reminded me of the dinner my holy teacher had prepared for a group of disabled people. One of them kept asking for different foods at different temperatures. He must have sent the holy teacher back and forth to the kitchen ten times with various requests. I not only saw in this a lack of *derech eretz* on the part of the recipient, but it also helped me to realize that even the most generous giver should sometimes say no.

This morning, I was asked by Benjamin S. to help him carry the tables that had been set up for the *azkarah* downstairs. I saw that he had difficulty in breathing. I told him to let me do it and did it on my own until another regular came at the end and helped me.

Rabbi Breitowitz spoke yesterday about a type of *avodat Hashem*, that of *gemilut chassadim*. He referred to Torah study as a supreme value because it enables the service of God through *gemilut chassadim*. He was asked about those in the Torah world who engage only in learning, while not lifting a finger to help others. As I was moving the tables from the *azkarah*, I came upon such a person, who was continuing his prayers after having prayed with the congregation. He saw me struggling with the tables but did not pause to help. This same person often concentrates on reciting his own individual prayers to their completion, rather than reciting the *birkhat kohanim*, despite the fact that he is the only *kohen* in the *shul*. My own sense, though I may be mistaken, is that he has his priorities wrong.

I am unsettled by a high level of resentment and negativity that is brimming within me. This frustration is directed against those supposedly "religious" people who think and act only for themselves and their own small groups without concern for society at large – the "takers." I am bothered by their smug manner. I begin to think of myself as the "last angry Jew." I am simply tired of self-righteous preaching by those who do not act in the best interests of others.

I have another lesson with my holy teacher today. I have work to do and would prefer to make it another time. This feeling is familiar. What normally happens, though, is that whenever I do go, I am glad that I went. Still, there are times – even with my holy teacher, who has given me so much – when I become tired and feel as though I have been hearing yet not really listening. This raises the general question of when one has the right to be a little selfish; one might make the argument that otherwise, not only will one fail to accomplish any good, one may even cause damage instead.

Strange. As I have been walking around lately, wondering how I can use my writing to help improve the situation in Israel, I have felt estranged and angry. Why? It's because I see people toss litter on the street without any consideration of others. Perhaps this is not the biggest thing in the world, but then again, it is a reflection of rudeness and selfishness of other types as well. This idea can be seen by the behavior of loudmouthed, vulgar teenagers on the public bus, of elderly people who push ahead in lines because of their perception that their discomfort gives them the right to do so, or of those who walk nonchalantly across the street in a way that could cause an accident. I remember now that when Rabbi Tropper was asked about our being "a light unto the nations," he spoke about the value of first learning to behave properly amongst ourselves. I understand this point so well now through many of the situations I witness of people relating considerately (or inconsiderately) to others. Paradoxically, it seems as though we could learn a lot from other "nations" when it comes to such matters.

I am reminded of another thing that makes me angry, an attitude that contradicts my conception of *derech eretz*. It is intellectual arrogance, a know-it-all disdain for others. I see and hear it all the time. I am especially offended when it comes from religious people, since I am a member of this camp. I am also bothered by the conceit of academic experts who, no matter how many times they have erred in the past, continue to sell the same flawed bill of goods again and again. I believe that *derech eretz* also enters into our intellectual and abstract discussions. A certain modesty and humility, as well as a readiness to listen to others, is called for.

Rabbi Breitowitz is, in my experience, the total opposite of this type of arrogant individual. He listens to everyone, and what's more, he can always find something positive even in foolish remarks. In doing so, he makes every person who he encounters feel of worth.

Wednesday, June 9
26 *Sivan*

I did not wait just now to walk Israel R. home from the morning prayer service. I assumed that he does not need accompanying in the light of day, yet I still feel slightly guilty. On the other hand, had I waited and taken another ten minutes to get back home and begin the day, I would probably have been resentful.

I picked up the litter around the *shul* on my way in, although I do not know if it is halachically proper to do so before prayer.

Yesterday, I went to the holy teacher and sensed my diminished enthusiasm in learning. Again, it seems to support the notion that there is superior value in doing a good deed when one's heart is truly in it, and not simply because it is a duty that one feels one is supposed to do. How often lately do I do the right thing with little enthusiasm?

I do not think I was right to tell the holy teacher about my sleeping difficulties. On the one hand, I am theoretically helping him by making him feel that he is helping me. On the other hand, I am drawing him into a whole realm of sickness, a realm from which he especially needs to escape now.

Should one help those who do not want to be helped? Trying to help can often result in achieving the opposite of the desired effect: interfering and burdening people.

One of the many daily irritations in the religious world here is the issue of men and women on the buses. On minibus no. 38 from the Jewish Quarter of the Old City to town yesterday, I not only had to get up myself, but also had to ask the person sitting next to me to stand up so that a woman who needed to sit down could do so. There were two other women waiting to sit. One man was sitting alone in another seat – he too could have sat down next to another man, thus vacating his seat for the women. At first he did not oblige, but then, somehow, just as I was chastising him in my mind, he got up and moved seats, following my example. It gave me the sense that perhaps persistently setting the right example can have a truly good effect on others.

Last night, I tried to stay until the end of a discussion on "Halachah and Artistic Creation." I wanted to exchange a few words with M., my former teacher, whom I had once interviewed. Had I been truly courteous, I would have forced myself to stay. I believe that my smile and warm greeting at least showed her that I am not angry at her for the insulting remark she had made about the published interview. Having said this, I believe that there was some justification for her remark, as the interview did somehow reveal more about her situation than she probably would have liked. This is a case in which, despite the fact that I was technically blameless, I could have acted with more consideration.

There are people who are comparable to saints. I think, for example, of Reb Aryeh Levin, of blessed memory. These are people who were intensely dedicated to the service of others. I am so far from being on that level that I should not even mention my name in the same breath as theirs.

There is a problem, though. Although I am inclined to respect and admire such a high level of generosity and goodness, I am also somewhat disturbed by it, since it can sometimes be excessive and sometimes even obsessive – especially in those cases where it leads to neglect of one's own family.

Friday, June 11
28 Sivan

I feel guilty for not going to Rabbi Eisen's class, but I just feel too tired after waking up at four-thirty this morning. This decision is a selfish one since by going there, aside from my help in payment, I also often assist in other minor ways such as in bringing in and setting up chairs. But I am falling asleep as I write this. I will try my best to make it next week.

Yesterday, I spoke to a young man in my class at Ohr Sameach Yeshiva who I had tried to help when he was caring for a lost dog. I listened to part of his story. His parents are divorced; his father is Basque and his mother is a Gypsy. A convert, he has been on his own since the age of seventeen. He seems to be a good person. I want to help him find a Hebrew class or, perhaps, to establish a work connection for him.

Helping others is what is most meaningful to me at this stage in my life, though at the same time, I understand that this can bring with it untold sacrifice of my time and pleasure. Prayer is also most meaningful when it is said on behalf of others.

What do I contribute to Rabbi Eisen's class when I am there? Support for him, a smiling face, an occasional question.

Today is my brother's *yahrtzeit*. I prayed and did as I should, but in the important task of helping my brother's children, I have sadly fallen short. It has been six years since his father's death and I believe that my nephew is in real trouble. He does not return my calls. Perhaps he is angry at me for not having been involved in the business and for not having helped his father and him financially.

Of course, it is always easier to help those who are not in one's own family, although we could offer help in a profound way to those with whom we are closest and care most about. However, to give deep, emotional support requires far more than simply helping someone walk across the street. Last week, I was overwhelmed by people's demands on me. Today, there are none, and I can just bemoan the loss of opportunities for helping others.

I was asked by the good, modest Mr. Leiberman to walk Israel R. home this morning. Of course I did it. This was at the time that I am usually most eager to get going and begin the day. When we reached his home, Israel R. said something to the effect of, "Excuse me for having inconvenienced you." I thanked him for his company.

Yesterday there was a substitute teacher for my regular class. A young man who appeared troubled asked questions about the biblical account of creation and the expanding universe. His questions were dismissed in a rude way. I proceeded to give the young man a list of books on the subject. As the teacher continued to ignore real questions, I thought for a moment of interrupting him, but I am a guest there, so instead, I simply left early. I wonder again if I did the right thing by being silent. This reminded me somewhat of my days in Rabbi M.'s class when he would make some outrageous statement and I would, in general, say nothing. Silence as a form of complicity is, I am sure, no great achievement in *derech eretz*.

My concern with my own problems makes me far less eager to think about those of others. This is in contradiction to the type of holy person who dedicates all of his time to the dilemmas of others, while neglecting his own personal problems. But I am not sure that halachically this is the right way either.

Monday, June 14
30 *Sivan*

Yesterday, I attended Rav Isaacs' *shiur* for the first time in a month. No one mentioned anything. Many times, true *derech eretz* is in restraining oneself and being silent. I could make a long list of the ways in which I do not show *derech eretz* to my full potential. So many times I decide that the benefit to the other person is really only marginal while the price to myself is far greater. But one totally devoted to placing others' well-beings before one's own would calculate differently.

Last night, I called Mel, only to learn that he had been in the emergency room in the hospital for four days. I offered to visit, but it was not a good time for his family.

My holy teacher helped me yesterday by assuring me that my son's decision to explore the world after three difficult army years is understandable. As I care for, and worry about, my children more than anything else in the world, this kind of assurance is of great help to me. My holy teacher is a true friend in providing this kind of emotional support.

I read in the book *Twerski On Spirituality* that the reason we do not make a blessing before giving *tzedakah* is so as not to delay the act of *chesed*, of loving-kindness.

There are so many small encounters with people that can involve *derech eretz*. Much of this depends upon our perception of the situation. There are many times when the proper course of action is not completely clear, and one must simply do one's best to come to the right decision. I find myself repeatedly making such judgment calls with regard to the *tzedakah* money I give.

I have not yet visited Dov, who has been absent from *shul* for four days. Once this would have been acceptable, but since I now walk him home almost every night and we've become much closer, I feel that I must pay him a visit. I asked the *gabbai*, Mr. Leiberman, about his condition and he said that he had spoken with him and that he is feeling better.

There is the perpetual question of which party has the obligation to call the other in order to keep up a friendship. I tend not to call. I have been troubled for some time by the fact that I have not spoken with certain friends who arrived in Israel just before Election Day. Perhaps this is because their reactions to the results differed greatly from mine. Last Friday I called another friend to find out if he had made any progress on a new project he is working on (I had given him a certain idea that I thought might help him). There was no answer – apparently, he is now in America.

I will go to Rabbi Eisen's class this morning, although I would rather stay home and work. Again, I feel obligated to my teacher, but there is another issue at stake. One great law of my life has been to maintain loyalty to people, and even to principles, beyond the time of their apparent practical usefulness. In certain kinds of relationships and friendships, this loyalty is clearly at the essence of the bond.

I saw a former publisher of mine at the supermarket last night. We had a short, friendly conversation. He had only two things in his basket and so I naturally let him go ahead of me in line. He did not ask, I offered. All this is perfectly fine, except that it stands in contradistinction to our past dealings with each other in which I believe he was really unfair to me. Again, am I a person who, by being "too nice," encourages bad behavior in others?

If one sits down and analyzes one's actions in detail, one will find that there are many incidents each day in which the correct course of action is not completely clear. Our freedom of choice comes into operation daily in regard to how to act appropriately towards others.

Even a small decision like whether to take off *tefillin* before or after I go to learn can be a real question of *derech eretz*. Suppose, for instance, I take them off and by doing so, I arrive at the *shiur* so late that my arrival causes a disruption.

If one is faced with the responsibility of helping two different people, one should weigh who is more likely to be at the greatest risk of injury.

I wrote my nephew a small note asking him to please call me. A clear example of my too-little, too-late nature is my failure to give real help to my late brother's children.

The cases of school violence that I hear about make me wonder how we can raise the next generation to be a just society, a light unto the nations. In my behavior in public, I try to do what is right and even to set a small example. However, I can recall an incident of typical teenage rowdiness that occurred on the bus in which I did not say anything on the grounds that it would be, at the very least, confrontational.

The ideal is that each person acts with modest righteousness in his or her own daily life. The real aim is to have a society in which people act like human beings towards one another in all aspects of life. That is to say, a society in which consideration for others can be taken for granted, and not one in which a caring act is an unusual, quixotic gesture. My idea is if each one of us sets an example of such consideration in our own way then, as the years progress, such compassion will be increasingly common. In this sense, a good deed is a seed planted for the gardens of the future.

Tuesday, June 15
Rosh Chodesh Tammuz

I do not greet everyone who I come across with *sever panim yafot*, a pleasant countenance. When I see Arabs – unless I know them personally – I pass by them without a word and with a blank expression on my face. I sense that an overly welcoming greeting would be seen as patronizing. Likewise, a greeting in their language would, I think, show (and here I might be wrong) a self-abnegating quality. More importantly, I sense that most Arabs would be more irritated than cheered by my greeting.

The press in Israel eagerly seeks to publicize all instances of *charedim* acting with disregard or contempt for the State of Israel, yet they tend to ignore Arab violations of this kind. One prominent example is during the sirens on our Memorial Days, when people stand in silence in remembrance of those killed in the Holocaust or in Israel's wars. The press focuses on the charedim's disregard for the siren, while failing to mention the Arabs who are also guilty of not standing in silence.

Last week, I was stopped by a lame, heavy Arab from Shuafat to whom I have given *tzedakah* in the past. He wanders around the Jewish neighborhoods and approaches people, asking if they speak English. I remember bringing him breakfast once after he said he was hungry. Last week he asked me for a certain sum of money. I gave him less and later regretted it: he did not ask for a large amount and if he needed a certain sum for something specific, I should have given it to him. Perhaps my reluctance to give him the full amount really reflects a deeper inner attitude of reluctance to help the potential enemy. But what kind of an enemy could such a guy be?

This reminds me that throughout the years there have been a number of street people to whom I have given money on a regular basis. I think specifically of the trombone player; of the man who sits in a wheelchair who does not appear to be angry if you do not give, and likewise does not look happy if you *do* give; of the beggar at the Western Wall who has six children and is always promising to stop begging and go to a *yeshiva*; and of the former physicist with eight children. Besides the importance of giving *tzedakah* with *derech eretz*, one should examine the *derech eretz* of those requesting and receiving the charity. I know that those who say thank-you or display some other human gesture are more likely to elicit a generous donation from me. There are a couple of beggars, and I hope God will forgive me for this, to whom I simply will not give money. One is the Arab disguised as a Jew who used to sit near the corner of Hillel and King George streets downtown. He is allegedly the father of a convicted terrorist. Another is the famous Luna, whose ugly speech and greed in collecting are legendary. Finally, there is the thin man in a wheelchair who curses those who do not give him anything as they pass.

My holy teacher maintains that it is absolutely wrong to make a list and a set amount of *tzedakah*, with the idea in mind that you will not exceed this limit. He says it might be conceivably correct to give to the same person ten times in one day. I write, and I am very aware of this, as one who can afford to give. But what of those who cannot? And here I am reminded of the man who comes on Sunday in search of *tzedakah*. He stops everyone, which brings to mind the contribution of the half-shekel that must be made by everyone. Even the poorest person must feel that he too can, to some degree, contribute. I had resented him for requesting money from a poor person, but now I understand it differently. Enabling the poor to give *tzedakah* may be seen as a great deed in that it promotes human dignity.

A significant share of my daily expenditures goes to *tzedakah*; my guess is that it constitutes a third to a half of what I spend on an average day. Here it is wise to remember the words of Rabbi Rabinovitch, who teaches that the money you spend on yourself is spent and gone, but what you give to others is taken with you as *zechut* in the World to Come. To be honest, I don't think that way most of the time. I am trying to do what God demands of us – to help others. I feel guilty all too often that I have more than I am giving away.

Yesterday, on Yavetz Street, I carried a man's wheelchair down the steps for him when I saw that he had difficulty carrying it himself. When he expressed his thanks in broken English I wondered, after all my years of living in Israel, if I still look like an Anglo-Saxon, or if he just presumed that such courtesy could only be expected from a non-Israeli. It is not true that Israelis do not help out in these situations; I see assistance of this kind from them all the time. In fact, I have witnessed many acts of consideration in Israel that I did not see in America. I think, in particular, of the way that people give up their seats for pregnant women or for the elderly on the buses here. The other day, I saw a young lady inconspicuously rise from her seat as she anticipated from a distance a middle-aged woman (who evidently had difficulty walking) making her way down the aisle of the bus. The young lady performed her good deed in such a way as to not be observed.

I try not to show my impatience when the early-morning, after-prayer learning session stretches out too long. Yet I wonder if it is not the task of the teacher to gauge a reasonable amount of time to allocate for these sessions. This teacher prefers to take his time and be thorough. There is another teacher who, conversely, goes so fast that most of the time, it is barely possible to sit down comfortably before he has already finished.

Aggressiveness and competitiveness are qualities that tend to go against the grain of *derech eretz*. Yet there can be fair-play in even the toughest competitions, which is a manifestation of *derech eretz*. I often have the sense that in Israel, it is as if simple interactions take on the quality of battles for survival, with no-holds-barred. I see this especially in economic claims made by various groups against the government.

Yesterday, I was planning to go see Rabbi Riskin when I got a call from Mel. I offered to come over at eight, but then sensed that he wanted me to come over immediately, which I did. This has been the second day that he is capable of sitting up and talking. His family is going through a very difficult time. One reason I may have responded so speedily to Mel (aside from the fact that he had been on my mind) is that I met Mrs. B. and her Philippino caretaker in the morning.

She asked me for the five hundredth time if I would come over and have breakfast with her now that her son has gone away for a couple of months. I told her that I would come over more frequently, but that I could not come in the morning. I saw her disappointment and felt guilty. I just know that were I to go there in the morning, I would lose a good share of my time allocated for work and would be irritated and impatient as a result. Another thing is that I do not find it at all enjoyable to be with her as she never stops complaining.

I so admire the F. family, who have so much to complain about, but never do. One of the bonuses of visiting the F. family is that during nearly every visit, I meet someone else from their long list of friends and acquaintances. Yesterday I met a teacher – a pregnant mother of two and a former neighbor. She was a truly positive woman, radiating energy and goodness. She took Mrs. F. to the market and back.

Yesterday, I was stopped by an Arab cleaner who asked me again about working in our building. I reluctantly gave him the apartment number of a neighbor who is in charge of apartment maintenance. I felt I could not remain silent once he had asked, but I prefer nonetheless that the cleaning be done by the woman who runs the *va'ad habayit*.

I chatted with my daughter's boyfriend last night. Although I try not to bother the young couple, I also do not want to ignore them or make them feel uncomfortable.

Tuesday, June 16
2 Tammuz

I led the prayers today for *Shacharit*. *Derech eretz* comes into play in this area, too. For instance, *derech eretz* can relate to the question of timing the prayers, waiting for others to catch up, or perhaps, as I did today, waiting slightly too long before beginning the repetition of the *amidah*. There are also questions of how to recite the prayers in such a way as to encourage maximum participation, identification and joy. Occasionally there are rude prayer leaders who care only about projecting their own voices. There are two things I try to do: pronounce each word clearly and be loud enough so that the elderly who have difficulty hearing can follow the prayers.

I think I should be more careful to make note in this journal of every incident in which I did not act in the correct manner.

The *siyyum* of *masechet Ta'anit* with Rabbi G. took place yesterday. I arrived in time to *davven Minchah* before the *siyyum*, but when I discovered that I was missing an important document, I was eager to go home and look for it. Fortunately, just as I was about to leave, someone else entered, so I felt less as if I were abandoning the group in the middle of the occasion. This is the kind of situation where technically I did nothing wrong, yet it would have been nicer had I acted differently. It was also a typical case in which I made a mountain out of a molehill. I am so particular about small things that I sometimes seem to lose myself in pettiness.

Last night, I tried to help a neighbor whose truck alarm went off. I tried to locate him and later, when the police came, I went down to the street and tried to discourage them from opening the truck by force in order to turn off the alarm. I do not know if I succeeded. What surprised me is that other neighbors who knew about the siren had not tried to inform him. Is this a sign that we are more selfish as a people than we once were?

I went to a play last night and did not demonstratively cry or walk out in protest when I found its content not to be to my religious taste. I think I was right for restraining myself, but am not sure.

My holy teacher made a remark to me to the effect of not knowing how long he will last. I have not pressed him about medical treatment. I believe I will ask him about this again today. He did something so nice yesterday – he remembered my Hebrew birthday and bought me *Likkutei Moharan* and a book of *midrashim* on *Eretz Yisrael* as a gift.

The thought of every one of those pieces of paper scattered around the city disturbs me. I have become slightly more fanatical about litter lately, cleaning up near bus stations. Yesterday I removed a carton that was lying on the road on the grounds that it might disturb drivers. This morning I stopped myself from beginning another small clean-up somewhere else. There has to be some limit to this.

Thursday, June 16
3 *Tammuz*

For a couple of years I have been bothered by the fact that on Thursday mornings, when I return home from *shul*, the Arab woman who cleans for a neighbor opens the door of the building for me. First of all, I like to open the door to my own house myself. Secondly, I do not like to disturb her. This morning she looked a bit sickly, so I found another means of entering the building, through the back door.

I was called to pray this morning. I said *kaddish* for my late father-in-law, whose *yahrtzeit* it is today. I believe his son is saying *kaddish* in America, but it doesn't hurt for someone else to say it also.

Yesterday or the day before, I witnessed a violent exchange between two vendors – one claimed that the other was occupying or blocking his allocated space. I said something to the more violent one to try and calm him down. Also, at the bus-stop the other day, I broke up an argument between a man who was illegally smoking and a woman who loves to quarrel. I have discovered that if you say something to someone in a friendly, light, humorous tone, it often reduces their level of anger.

There is a fine line to be drawn between being truly helpful and being a person who interferes in other people's business. As in so many of these incidents, much depends on the context of the situation.

I am troubled by the question of whether or not it is sometimes correct to cross the street on a red light. My rule is never to cross on a red light when a young person might see me. However, there are times when it can be extremely unpleasant to wait for a prolonged period of time. In such a case, after looking in both directions fifty times and making sure no cars are coming, it may be possible to cross the street. I am generally cautious, but there admittedly are times when I run across the street, and this sets a bad example for others.

Friday, June 18
4 Tammuz

My son asked me about a problem he and his friend are having with their third business partner, who contributes little to their work. I told him in a general way to be a human being by showing consideration for the inept third partner. However, I am not really familiar with the situation. There are times when today's mistaken kindness becomes tomorrow's cruelty.

Last night, a woman from a financial consulting office called to ask if I wanted to make an appointment. I hemmed and hawed – I did not know how to say no until she helped me. Then I regretted it because it might have been of help to her had I said yes. I just did not want to be presented with more options, complications and decisions that would distract me from my work. I probably would have done better to have said a quick decisive no from the beginning.

Monday, June 21
7 Tammuz

I did something nice today. One of the guest prayer leaders was offended the other day by the way one of the regulars, upon returning the Torah back to the Ark, showed disregard to others by failing to give them the opportunity to kiss the Torah. I deliberately waited a second or two when I saw the offended man approaching and held the door of the *shul* open for him. He said thank-you, as if grateful for having been acknowledged.

My holy teacher lights up the face of each person he meets. Walking with him in the Jewish Quarter of the Old City is like walking with the mayor – he has a good word for everyone.

Just now I had a chance to walk Israel R. home but I did not do it. I thought it better for him to not get into the habit of always having someone to lean on, so that he will retain as much independence as he can. On Shabbat I sat next to him at *seudah shlishit*, helped him with the food, with *zemirot* and whatever else I could.

Since the regulars were not there, I helped clean up after *seudah shlishit*. The *seudah* truly helped me, not only because it gave me a chance to do a few things to help others, but because of the singing led by Yitzhak M. He lifted our spirits and it was a joy to sing along with him.

I had another wonderful class with Rabbi Breitowitz today. His method of teaching embodies *derech eretz* in a true and, I would even say, complete way. He explains with care and intelligence. He responds to each question, always finding something of value in it. He truly answers each and every person. And he does everything on such a profound level, with such depth of understanding. He is a master of the subject of *derech eretz*, yet he is also modest and pleasant. He seems to be the embodiment of what might be called the *darchei noam* approach, the way of pleasantness. He is a wonderful storyteller and a master of emphasis and tone. He is never boring; he speaks with interest and knowledge on every topic and is always bringing in something new. I feel it is a special blessing that I have been able to learn from him this year.

I went to the home of the F. family tonight. They are always so welcoming. I did my best to be in good cheer during the visit. I can see how difficult it is for Mel to be up all the time. Nonetheless, I believe my company gives him something positive.

Last night I called Rabbi Tzvi Weinman, the rabbi from my hometown, who is in Israel for a few weeks. I did not wait for his call. I believe I helped pass what might have been a lonely evening for him. We spoke about the old hometown. I gave him a copy of my second interview book with teachers of Torah. I remember how, during visits, he tried to comfort me in times of grief. A good man. *Hakarat hatov.*

Tuesday, June 22
8 Tammuz

I wonder if a person is obliged to say hello whenever he sees someone he knows, even if they do not see him. In other words, to give a friendly smile or word of greeting. I don't know. I sometimes avoid saying hello to people who I believe have not seen me. This could be out of haste or shyness, or simply not really having anything to say. But always some small tinge of guilt remains as if I have not really acted in the best possible way. I am sure that, at least in part, the answer is determined by the kind of reaction the other person is expected to have. If it is going to disturb, irritate or delay, then why do it?

Impatience is a significant source of violations of *derech eretz*. Thus the busy, the young and the ones involved in competitive activities, are more likely to suffer from errors of this kind. I am going to try and keep in mind models of *derech eretz* provided by others. I think the F. family is one example. Despite Mel's illness and all they have endured, they do not complain or accuse. They continue to be as friendly and cheerful as possible. They do not focus on the illness, nor do they treat it as a taboo subject. They make the best they can out of a difficult situation. This is a kind of quiet heroism.

I hear how careful Rabbi Breitowitz is in leveling criticism. He does not rebuke in an ad hominem manner, but rather always conveys his criticism in general terms in order that he will not personally insult the offending person.

I feel a certain failure in regard to three *shiurim* I used to attend much more frequently. One reason I go less is that I always give priority to my holy teacher as our time is on a one-to-one basis and I am closer with him. But another reason that I have stopped attending certain *shiurim* is that I often sit through the hour and learn nothing. In any case, I could apologize to the lecturers for my absence, but I don't want to lie to them.

There is an old Sephardi blind man who regularly sits at the front entrance of the *shul* opposite the Machane Yehuda market. He gives blessings and collects *tzedakah*. After giving him money and asking him to make a blessing for the children, he asked me to go to the market and buy him bananas. I was in a hurry but of course did it.

I came home and there was a message on the phone from a person I do not know requesting that I call back. I did not. I believe it is probably a person requesting money. I feel guilty for not calling back.

At the bookfair, I saw Eva Shaltiel and remembered a wonderful poem of hers about the character traits of family members that are revealed as they slice tomatoes. I bought her book, which I then skimmed through. I always try to buy the book of a writer when they themselves are selling it.

Wednesday, June 23
9 Tammuz

I said *yashar koach* to the *shaliach tsibbur* after the prayers this morning, although I feel that he didn't deserve it as he went far too fast during the prayers. This is hypocritical of me. However, I could not have asked him to slow down since he is much more of a veteran in the *shul* than I am. Still, I know that some others feel as I do. I am not sure if I am doing the right thing, but I know that even one word can spoil a relationship by creating bad feelings.

Moshe B. asked me to help him carry *tzedakah* money to the house of another *gabbai* this morning. I did so, but then I learned something that could make me suspicious of the other gabbai's honesty. However, as I have no real solid evidence that might confirm my reservations, the suspiciousness in itself does not seem to be very commendable.

I saw one of my quiet, unsung heroes yesterday: a former partisan veteran of Israel's wars, a *gabbai* from Ramat Eshkol. He told me that his wife had had a bad fall and that he had not come to *shul* for some time because he had been caring for her. He takes me into his confidence whenever I see him. I believe this is a quality of *derech eretz*. I myself have great difficulty in attaining this *middah*.

I once listened at length to the story – which he reluctantly related – of the unimaginable hell that he endured in the Holocaust, and then of how he was consequently thrown into the wars here afterwards. Perhaps my listening to his story won his trust.

Being aware of the long-term consequences of our actions are an element of *derech eretz*. I learned from Rabbi Breitowitz that the pain we inflict on others may end up coming back to us, even if it is for a righteous cause. My Bubbe also taught me that the good we put into the life of others comes back into our own.

Thursday, June 24
10 *Tammuz*

I am wondering whether or not to date this journal. I am trying to think of what is best for the reader. Consideration for the reader is something to which, in my writing up until now, I perhaps have not paid adequate attention. I may have been misled by the Joycean proposition of being the solitary star who it is the reader's task to follow. So, I will begin backdating the journal now out of the sense that some readers might take interest in this. Today is June 24, 1999; 10 *Tammuz*, 5759.

I tried not to push or sell my work at the Jerusalem International Bookfair yesterday. I met with those editors who have "the power." I always feel ashamed when I perceive over-ambition in myself. At this stage in my life, it is not as if I have no work published. Perhaps because I am older, more experienced and have been through this before, I was neither overly anxious nor eager. I debated in my head, as I constantly do, whether or not I should try to sell myself and my works to others. In the end I decided that I should. In a couple of instances, I introduced myself to a few editors.

At the bookfair, I spoke from the audience at the seminar on "The Books Which Had the Greatest Influence on Life in This Century." I did not say what I thought the panelists would like to hear, but rather what I believed. I inadvertently rebuked the Israeli panelist (who, by the way, gave the best aesthetic presentation) for his statement that books have had no real influence on the State of Israel. I reminded him that the State of Israel was founded, in part, thanks to the book *The Jewish State* by Theodor Herzl. I had no intention of insulting him or even contradicting him – I simply wanted to make a general point about the power of books. But deep down, I wanted to somehow criticize the post-Zionist, anti-Israel line that has been the stance of this person in the past.

The question of how one contradicts a person, especially when they are engaged in a public debate, while still maintaining a certain level of *derech eretz*, is a difficult one. Perhaps the emphasis should be placed on concentrating on the matters being discussed and not on the characters or personalities of one's rivals. I do not, however, know if this is possible. I have to study this question more. I think that one of the dangers of writing in the way that I am doing so now is the pretense of knowing more than I do about these questions and somehow being misleading as a result.

Did I act with *derech eretz* yesterday in contradicting the anti-Israel majority at the bookfair? I don't know. I took them all on. Is personal courage (of which I admittedly have not had enough in the past) an aspect of *derech eretz*? I believe it should be, for what we are talking about is being a mensch and behaving in an appropriate manner. The responsibility of speaking out is one I do not relish, but am nonetheless sometimes forced into.

Monday, June 28
14 *Tammuz*

This morning, I saw Renee S. on the bus. She acted as if she did not want to see me, so instead of going to sit next to her, I simply said a brief hello and carried on. I then sensed she may have been disappointed that I did not sit down next to her. In other words, she may have changed her mind as she saw me approaching. In any case, I feel regret at having given her the impression of indifference. I have known her and her husband for years. In fact, her husband was my teacher years ago, and I respect and like them both.

Tuesday, June 29
15 *Tammuz*

On the way to Rabbi Breitowitz's class, I saw a woman who really seemed to be having difficulty carrying her things. I asked her if she needed help. She is a Russian woman who moved to Jerusalem only two years ago from somewhere else in Israel. She has difficulty in walking up hills. I helped her and we had a friendly, brief conversation.

Wednesday, June 30
16 *Tammuz*

Yesterday, I helped to complete a *minyan* at the Kushta Synagogue near Yoel Solomon Street. I have always responded affirmatively when asked to help them complete a *minyan* for *Maariv* in the evening.

Thursday, July 1
17 *Tammuz*

I just came from the emergency room at Har Hatsofim where I visited Mel. I saw how much he enjoys my company. I hope he will be able to go home tomorrow. Today, I also said good-bye to a friend and did him a favor – I returned the cane he had borrowed from Mrs. B. While I was at her house, Mrs. B. explained to me why she does not want to give money from the *tzedakah* funds she raises to a potential convert. She claims that the woman recently received a grant of seven thousand dollars from another fund. I tried to help her figure out how to increase contributions to the *tzedakah* fund. I did this even though I object to the way in which she interrogates potential *tzedakah* recipients, often only to subsequently refuse them. Nonetheless, she does much good which would not be achieved without her.

I sense that Dov no longer needs me to walk him home, although he generally seems to enjoy it.

Friday, July 2
18 *Tammuz*

I read in Rabbi Wagschall's work on *derech eretz* that *derech eretz* has to do with making others happy. One must cultivate humility, impartiality, a sense of justice and a sensitivity to the needs and concerns of others in order to achieve this.

Today, in Rabbi Eisen's *shiur*, I acted in accordance with known prescriptions for *derech eretz*, but failed the test of having a positive attitude in what I was doing. As is often the case when I force myself to do the "right thing," I felt inwardly impatient.

Sunday, July 4
20 *Tammuz*

I failed yesterday. I thought of going to visit Mel at home but I did not go. In the evening, I called Mel's house and his wife told me that it had been a long day – he had been hospitalized with a suspected touch of pneumonia. I will do my best to go to the hospital today.

When people are engrossed in their own worries, it is difficult for them to demonstrate real *derech eretz* in their actions. But this is, of course, one of the tests of *derech eretz*. It is during the moments of strain in one's life that one is most required to overcome one's self-absorbed inclinations in order to help others. Life has a feeling of emptiness when one is living and acting only for oneself.

Monday, July 5
21 *Tammuz*

I did something that I generally do not like to do today: I walked out of a lecture before it was over. I tried to be as inconspicuous as possible. I got up as a questioner from the audience was addressing the speaker who was, among other things, boring, smug, and unable or unwilling to truly address the questions he was being asked.

Rabbi Breitowitz spoke today about some of the essential qualities of Jewish spirituality. It seems to me that they are also essential to *derech eretz*. He spoke of the gratitude and sense of blessing a person should have for the gifts he receives. He spoke of how the Hebrew word for "love" has the same root as the Hebrew word for "giving," and how to love is ultimately to give. He spoke of empathy and feeling for others in times of sorrow and joy. He spoke of flexibility and the ability to not be defeated, but to rise up from one's disappointments in the pursuit of one's goals. He spoke of the ability to channel one's anger constructively, not allowing oneself to be governed by it. In other words, he presented a portrait of a human being who can maintain a positive attitude towards life and is devoted to bringing goodness into the life of others.

I have not really thanked Rabbi Breitowitz for the Torah he has taught me. At some point, I plan to make a donation to Ohr Sameach Yeshiva, where he teaches. I do not know what else I can do to show my gratitude.

I visited Mel in the evening, before the lecture. He is to undergo a special procedure for stabilizing his heart rhythm on Thursday. In the bed next to his lies an Indian man. Two of the man's sons are doctors who were trained in Israel, and are now are now working in Australia, and the man has no one by his side at the hospital. Mel said that he was crying out, "God, take me." The man is blind and has difficulty breathing.

Thursday, July 8
24 Tammuz

I urged my daughter to go to the funeral of a mother of a former friend of hers, with whom she has not spoken in some time. I think that it is the right thing to do.

I visited Mel again yesterday. I took him for a walk in his wheelchair. They are not going to do the procedure to stabilize his heartbeat, but instead intend to treat it with drugs. He will hopefully be home by Shabbat.

I have been thinking about the articles I wrote the other day and their possible publication. They will surely be greeted with outrage. In them, I call for some *derech eretz* from the Palestinian Arabs in their daily interactions with us. This made me wonder again about the role of courage in *derech eretz*, and also about those times and situations in life when consideration for the feelings of others cannot be one's first priority. In other words, it made me ponder the natural limitations of the concept of *derech eretz* and the possibility that it cannot be the single value that guides our actions. I could go beyond this and ask: aren't there times when excessive consideration for the feelings of others is simply a betrayal of the way of righteousness? When others are evil, isn't it our duty to oppose them with all our strength? Doesn't placing total emphasis on kindness and goodness also result in the development of a weak character, incapable of combating evil?

It is simply not enough for me to tell the truth, to express my feelings in these articles. It is necessary for me to try and have a certain positive effect on others and, in doing so, be careful to consider the overall effect of my words and measure their benefit. But how can I possibly determine this?

Sunday, July 11
27 Tammuz

Yesterday, I stopped to speak with an elderly man who I have not seen in a long time. He has lost a great deal of his eyesight. I do not particularly like this man but attempted to lift his spirits nonetheless. I did not, however, offer to take him to *shul*. I instead told him that if I happen to be passing by his building on Friday night and he would like to come (which he did not verify), I would accompany him to and from *shul*. His wife, who I had never before met, thanked me. She is in a wheelchair.

I remember this man's terrible story about his quarrels with his son over money. *Hashem yirachem.*

How often a warm smile or greeting melts even the most hostile face! I often see such mode of behavior from my holy teacher. Unlike him, I have difficulty in being so generous. Perhaps it is because I am a more private person and therefore find it awkward to simply greet strangers. Then, too, there are those who want to be left alone – nothing will bring a smile to their face.

I still have not made the transition to writing this journal in Hebrew. Keeping promises is certainly a part of *derech eretz*, including promises made to oneself.

I do not enjoy the services led by two of the regular prayer leaders in the first *minyan*. It is not simply the music that is jarring, but also the speed of their prayers. They do not allow people the opportunity to complete their prayers fully. I do not, however, say anything because they have been there much longer than I. I think that if I said something, they would be insulted, even if they pretended not to be. Besides, while I know that many other people do not like the way they conduct the prayers, there are some – perhaps even the majority of people – who actually prefer the faster tempo and who probably resent my slow pace.

Monday, July 12
28 *Tammuz*

Yesterday, I stood outside the *shul* on Yoel Salomon Street and called people in to complete a *minyan*. In the end, the *minyan* was completed by an American tourist with two sons who had already prayed.

There is *derech eretz* involved in the way we look, and do *not* look, at others. I try my best not to look at women in a way that I sense might offend them. I do not stare or look intently at certain body parts, even if they are prominently displayed. On the other hand, I do not adopt the *charedi* strategy of walking with one's head down, although I will admit that I often lower my eyes so as not to stare. I especially try to avoid looking too closely at women who I might be attracted to. The question is, of course, how can I be talking about not looking at something which I have obviously already seen? I think that there is a way of glimpsing at something from a distance and getting a general feeling about it, and then wanting to get a closer look. But it seems to me that what is most essential is not to embarrass or cause discomfort to a stranger by making her feel as though she is being ogled. Real *derech eretz* is, first and foremost, concern for the other person.

What about those women who clearly want to be looked at? Why don't I consider their signals, such as wearing revealing clothing or an inviting expression? I usually do not look in such instances because of the religious prohibition against "searching after them."

There is another reason I do not stare at women – I respect their privacy, and believe that each person has the right to walk in the public domain with a certain sense of security and freedom. This also explains my anger when I see outright violations of this type of respect – staring or, even worse, what might be termed as verbal harassment of women. I rarely interfere and make any scenes because it is a delicate matter of judgment, but if I really sensed that a woman was being threatened, I would interfere.

Tuesday, July 13
29 *Tammuz*

Small favors performed for others. This morning I helped a *gabbai* by reading a meter for him. A neighbor just asked me to pick up the mail for him for three months.

As I am writing this, I wonder about the appropriateness of relating minor acts of kindness that I perform for others. Is it *derech eretz* to write about my actions? It seems to me that it is more modest and fitting to perform small deeds of kindness without receiving any recognition or credit, except perhaps that given in the world to come. On the other hand, if by relating one's own deeds one can help others improve *their* level of *derech eretz*, then there is a constructive benefit in doing so.

I read a book by Rabbi Wagschall yesterday in which he discusses hierarchies in *tzedakah* – for example, one's children have priority over one's parents until they reach the age of six. After this point, one's parents come before one's children. I do not understand this.

Thursday, July 15
2 *Av*

I went over to the F. family's house this morning. I waited there with them until the special ambulance arrived, and then I helped lift Mel into it.. Their daughter was helpful – she enlisted the assistance of another person who helped me to lift him. Ruth F. is worried about how they are going to manage with Mel in the future. I told her that she could call me at any time.

I just said good-bye to a neighbor who lived here for fifteen years. I regret now that I did not convey to him my appreciation for what good neighbors he and his family have been. But perhaps it was better that I refrained. I would have reminded him – as if he needs to be reminded – of his wife who died here at a very young age, leaving him with two young children.

I did not act correctly yesterday. I could have invited myself over to the F. family to help. Instead, I made a selfish excursion downtown. Perhaps one reason for my having done this is my perception that my talking to Mel no longer really helps him very much. He is at a stage where he has difficulty really listening. His mind is elsewhere, perhaps focused on his discomfort.

I just picked up the neighbor's mail for him. I felt an instant rush of gladness after doing this. How much a person needs to feel useful!

Yesterday, I reread the book on *derech eretz* by Rabbi Wagschall. He elucidates many areas and ideas within *derech eretz* with which I was not really familiar, and yet, somehow, had vaguely thought about. For instance, he makes the point that one should not be haughty while doing a *mitzvah*, that a certain kind of superior smugness should be avoided.

There is a cautionary word about the way one gives *tzedakah*. Clearly, one should not humiliate others. Also, when donating a large sum to *tzedakah*, I endeavor to be as inconspicuous as possible. Unfortunately, the *tzedakah* boxes are placed in the middle of the *shul*, within everyone's field of vision. I try to seek an opportune moment, when no one is looking, to put money in the box.

I think that there is also *derech eretz* involved in the way we act and relate to God. A simple example of this is that, as far as I know, there is no outright prohibition against praying in an old rumpled shirt. However, it is *derech eretz* to take the trouble to put on a clean shirt that is befitting of prayer.

An inclusion of a list of some of the topics in Rabbi Wagschall's work can lead to a broader perception of *derech eretz* in its entirety. Here are some of his chapter titles: "Welcoming Others with a Pleasant Countenance"; "Bending One's Will for the Sake of Others"; "Fulfilling Another's Needs"; "Developing Love for Other People"; "The Importance of Impartiality in Interpersonal Relations"; "Bending the Truth for the Sake of Peace and *Derech Eretz*"; "The Prohibition Against Startling a Person"; "Obtaining the Permission from the *Ba'al Habayis*"; "Refraining from Causing Pain to a Person through One's Speech"; "Avoiding Arousing Others' Envy"; "Extending Hospitality"; "The Prohibition Against Eating in Public"; "Maintaining a Joyful Attitude"; "Refraining from Being Overly Critical"; "The Prohibition Against Divulging Another's Secret"; "The Necessity to Prepare Oneself in Advance"; "Behaving Beyond the Letter of the Law"; "The Merit of Being Consistent"; "Refraining from Laughing at Friends."

Rabbi Wagschall also recommends saying *shalom* in acknowledgement of another's presence. I think now of how I do not do this all the time. Why is this? Sometimes it is because I sense that the person does not want my "*shalom*." It could also be because I sense the person will simply not respond. I think that, once again, the element of evaluating in an attempt to understand a particular situation is crucial. To be a person with true *derech eretz* requires perceptive understanding and sensitive judgment. It means being able to transcend the mere formulistic response, and in turn enduring the anguish that true freedom of choice often entails.

I have an acquaintance, a *gabbai* at a local Jerusalem *shul*, who is essentially a good person, but does not know when to stop in his expression of words of condolence. He sometimes inadvertently reminds others of their sorrow when they do not wish to be reminded of it.

Sunday, July 18
5 *Av*

I cannot think of anything special that I have done in the last couple of days that has reflected *derech eretz*. This raises the question of how much time one is permitted to be by oneself, acting in one's own interests, without sinning in some way.

Monday, July 19
6 *Av*

Yesterday, a closet I did not want had to be moved from my house. In the end, I moved it together with three Arabs. We played the game of who names the price. When one of the workers named a low price, I raised it. I saw that they were satisfied with my offer. After they had finished working, I immediately gave them drinks. The truth is that when it comes to personal relations, I always try to treat a person with respect, regardless of any ideological hostility. Special dilemmas involving *derech eretz* arise when one is dealing with those from different cultures with different expectations.

Tuesday, July 20
7 *Av*

When I returned to my home yesterday, I saw that my daughter's boyfriend had completed a job that I thought would be too physically difficult for me – taking apart an old cabinet. He then worked on assembling the new one. He did not finish and I am not sure that he will be able to. Still, I will give him the benefit of the doubt and therefore will not call the contractor who had said he would send a carpenter over to do the job. The contractor could not care less about this small job, and I do not want to insult the young man who helped and seems to enjoy the work.

I received a call from Andy M., an old American friend. He was depressed and discouraged. I tried not to let him hear that I had noticed and attempted to cheer him up.

I went to see Mel last night at the time that he had requested, but I was not really needed as other guests appeared, including his daughter and two of his grandchildren. When I saw it was becoming crowded, I cut the visit short. He now has to be given oxygen all of the time. I see that his situation has deteriorated. *Hashem yirachem*.

Perhaps what I primarily mean by *derech eretz* is simple decency and kindness. In this sense, it is not something of which to make a big deal, but rather something that one does naturally and comes to expect of others, as basic civilized human behavior.

It is possible to think that one is being kind when offering help to another person, while the one being offered help feels as though they are being patronized or stripped of their freedom and dignity, and therefore rejects the offered help. There are also those who, even in times of deep need, place such great pride in their independence that any offer of help to them is rejected. Or worse still, there are those who, upon receiving offers of help, might come to hate those who are extending it, for they see in those people a freedom and power that they themselves do not possess. So the whole issue of doing good deeds and being kind is not so straightforward in many cases. One cannot simply assume that there will be an automatic solution and benefit when they offer help. A person can try to do the right thing in total innocence but end up feeling blamed as a result.

There is a danger in performing acts of kindness, in being involved in *derech eretz*, to the extent that one becomes immersed in one's own pride and ego. This is why it is *derech eretz* for the one who is giving to be filled with humility. It means having a sense that one is not eternally in possession of the means through which one gives, but that one has been temporarily blessed by God and is now sharing this blessing with others. In other words, the path to humility relates not only to your relationship with the one to whom you are giving, but also to your relationship with God. In giving to another person, one must always be aware that the gift is only possible because God is giving to us all of the time. Once one understands this, there is far less danger of becoming a victim of one's own good deeds.

There are many, many small ways in which I am lacking with regard to *derech eretz*. For instance, I could have put everything else aside yesterday and run to be on time for Rav Halperin's *shiur*. I know it is more correct to be there from the beginning, yet I let other commitments – that of speaking with my daughter and saying a proper good-bye to her friend – come before this. I generally do my best to be on time for *shiurim*, except those in which I know I will "switch off" so early on that I will just sit there, pretending to concentrate. This indicates that a certain pretence is sometimes necessary for *derech eretz*.

I think of a few people I have not called, especially my friend Larry B., but also Mrs. B., Anita P. and Mrs. R. The last three women are widows. Again, I am faced with the whole business of hating to be reminded of death, loss and loneliness. It is precisely when I feel my own suffering, loneliness and inadequacy – in not having a wife, not achieving what I want with my work, not going anywhere, and never being around young people – that I find it difficult to regain some control and perspective and visit these elderly people. Yet most often when I do visit them, I feel gratified by it and feel glad that I may have helped in some way. But I also know that such visits may not achieve this and might also make the person I am visiting feel even worse.

Wednesday, July 21
Erev Tisha B'Av

Last night, I went to the *shiur* of my holy teacher. I found out that it was his birthday; I should have remembered. I also enjoyed the *shiur*. Going there is an illustration of a principle that recurs repeatedly: when you do the right thing, you inevitably feel better afterwards. Or perhaps another variant of this is the idea that doing the right thing pays. Of course, having this in mind when performing a good deed diminishes from the righteousness of the act.

One of the most difficult tasks I face with regard to my service of God has to do with my relationship with my former wife. The rule here, however, is simple, and I have tried to adhere to it from the beginning: the understanding that what is at stake is the well-being of one's children, and that as a result, any insult or injury to either of their parents is an injury or insult to them. And so, whatever the personal anger or resentment, one must always take the high road of showing respect and consideration for one's former spouse. This means overcoming one's feelings at times. It means striving towards cooperation. It means overcoming oneself by responding and replying when one no longer wishes to. For me, it also means going through many uncomfortable moments where decisions must be made mutually, and not relying on my own will and judgment alone. It also means confronting, again and again, something I do not really wish to think about – that because I am divorced and have therefore been rejected, I have failed. But again, all my own feelings are secondary to one overwhelming consideration – the well-being of my children.

There is another point to be made here. I see this situation as something I never wanted and, at the same time, as a test from God. In life, God does not always give us what we ask for and we are often forced to face realities that we never wanted to confront. In such situations, acting with *derech eretz* may be especially difficult.

Initially, this test was almost impossible for me as I was so broken by the whole experience. Yet, with time, I simply acted with a kind of consideration, which in many ways comes naturally to me. Above all, I was helped in this by my children, who continued to show their love for me. By this time, there has been a certain kind of cooperation built up between myself and my former wife, which is hopefully the best that can be done for our children.

My contributions to Rabbi Isaacs' *shiur* yesterday were finding additional *gemarot* for people who came in late, passing out some of the *kibbud*, and greeting all with a pleasant countenance.

Yesterday, I helped someone out for five hours by driving a car from the Hyatt Hotel to the Old City. My holy teacher and friend asked me to do it so I agreed. It turned out to be complicated, with the car stalling in the middle of a main traffic area. The policeman there showed true *derech eretz* and patience by helping us move the car and find appropriate help.

I gave *tzedakah* to an Arab woman with small children by her side on the walkway near Jaffa Gate yesterday. I did not give her today, but rather saved the *tzedakah* for the Jewish beggars and felt guilty as a result. I do not know what God wants of me here. I have read that these women are "run" by some kind of criminal group. I also know the injunction about not being kind to the cruel. On the other hand, they may just be poor people in need, in which case it would seem to be a crime for me *not* to give them money. The rule is to err on the side of mercy. The problem, though, is our day-to-day suffering, and also the fact that they belong to our rival group, even enemy, who are fighting for control of the city. However, this is another argument in favor of giving *tzedakah* to these Arab women, for if we control the city, it is our responsibility to care for all those who are a part of it.

Thursday, July 22
Tisha B'Av

Fasting, thinking of the history of our people. Repenting. This would all seem to involve my personal relationship with God without much of an element of my relationship with others. Yet it is possible to say that when one joins others in prayer, in a collective experience, one strengthens them.

Perhaps there is a certain *derech eretz* at times in just being part of the community.

Friday, July 23
10 *Av*

I prayed from *yishtabach* before the *amud*. The *shaliach tsibbur* who preceded me is a holy Jew with real *kavvanah*, but he has a poor voice with poor enunciation. This morning I was blessed with an especially good voice. My whole soul was longing to pray. I believe I may have helped others be uplifted through the prayers.

There are complicated questions of *derech eretz* with regard to performing the will of God. For instance, as I was thinking today about which course of action would truly fulfill the will of God, it occurred to me that when it comes to very minor acts, entreating God might be a wrongful imposition.

We should perhaps save our requests for when we find ourselves in truly urgent times of need. Of course, in adopting this approach, we may not be doing at all what God wants from us. I do not know. But there is an element of consideration in this idea that I think is probably fitting.

Monday, July 26
13 *Av*

I did my best to show consideration for Rabbanit Goren at our meeting today. I deliberately put on a long-sleeved shirt. I came and left on time. I listened. She herself made all this easy as she is a very intelligent, interesting woman. One of my main dilemmas is nonetheless whether or not I will write the work on the life and teachings of Rabbi Goren. I want to write a work largely appreciative of this great man, but I do not want to write a false work; and so I must include something the family will not like, a consideration of criticism of him made by others.

Wednesday, July 28
Tu B'Av

A few hours ago, when I did not feel like speaking to anyone and was in a hurry, I forced myself to stop and talk with my ninety-year-old neighbor. I thought he had been away. In fact, he had been house-sitting for his niece for a month while she was away.

Thursday, July 29
16 *Av*

I went to see Mel last night. It has become increasingly difficult for him to speak and to take an active interest in what is going on around him, so I feel that my visits mean less. His body is swollen with liquid that cannot be drained. He said, "Whatever the *Ribbono Shel Olam* wants" a couple of times. This is the first time I heard him talk in such a fatalistic way. I did not know what to say, so I decided that it was best to say nothing. I sat there for two hours and was relieved when his married daughter, her husband, and his youngest grandchild finally arrived.

Yesterday I switched buses because I had the feeling that the person I was speaking with on the first bus would have felt obliged to continue speaking with me had I stayed, when he obviously wanted to be alone.

Today, I moved a very heavy bag for a female soldier. She thanked me profusely. Sometimes people need only a small sign that someone is willing to help them in order to be strengthened in what they are doing.

Life is filled with all kinds of opportunities for small, almost unnoticeable, acts of kindness and help, and with our initiative these types of acts can be multiplied.

Friday, July 30
17 *Av*

I spoke to Dr. Veschler's widow this morning. At first we merely nodded at each other from a distance, but then I went over to ask her about her daughter. Her daughter, who is the same age as my daughter, is going into the army and will work at the Air Force magazine. I mentioned her daughter and her accomplishment because I knew that this would be a subject she would be happy to talk about. But I saw how distraught she was. At the end of our conversation, after my attempt to cheer her up, I said, "Be strong" to her. I now regret this. Instead, I should have empathized with her about how difficult all this must be for her. I just thought it might hurt her more to do this, but I think on this occasion I misjudged the situation. She told me twice that what is most difficult to contend with is oneself. I should have asked her what she meant, giving her the opportunity to elaborate.

One of the people I ordinarily converse with at great length whenever I meet him, Danny V., gave me short shrift this morning. It was clear that he was on his way to run errands, and was evidently in a hurry. However, had he said a word to this effect it would have eliminated any possible insult. But now that I think of it, I said quick hellos to two people in the bank I ordinarily chat with. As for Danny V., he is an old army friend with whom I have maintained friendly relations over the years.

Once upon a time, in Israel, you would say "Shabbat *shalom*" to every Jew you came across on Friday. Now there are the "have a pleasant weekend" people. There are even those who seem to be insulted by the Shabbat *shalom* greeting. Should one try to attune oneself to the latest mode of behavior or should one remain true to one's way? I will always say Shabbat *shalom*.

Sunday, August 1
19 *Av*

An interesting question presents itself with regard to my proposed visit to the doctor today. I have not told him the complete truth about my medical condition – he does not know about the urgency problem, nor does he know about my blurred vision. I have not wanted to be referred to other doctors. Is there an obligation on the part of the patient (as a form of *derech eretz*) to tell the doctor the whole truth? I believe there must be, for there is an obligation to be honest in all of one's dealings. Again, though, the truth and peace (in my case, my own peace of mind) often conflict. I simply cannot allow myself to become overly involved with doctors. I believe it will do more harm than it will achieve good. On the other hand, if something bad happens to me and the doctor feels at fault when it is not due to his negligence, then I will truly have done him a great injustice.

I once again cleaned up the garbage after *seudah shlishit* yesterday. I had two youngsters enlisted as helpers. Perhaps I should have let them do more.

I derived a small lesson in *derech eretz* from my favorite young teacher, Rav Yoni Berlin. A *siddur* was dropped. Both of us bent down to pick it up. I was sitting closer to the *siddur*, but he was quicker. He let me pick it up, enabling me to feel that I had performed a valuable deed.

I did let the doctor know about the symptoms I have been experiencing. I did not tell him directly, but rather gave him a sign which enabled him to read it and understand, so I am free of the sin of concealing information. There still remains one more problem that I have not yet mentioned to him. I will bring it up when the opportunity presents itself.

Last year, when Hanoch Mandelbaum went on vacation, I had the *zechut* of saying *berachot* in the second *minyan* of the morning in his place. I now pray in the first *minyan*, where they are missing a *gabbai* and need people to help complete a *minyan* before *kiddush d'rabbanan*. This morning, Hanoch was not in *shul* and the second *minyan* began late. Do I leave the first *minyan* and volunteer again to lead the second one while Hanoch is on vacation? Answer: I certainly do not volunteer. If asked, I will consider it. However they will not ask, for there will be other people available. This reminds me of a frequent error a certain kind of do-gooder like myself often makes – I overestimate my own importance.

The *derech eretz* of the carpenter working here now: upon deciding which way to construct a cabinet, he said that he would not use his own innovation but rather will construct it as closely as possible to the original system. He did it in this way so that anyone else who wants to move it in the future can do so. One should not approach a job with the mindset of doing it in any old way so as to just get it done, but rather one must do it in the best possible way for the other person, with real consideration.

Tuesday, August 3
21 *Av*

The carpenter asked for a price that I thought was too modest, so I gave him what I thought was fair. Again, I think of the lessons I learned from my father of how to treat workers in the right way, of observing the Torah's injunction of not withholding the wages of the day-laborer. I have a certain sympathy for the poor, honest, hardworking person. This feeling is partially due to my sense of guilt for not having worked in a way that achieves clear and definite good for others, but primarily arises from an appreciation of those who do perform such good.

Wednesday, August 4
22 *Av*

Late yesterday, I checked my messages and saw that I had a call from Rav A., a last minute invitation to his son's wedding. I was unable to hear the address properly. I went out and while I was on the bus, I saw someone who might have been going to the wedding, yet I did not ask him for the address. Later, I came to Meah Shearim and asked for what I thought was the name of the wedding hall. I never made it there in the end. I had given Rav A. a substantial check when he had asked for it – he told me he needed it for the wedding. He should have sent me an invitation. But the fact that he called and asked me to come means that I should perhaps have made more of an effort to actually get there. It seems to me that there was less than perfect *derech eretz* displayed by all concerned. In any case, when I see him I will greet him with a *"mazal tov"* and will wish the newlyweds a life filled with blessings.

The decision of who to call next when I do not truly feel like calling anyone. *Derech eretz* often means struggling with one's feelings – and sometimes overcoming them.

Thursday, August 5
23 *Av*

Today, a young religious man with heavy bundles got on the bus and approached the seat where an elderly woman was already sitting. He motioned for her to get up and move to sit next to another woman nearby. He then sat down, placing his bags by his side. Causing an elderly woman discomfort for the sake of one's own comfort is hardly what one would expect of any decent person, much less a religious one.

The neighbors upstairs are moving. They are respectable people. However they always hogged the elevator, sometimes poured water down onto our windows after cleaning, and often made renovations at less than convenient times, including during holiday periods. I never brought any of this up with them at the time because I thought it would do more harm than good. I also remembered how committed they were in their role on the *va'ad habayit*, doing things for the whole building that I did not do. In addition, I did not want to risk spoiling relations with them for no reason, especially since we have been on friendlier terms in the last couple of years. They especially helped me the day I could not get into my house because my daughter had locked herself in and had gone to sleep. I think that they became more friendly to me as the old-time neighbors were becoming scarcer and scarcer.

Friday, August 6
24 *Av*

I spent the evening with Mel, his wife, his daughter, two of their neighbors and their Philippino helper. When I called, I was both saddened and moved. For the first time, Mel said that he was "not so well" when I asked him how he was feeling. I am amazed at his composure, courage and consideration. His whole body is filled with fluid. He is truly bone-thin. He needs help in order to move. He can no longer walk outside. He falls asleep on and off all the time. And yet his mind is perfectly lucid. I left when I sensed that his daughter wanted to be alone with him.

Yesterday, I spoke with Israel G., who is the father of four small children. It also turns out that he cares for two older children from his wife's first marriage. When I saw how troubled he looked I began to speak with him. He has real money problems. Thinking of their four small children, I offered to give a certain monthly sum. He said that he did not want to be dependent upon anyone. I think that what he has in mind is a much larger sum for the production of a record he has made (he is an excellent pianist). I believe that he will, at some point, request a loan. However, I will not lend him money, especially after a bad experience I had with an old childhood friend who would not even speak to me when the time came to repay a loan. Instead, I will give him a certain sum of money.

This morning, I did not say hello to the divorce lawyer who sat directly in front of me on the bus, even though I know she must have seen me. I suppose this was impolite and not in keeping with the principles of *derech eretz*. Deep down, I blame her for I feel that she was too hasty in pushing my divorce. This is perhaps not entirely fair as she is certainly not to blame for my former wife's decision, and she could not really have changed her mind. But I believe that as a religious woman, she should have not been as eager to push the divorce as she was.

Sunday, August 8
26 *Av*

On Friday I spoke to the person who had supervised the installation of my boiler. I thought there was a leak, as there was some dripping. He told me to close a certain faucet. He also said that he could not help me in any other way as he was out of town but that I should call him on Sunday. I see today that there has been no leaking so I did not call him, even though he had booked me in his work diary. Just now I called another person, a plumber, about a different problem. I could have called the supervisor who oversaw the initial installation and he most likely would have sent workers, but I did not. I suppose that there is nothing wrong with what I have done, except that I showed a certain lack of trust for the supervisor. The underlying reason is my suspicion that he would not do the work himself, but would send other people to do it instead. Also, my guess is that he would have been more expensive. Again, I did nothing wrong technically, but I suppose that I should have trusted him. Last time, he sent two Arab workers to install the boiler and I had a difficult time communicating with them. So this time, I called a person who had written on his card that he did not work on Shabbat, in line with the halachic imperative to give a Jew *parnasah*. But also, practically speaking, I wanted someone with whom I could at least speak and ask questions.

My daughter lost her wallet. The man who found it called to let her know. *Derech eretz*.

Monday, August 9
27 Av

The telephone message I received last night canceling tomorrow's meeting in Tel Aviv was repeated this morning. The person with whom I was scheduled to have the meeting wanted to confirm that I had received the message and would not travel unnecessarily to Tel Aviv. This kind of consideration is a demonstration of *derech eretz*.

Tonight, Israel G., the man who is raising six children, four of them his own, called and asked me for a loan. He told me the sum of money he wants. I told him I could not fulfill his request because of my negative past experiences with loans. I told him to consider accepting a gift instead. He called me back to accept my offer after he had spoken with his wife. I then went to meet him. To my surprise, he did not expect to receive a check – he had expected cash. I learned that he is apparently cut off from bank service. After telling him that I could cash the check for him the next day, he decided nonetheless to take the check. I do not know if I have helped or aggravated the situation. Clearly, I will not save them from their debtors, the bank. I am afraid of getting into a situation where they will ask for larger sums than I am able to give. He mentioned, however, that they owe money at the *makolet*, so perhaps my contribution will help them with that debt.

Of course, the best assistance would be to help him find work. The advantage of assistance in the form of a loan is that it expresses confidence in the ability of the person to pay it back. In other words, I am aware of the possible negative educational effects of my action in denying them the loan. I pray that they will be helped and not hurt by my gift.

This morning, I raced across the street to catch a bus and, in doing so, I forced the driver coming in the other direction to slow down. I should not have done this. Again, the question of whether or not to cross the street on a red light is not so clear cut. I try very hard not to do it when others are near. However, there are certain lights and crossings at which waiting for a long time means having cars and trucks rush by at breakneck speed, which means dirt and noise. I do cross in such places when I feel it is absolutely safe, have looked both ways carefully, and can see that I am not in danger of setting a bad example. If there is a person who is not used to a particular crossing who comes and waits to cross next to me, I restrain myself and wait with them.

Tuesday, August 10
28 Av

Last night, after the learning session, I did not abandon a woman who I sensed had come in part because I was there. I went with her to have a light supper and listened to her speak, but said nothing that might have given her a false impression of desire for a deeper relationship.

Thursday, August 12
Rosh Chodesh Elul

There are certain people (I sense it is a minority) who have real consideration for others, based not only on compassion and a genuine desire to help, but on tact and intelligence. There are many who help others but do so more out of their own fixed ideas rather than a real understanding of the other person.

Friday, August 13
Rosh Chodesh Elul Bet

I did not give the carpenter more money than was stipulated in the contract for the second work he did for me, as I had originally intended to do. It simply worked out that way – he worked for two hours instead of the four he had said would be needed. I did give him a choice of children's' books from those my children have long outgrown, and he took several. Nonetheless, I believe I disappointed him, as my generosity on the previous occasion probably created an expectation of similar treatment this time.

I went to see Mel. I spoke with his hospital roommate who, it turns out, was one of the editors of a writing project that I worked on many years ago. As I was leaving the room, I asked Mel if he needed or wanted anything from the store downstairs. I now realize that I should have asked his roommate as well.

Sunday, August 15
3 Elul

I thought I was being helpful the other day in passing on a message to the family of one of my son's friends. I had relayed the message to the youngest son because both of the parents were busy. This is a case of not doing the correct thing in the best possible way, but doing it just to get it done, thereby creating a potential misunderstanding.

My expression of gratitude to Rabbi Breitowitz was also somehow conveyed in an inadequate way. I could not give him money – it would not have been appropriate. Perhaps I will try to go there today to say good-bye again, or at least to be present at what is scheduled to be his last class of the year. There has been an interruption of his classes recently and I, who have faithfully attended his classes throughout the year, was not there when they resumed. An unintentional error. Now that I come to think of it, it is interesting to note that the Torah portion of the week, *Shoftim*, deals with a *shogeg*, one who commits a mistaken, unintentional crime. And I myself begin the week with two instances of acting as a *shogeg*. Apparently, there are cases in which our failure in the realm of *derech eretz* happens despite our best intentions.

I did something that I am ashamed of a few hours ago. As I walked out the back door of my building, a dog from the building next door raced out in front of me. This dog has bothered me in the past, startling me as I was walking and dreaming many times over the years. I turned and, with a raised hand, made the dog move away. It came back a second time and I chased it away again. Not content with this, I picked up a pine-cone and threw it at the dog. A teenaged boy who emerged from the building at the same time with another dog and a middle-aged woman shouted "Maniac!" at me. I turned to him and said, "Come here for a second," but he and the middle-aged woman raced away.

I do not know what the correct course of action should have been in such a circumstance – perhaps a different person would have made friends with the dog. I am most ashamed at having shouted out to the teenager in the presence of what was most likely his mother.

The great heat of summer throws people off balance, making them more irritable than usual. Last week there was a large number of traffic fatalities, many of which resulted from such irritability. Ideally, one should be especially careful and conscious of controlling one's temper during this time of year.

Monday, August 16
4 *Elul*

There are times when you try to do the right thing, yet it seems as though there is no way for it to be done. Yesterday was filled with incidents in which I somehow did not respond to situations in the right way. This was based on some misinformation I had received. In one case, I gave someone some wrong information. In the most serious case, and the one which troubles me now, there was simply no right response. I wanted to encourage my brother-in-law in his struggle against his illness, but I fumbled and ended up making a stupid remark. My brother-in-law, in response, said that any expression of concern was deeply appreciated.

There is *derech eretz* involved in performing an act in the right way.

Tuesday, August 17
5 *Elul*

The refrigerator repairman came at the time he had told me he would come. He checked everything thoroughly and, although he could not determine the problem, the motor resumed working as a result of his checks. I offered to pay him but he said that he would accept payment the next time I called. But what if the refrigerator is in working order and was only not working as a one-time occurrence, related to accumulated moisture, which he wiped up in the course of checking it? I will wait, and if that is the case, I will probably send him a check. However, the true *derech eretz* lies in the way he treated the problem. On a previous occasion in which there was a problem with the refrigerator, I had a very different kind of repairman who insisted upon the maximum repair (the replacement of the motor) before he had even looked at the machine. Basic honesty is the first principle of *derech eretz*.

Wednesday, August 18
6 *Elul*

I fell asleep during the meditation exercise in the class I attended yesterday. This demonstrated a lack of respect for the teacher.

Today, a book that I had lent out was returned to me. The package included some articles I had requested. I had in fact given up on this woman's response, but she proved herself to be what I had always sensed about her – a person of integrity.

Thursday, August 19
7 E*lul*

I do not know if I acted correctly. I went to see Mel last night. I spent time talking with him and his son but perhaps they had wanted to be alone. Mel said that he might be going to a hospice in Har Hatsofim soon. I resisted this thought and said that I would see him at his home, to where he is supposed to return today. The grief of this!

Monday, August 23
11 E*lul*

The *gabbai* Sharlo asked me to arrange the seats in the women's section for Rosh Hashanah. I knew he wanted it done immediately yet I did not do it right away. Now I feel guilty. I will try to do it today even though I know it will have to be redone before the holiday because there is still sufficient time for the seats to get mixed up again.

Just as there is *avak lashon harah*, something which is not actually evil speech but somehow has some trace of it, so too there can be a violation of *derech eretz* which is not so terrible and obvious, but at the same time goes against the spirit of the concept.

A letter appeared in the paper today about the litter crisis in Jerusalem. It feels good to know that I am not simply "crazy" about this, but that there are others who share my concern as well.

There is a kind of criticism that is intended to hurt and insult, and then there is a kind of criticism that stems from a desire to help. Yesterday I tried to prevent someone from making the first kind of criticism and attempted to persuade him to make the second kind instead, but something inside him had difficulty accepting that this is what the goal of criticism should really be.

I have not yet been able to bring myself to visit Mel at the hospice. Since not that much time has passed since my last visit, I am not really obliged. I am reluctant to go because I do not want to confront the truth of his sordid condition. Also, I do not want to enter a place of mourning.

Wednesday, August 25
13 *Elul*

Somehow, the streets appear cleaner this morning. I think of my apprehension regarding the city's cleaning crews and wonder if that too does not constitute a kind of bad will, a sin. And yet the question is how far should we go in saying that things are good in the hope of engendering good as an outcome when the reality is clearly otherwise? Again, I suppose that the real dividing line is between criticism that is simply malicious and criticism that has a corrective and constructive aim.

I think that I was lacking in tact yesterday when speaking to my holy teacher about his illness. I had wanted to help my brother-in-law, so I spoke with the holy teacher about ways of contending with his illness. This, of course, could only remind him of his own illness. He was very tired yesterday, and I did not notice it until the very end of the *shiur*. After talking about my brother-in-law's problem, I showed even greater insensitivity. I spoke about my reluctance to visit Mel now that he is in a hospice.

Thursday, August 26
14 *Elul*

It is a fact that wherever people go they encounter situations that – even if only to a small degree – give them opportunities to act with *derech eretz*, to be of real help to others.

Friday, August 27
15 *Elul*

I went to see Mel at the hospice yesterday. His wife, son and one of his daughters were there. I sat and spoke with them. The rules have changed.

Everything seems to have slowed down. He told me that he is not in pain. He smiles faintly and does not complain. I asked him (perhaps stupidly) if there was anything I could do for him. Nothing. I left him surrounded by his family and other visitors. At one point, I sat with him and his wife and saw how she helped him find the threads of a story which is one of their family favorites. Aside from the tears in the daughter's eyes, I did not see signs of grief from the family. Only a subduedness. I myself, only a peripheral figure in their family dynamic, was shaken up inside and depressed from grief nonetheless. I left without saying good-bye, as perhaps I should have, to the family. I did not have it in me to be cheery.

There is a man who stands on the corner of Jaffa and King George Streets near Sbarro's restaurant on Friday mornings and begs for money, yet he does not look like a beggar. His posture is upright; he looks like a respectable gentleman who has come upon hard times. I give him more money than I usually give to the other beggars on the street. I spoke to him once and he told me that he had been a dentist in Russia. There is something about the way he says thank-you which makes me want to truly help him. I spoke to him once about finding work, but it was a really problematic, given his age. I would like to help him more. After hearing his greetings of "Shabbat *shalom*" and "*shanah tovah*," I began to cry inside. Perhaps this emotional response was connected with my visit to Mel. Perhaps it was also related to my guilt over having material means while others around me, no less worthy, do not. I think it also had to do with the fact that this man looks considerably worse than the first time I saw him some weeks ago.

Sunday, August 29
17 *Elul*

Yesterday, on Shabbat, I was at the hospice with the F. family. I displayed a kind of patience which I feel made it all easier for them. I helped with some small physical tasks. I later walked Ruth F. part of the way back home, up until the point when she expressed that she would like to continue on alone. I tried to do what would be best for them.

I somehow feel less outraged by the lack of *derech eretz* in the world around me. I have a sense of having exaggerated the faults of others, of having ignored the good deeds that are being performed all the time. I read yesterday of two volunteers at the hospice who have been helping families through their difficult times for years.

Monday, August 30
18 *Elul*

I was at the hospice yesterday as Mel slept. He did not have the strength to talk. I waited until his wife came. I spoke with her and then left when there seemed to be no point in my staying. I will try to go again today, as their son was supposed to leave the country last night, and their youngest daughter comes only on Fridays. I know that I am doing the right thing by visiting each day but this good deed comes at a price – the visits make me depressed and even frightened.

Tuesday, August 31
19 *Elul*

I always want to be thanked for the good that I do. Is this so wrong? Expecting gratitude seems to be justified. It is important that people should be grateful and appreciative of kindness shown to them.

I feel that I have a duty to attend the prayers in the main *shul* for Rosh Hashanah because there are people there who require my help on a personal level. Another gabbai's assistant, Mr. Leiberman, who also helps people, will be in Uman for the holiday. However, if I do not pray in my regular *minyan*, I am concerned that there will not be anyone to walk home an elderly, unwell couple who are friends of mine. I am also worried about who will provide company for Menahem, with whom I have prayed alongside for many years.

Wednesday, September 1
20 *Elul*

Yesterday, I went to see Mel because I had promised that I would the day before. I doubt that he remembered the promise, but I kept it because I made it.

I am troubled by what I am writing in this journal. It seems to me as though I am often criticizing others (even if they are unnamed), while I am extolling my own deeds of virtue. Is this *lashon harah* against my fellow man? In my own defense, I would say that I am not being critical with the intent to slander, but rather in the hope that I can contribute to the improvement and refinement of our actions and treatment of others.

Yesterday, I saw some Arab women in ragged clothes with some children in even more ragged clothes begging on the promenade leading to the Jaffa Gate. It has been claimed in newspaper reports that these women are not truly the real mothers of the children. They are run by a "businessman," who uses the money collected for his own means. With this in mind, it seems wrong to give charity to these women. On the other hand, there are people there with their hands out. I walked past two of them, but a third one was sitting right near the gate where I kiss the *mezuzah* before entering the Old City. I could not kiss the scroll upon which are written biblical verses while ignoring one of God's creatures at the same time, so I gave the Arab woman a small amount of money. As I walked into the gate, I noticed that one of the scruffy looking children, perhaps six or seven-years-old, was following me. He pointed to my cola bottle and made a wailing sound, indicating how much he wanted it. I hesitated, went over to an Arab stand, took a plastic cup (I thought it would be an insult to offer to pay for it), poured cola into the cup until it was full, and gave it to the child to drink. I saw that the Arab vendor approved. The child took the drink and I continued on my way. Only later did it occur to me that he might have wanted the bottle also for the woman and the other children sitting there.

What I *should* have done was give him the bottle and simply buy another one for myself.

Mel had a problem with his radio yesterday. I went and bought him batteries but it turned out that the batteries were not the problem. He wanted to hear F.M. and it was only an A.M. radio. I have a small radio in working order which I use everyday. I think I will give it to him, even though I need it. I can always buy another one.

If not for the money left to me by my family, I would not be able to give *tzedakah* in the way that I do now. I hope it contributes in some way to their souls' spiritual benefit, their *ilui neshamah*.

Another incident happened on the bus. I got up from my seat a couple of stops before I needed to in order to allow a *charedi* couple to sit together. A man with a knitted *kippah* dressed in a business suit clearly saw what I was doing, yet quickly moved to my seat from where he was sitting so that he could sit alone. The *charedi* couple, who had begun to move towards my seat, remained standing. I was going to say something to the offensive man but did not.

Yet another incident occurred yesterday where I could have criticized someone but did not. A *charedi* man threw a food wrapper onto the ground just as I was passing by. I stopped and picked it up without saying anything. Also, the day before, I did not say anything to a young Arab man on the bus who had his feet up on a chair that someone else would surely sit on soon. In many of these types of instances I choose not to risk an argument or to embarrass someone when I do not believe that a reproach will have a constructive benefit. I also shy away from coming across as an interfering do-gooder.

Thursday, September 2
21 *Elul*

The truth is that when we do good for others without any thought of reward, we often ultimately do receive an unexpected reward. I remember once being kind to Moshe S., who, when I met him yesterday, truly helped me in understanding Rabbi Goren's approach on a number of issues. He also gave me contact information for people who might be able to help me with my project on Rabbi Goren's life and work.

Yesterday, I was in the post office in Tel Aviv's Central Bus Station. The line was long and the clerks seemed to be working in slow motion. I made some kind of noise, expressing my discontent and impatience. As is often the case, there was a logjam which, when cleared, let the line flow rapidly on. I feel I was slightly rude in my gesture of impatience, even though it was not heard by the clerks.

Is there such a thing as *derech eretz* with regard to one's own private thoughts? In one sense, *derech eretz* relates to our *actions* towards others. Yet *derech eretz* also applies to our thoughts, to being respectful in all facets of life. My own thoughts often contain meaningless, vulgar meanderings that sometimes include mockery of others. I have to work at reducing such thoughts to a minimum and so, as it were, have greater *derech eretz* within my own mind.

Friday, September 3
22 Elul

I met Israel R. this morning when I was in a hurry. Nonetheless I stopped, listened to him complain, and took some money from him to give to the *gabbai* for his seat in *shul* for Rosh Hashanah.

This morning, I went to see the dignified man, the Russian former dentist, who begs on the corner of King George and Jaffa Streets. He was so moved to see me that he did not even look at the money I gave him. He said that he wanted to help me in any way he could. I got the impression from what he said that his monetary situation is not as bad as I had thought. But above all, I got the sense that he is a person who wants to give to and help others, and that his biggest deprivation is in not being able to do so. I understood that the greatest assistance I could provide him would be, as Rambam teaches, to help him find a way to help himself become self-sufficient. This is another case where money is not the answer, yet I have no way at the present time to provide him with the answer he needs.

In class this morning, Rabbi Eisen, who is the most polite and considerate person one might think of, asked the class for forgiveness if he had insulted anyone by not truly listening to their comments or not answering their questions fully. After the class, I gave him a check as a gesture of thanks and likewise asked for his forgiveness. He may not know why I asked for his forgiveness, but I do: my anthology in which his interview appeared, and on which he worked so hard, has not really helped him professionally. I feel that this might be because I have not promoted the book as I well as I could have.

Sunday, September 5
24 *Elul*

The carpenter who assembled the closet in my daughter's room and who made the new bookcase in my workroom was here again this morning. He came earlier than expected, just as I was making breakfast. He brought the extra shelf and the rungs that I had requested. I asked him what I owed him and he said, "Nothing." I then said that I wanted to give him something for his family for the upcoming holiday, but he replied, "No thankyou." I had wanted to give him *tzedakah* money but this is a man who works and earns. I did give him a storybook on the life of Rav Kook for his children. What struck me most was his *derech eretz*. He made the special trip to give me something extra and I suspect that his abruptness was due to his rushing to another job. In any case, his actions strengthen my faith that there *are* numerous people who quietly conduct their lives with *derech eretz* and perform good deeds. It is paradoxical that those who I want to give to most, those who are struggling to earn their way, are those who do not wish to be weakened by accepting *tzedakah*. Instead, it is to those people whose hands are always out, that I, somewhat grudgingly, give.

Monday, September 6
25 *Elul*

A strange incident occurred yesterday. After the Gemarah lesson in *shul*, I noticed that Dov had forgotten his cane there. The *shul* was about to be closed and I could not decide whether or not to take the cane to his home. In the end I decided that I had better do it. He was not at home but his wife was. She told me that Dov had gone to the bank on the way home from *shul*, and she suggested that he had not wanted to be seen there with the cane. I offered to go to the bank with the cane but she declined and said that she would take it to him herself.

Dov was very late for davvaning this morning and I wondered if something might have happened, some mix-up which might have caused him trouble. I worried and prayed. Dov is a person for whom I feel a special affection and admiration, due to his modesty, good humor, superior learning skills, and the fact that he fought in the War of Independence. His wife is also a great favorite of mine, a modest woman of spiritual strength and beauty.

While I was worrying about Dov, I thought to myself about the danger of trying to be good, *too* good, and by doing so, actually interfering and doing harm. I should have had the sense to realize that Dov is not the kind of person who would mistakenly leave his cane somewhere. He is a person who is always aware of what he is doing and I should have trusted him more.

I am sadly aware of my shortcomings as a father. I feel as though I lack *derech eretz* in regard to my treatment of my children. In revealing my reservations about my children's activities to others, it is as if I wish to gain their sympathy, and worse, prove that I am the good guy and that it is my children who are the perpetrators. This is contemptible. Of course, another interpretation, which I believe has some truth to it, might also be given: I am trying to protect them from the envy of others so I downplay their achievements. But this is also wrong. A third possible interpretation is that I am looking for advice on how to help them. Nonetheless, I have decided to take a different tack in the future. First of all, I will continue to adhere to my mother's rule of not boasting about my children. I will also endeavor to support them more and show them how much I believe in them. This means believing even more strongly than I already do that they really are good human beings. I pray with all my heart to God that they will both find their way towards leading good lives.

Tuesday, September 7
26 *Elul*

The garbage strike in Jerusalem continues. I wonder if any of the striking workers feel any remorse for bringing such unpleasantness to the general population. It seems to me that these wage struggles – in which the good of the general public is ignored – are characteristic of much of the group mentality in Israel.

Mel shows every sign of wanting to live. He is constantly battling against his illness. I doubt that I would have the same attitude in a similar situation. Certainly, from a traditional point of view, his attitude is correct.

I just shared all my complaints about the present government's actions with a friend who I know shares my views. I feel there is a certain "uncleanness" in the kind of talk I just engaged in, which consisted of, in part, both ridicule and mockery. I feel that my freedom of expression has been limited as a result of my attempts to achieve greater *derech eretz*. Even though I found that venting my anger released my frustrations with the government, I nonetheless feel guilty that I indulged in this kind of talk. From a psychological perspective, I found it to be therapeutic, but I am not sure how justified it was from the point of view of *derech eretz*.

Wednesday, September 8
27 *Elul*

My holy teacher sets such a wonderful example by greeting everyone he meets with a warm and welcoming countenance. He makes no exceptions;

those ignored and out of favor with others are likewise greeted by him in kindness. He and his wife excel in the *mitzvah* of *hachnasat orchim*, of inviting guests to their family table (something in which I am greatly deficient). When I learn with him, I am uplifted merely from being in his presence.

I learned a *mishnah* in *masechet Sukkot* from Rabbi Meir Schweiger this morning which I think is pivotal to *derech eretz*: this *mishnah* teaches us that we are to thank God for the joy we have in serving Him.

Instead of waiting for them to call me, I called the house of my friends who have just returned from America. In the course of the conversation, however, when we moved to the topic of davvaning in different shuls, I said that the *shul* that I *davvan* in is considered to be in the "big leagues." Intentional or not, this was a kind of a slight against the *minyan* of which I was once a stalwart, and which my friends still attend. I also suspect that my statement was a kind of mild revenge against my friends' having supported the opposing side in a *shul* dispute. In any case, I regret my words.

I went to the early service at the university to pray today so that I could *davvan* slowly and without pressure. I did not go to visit Mel as I had intended. Instead, I came back home to work. I *do* feel guilty, but I know that there is a large and dedicated nursing staff at the hospice, as well as many others who come to visit. Why am I constantly making excuses for myself in an attempt to justify my behavior?

If anything indicates a lack of *derech eretz*, it is this garbage strike. Israel needs to do something about the situation here, in which public service unions blackmail the public by denying us vital services. The streets are a disgrace. Garbage is everywhere. It is a real health hazard. I could not walk on Shmuel HaNavi Street yesterday without holding my nose.

Thursday, September 9
28 *Elul*

There are people who act so strangely that it is impossible to understand exactly what *derech eretz* means with regard to them. For example, I was in a taxi yesterday and the driver drove with only one hand. When I asked him to drive more carefully, he launched into a long speech about his impeccable driving skills. He also told me that the only three times that he had accidents in his twenty-five years of driving a taxi were after passengers irritated him by telling him how to drive.

I thought of reacting angrily, but it was impossible. He was so good-natured, so filled with life and exuberance. I could have been angry at him for other things, though; for example, the fact that he engaged me in non-stop conversation. Also, the presence of an extra passenger, his alleged wife, who looked thirty years younger than him, and to whom he spoke in a way that no married man would speak after so many years of marriage. When he questioned me, and drew out of me that I am a writer, he began to tell the woman next to him that the person sitting in the back was an important writer, an intellectual. I simply laughed.

I would have been happy to have had a driver who simply drove the vehicle as it should be driven and minded his own business. From my point of view, that would have been true *derech eretz* on the part of the driver.

There are times when the action of an individual is so good, so beyond what one could possibly have expected it to be, that it cancels out all complaints one might have had about a lack of *derech eretz* and makes all these judgments seem petty.

I read the following story in today's paper: the father of the army commander who was killed yesterday had been trying to reach his son's unit that whole morning. Not knowing how to break the tragic news of his son's death to him, various people referred the father to others, until he finally reached the deputy commander. The father surprised the deputy commander by telling him that he already knew what had happened. He was calling to ask the deputy commander to send someone to be with the mother of another soldier who had been killed earlier that year. His own son had been very close to his friend's mother, and the father knew how painful and difficult it would be for her to hear the news of his son's death.

There are many stories of Israelis who courageously volunteer abroad. The recent rescue operation by the Israeli relief team in Turkey is one example of this. These extraordinary actions seem to be incongruous with the stereotypical impatience, rudeness and lack of consideration that Israelis are often accused of displaying.

There is *derech eretz* involved in how one reacts when someone mistakenly calls them, a "wrong number." I usually ask the person what number they are trying to call so that I can tell them whether or not their error is a dialing error. However many people, like the person I mistakenly called yesterday, are too impatient and slam the phone down, showing no consideration for the caller.

Last night, I helped the rabbi move benches and tables in the *shul*. He thanked me for all the work that I do. I was embarrassed by his thanks because I feel that it is only natural and right for me to help in this way. This is part of the education that I received.

This morning, after the long prayer service, Moshe B. asked me to change the curtain on the Torah ark. I gave an answer I rarely give: that if he could find someone else, I would rather not do it. I then proceeded to begin to do it while he was still talking. At that point I saw that the rabbi had asked someone else to do it and that I was not needed after all. I pointed this out to Moshe B. and left, but the truth is that I felt bad that I had not helped.

Last night, I went for a walk at around ten o'clock and saw that our car was surrounded by garbage so I cleaned up around it. And then I had the thought that instead of walking for exercise, I should clean up the street instead. I went upstairs, got a broom and a carton for the garbage, and began working. I cleaned up one whole length of sidewalk in a far less than perfect way. As I was doing this, I wondered why there isn't more initiative for citizen action. The garbage was strewn around everyone's houses yet the only reaction from the residents was to just sit and wait for the strike to be over.

Monday, September 13
3 Tishrei, Tzom Gedaliah

Baruch Dayan ha-emet. Mel is gone. I am trying to summon some consoling words to say at the funeral. I would like to say something that will act as a solace to the family. I will probably end up listening to the other speakers, and will then add what I feel might have been missed. Nonetheless I would like to write something down because it will enable me to speak if I fall silent.

The funeral was conducted in a dignified manner. I spoke at the cemetery. The people there were of the same caliber of considerate people as the F. family. Life is so difficult when one sees how even the kindest people suffer.

Tuesday, September 14
4 Tishrei

I went to visit the F. family last night. This morning I met two of the children outside the supermarket. Speaking with them is simply a pleasure. Their consideration and intelligence make it easy on those who would like to console them.

Wednesday, September 15
5 Tishrei

I did not go to the F. family's afternoon prayer service simply because I did not wanted to be part of an egalitarian prayer service. In any case, I would feel guilty if they were short of a *minyan* because I was not there. In the old days, when I was the driving force behind the *minyan*, I would round people up for *shivah minyanim*. I did not get there in time for today's service, but if I hear that they were short of people in completing the *minyan*, I will probably go tomorrow, lower my head, and pray.

Thursday, September 16
6 *Tishrei*

This morning, as I led the prayer service, I was corrected for not pausing enough between blessings to allow the public to respond *"amen."* I thanked the person who corrected me. He is a strange character, with totally decrepit clothing. He looks like a *timhoni*, a naïve, innocent person. However, he is a very nice person, and also seems intelligent. He seems to be one of those kind of people my father used to visit regularly and befriend, an "oddball." I believe we should take special care to be nice to those who are generally ignored by others.

Yesterday, my holy teacher wanted to learn in the restaurant at the entrance to the Muslim quarter. The owner, a friend of his, always charges him much less than the menu price. We ate for two and paid for one. I was uncomfortable, however, with this arrangement because I can afford to pay full price (although I did not have spare money at the time). Also, the owner knows this, as I was a client of his when he owned a laundry service in Ramat Eshkol. This is the second time that this has happened. The next time we go to this restaurant, I will insist on paying full price.

Friday, September 19
7 *Tishrei*

Yesterday, I went with Menahem to the *shivah* house. My accompanying him made it easier for him to come. My son drove us there. Menahem was also upset by the news that a childhood friend of his, who he had studied with in Warsaw sixty years ago, had died. I walked him back home before returning to the *shivah* house. Both he and his wife have severe health problems. I pray that they will both have a year of well-being.

I believe that I was right in overcoming my resistance to go to the mixed *minyan* at the *shivah* house. I helped Ruth F. find the place in her *siddur* a couple of times. I also remembered that Mel had responded to my calls to help complete the morning *minyan* many times. Had I boycotted his *shivah minyan*, I would have felt terrible.

Professor Lee Levine taught us that the concept of *derech eretz* was, according to the Mishnaic fathers, "work" (*malachah*) – to provide material support for oneself and one's family. According to Rav Hirsch, *derech eretz* also means knowledge of Western learning and culture. Today, we tend to think of it merely as good deeds done for others.

I went to a lecture at Pardes on the book of *Yonah*. I was considering leaving before the second lecture, which was to be given by Rabbi Meir Schweiger, one of my all-time favorite teachers and an especially good, learned, humble and holy Jew. But then I met Meir, and after he had seen me there was no way for me to leave. It was an especially good talk and, to my surprise, I stayed awake for the whole time. The subject was the *Mussaf* prayer of Yom Kippur, the *avodah* service.

I appear to many to be a carefree person who has all the time in the world to pursue all of my heart's desires. However, inside, I am a driven person who never feels as though I have enough time for the work I need to do. Nonetheless, I try very hard to always show others that their time is as valuable, if not more so, than mine. I try very hard not to claim that I have "urgent appointments," which make it seem as though I am busy or needed.

I heard on the radio that there is a special effort involving the Nature Society and other groups to clean up the beaches here. Finally, a little initiative! I also heard that this endeavor is in conjunction with a similar effort in seventy other nations. This display of respect, not only for God's greatest creation, humanity, but also for the environment as a whole, will no doubt be vital for the future of mankind.

The other night, when we were pushing my son's car (it had died), a young Arab stopped and offered to help us. He even let us try to jump-start the car with his battery. I found the whole incident, in which an Arab volunteered to help Jews, an encouraging exception, a hint that perhaps there are better days ahead.

When we help others, we sometimes feel a kind of power and sense the vulnerability of the person we are helping. With regard to this, the ongoing story of the relationship between the Jews and the African-Americans in the United States is well known. The former "helpers" eventually become resented and even hated.

It is hard to know when one should – or should not – intervene with the intention of helping others. There can be a *derech eretz* in minding one's own business.

Sunday, September 19
9 *Tishrei, Erev Yom Kippur,*

Last night, instead of going to hear Rabbi Riskin speak or to visit the B. family, I went to visit the F. family. I chose to be of help to others rather than advancing in my own learning, or perhaps pleasure. In turn, I was rewarded with the pleasure of feeling I had done the right thing. This is one of the greatest blessings of *derech eretz*: by doing the right thing, one gains a sense of inner satisfaction, a feeling of wholeness and closeness to God that gives meaning to life.

Monday, September 20
10 *Tishrei, Motzei Yom Kippur*

Our Arab neighbors behaved despicably over Yom Kippur. Hecklers formed on the streets and bands of youngsters harassed some young girls, who then needed to be escorted to their destination. It is unfortunate if the only way there can be respect from them is by instilling fear in them.

September 21
11 *Tishrei*

I chose not to go, after breaking the fast, to a celebratory meal at the house of a cousin of the F. family. This is a case of putting myself and my family before others. Of course, I did not insult anyone by doing this. I am not sure anyone really cared very much if I was there or not. I do not believe that there is really a violation of *derech eretz* in what I did. On the contrary, *derech eretz* equally relates to the way we meet our obligations to ourselves and to our families. There are people who are so dedicated to others that they completely neglect their own families – that cannot be *derech eretz*.

This morning, someone asked me why I was not in the regular *shul* for the High Holidays. This made me think again about the fact that there are some people in the *shul* who enjoy my presence, who would feel better if I were there. Did I show a lack of consideration by not answering them? Or is this just too trivial of a thing to really think about?

There is a danger of being *too* helpful and, in behaving this way, achieving the opposite outcome from the one intended. I think of my *gabbai* friend who knows people's *yahrtzeit* dates better than they themselves do. He often reminds and intrudes into congregants' affairs when it is the last thing they want. A person may feel inadequate and helpless if he is the recipient of too much help.

Wednesday, September 22
12 *Tishrei*

This morning, I went to the *yahrtzeit minyan* for my great teacher of daily prayer, Rabbi Eliyahu ben Reuven Barneis, of blessed memory. I did not want to go back to pray with the *minyan* I had helped run for many years and was, in effect, forced out of. I went, however, out of respect for his memory and a feeling of sympathy for his widow. I ended up feeling guilty about being absent from my own daily *minyan*.

I have not visited Mrs. B. in quite some time. I also think that I will not see the F. family for a while. Part of the compassion in comforting a family in mourning is not abandoning them when the official mourning period is over. But what do you do when the one with whom you have been truly friendly is the one who passed away?

I will go to the holy teacher today and bring *tzedakah* money for him to distribute to a woman in need. I doubt very much that this is what the woman needs most right now – she just lost her husband and has two small children who are in the hospital and three others at home. *Hashem yirachem* and give her the strength to go on.

In all the good things that I do, I feel that I am only helping others in a very small way. I have a longing to do something more significant for the good of others, but I do not know exactly what. I feel that I will never be in a position of power that might enable me to harness and utilize large-scale resources for the benefit of others.

Thursday, September 23
13 *Tishrei*

There are situations in which it seems that a lot more than mere *derech eretz* is required. I am thinking of great and acute suffering, extreme situations where extraordinary help is needed. I am thinking of situations where huge sacrifices might be required.

Sunday, September 26
16 *Tishrei, First Day of Chol Hamoed Sukkot*

I have been reading about the problem of road rage in Israel. The frustrations of having powerful instruments of speed yet being confined to crawling along in traffic jams, the exaggerated sense of power felt by some when behind the wheel, the overall tension in this society – all of these factors are said to contribute to an increase in the road rage phenomenon. I sometimes fault myself for not taking up the challenge of driving in Israel and applying certain principles of *derech eretz* (such as patience and giving others the right of way) in order to set a positive example. But the truth is that I find driving unpleasant. And, even more importantly, it would detract from the time I now spend walking, which is both enjoyable and healthy.

It is logical to predict that in a place where there is much crowding there will be poor *derech eretz*. When I was on the way to the *shuk* to buy my *arbah minim*, it was impossibly crowded and a young man pushed me hard to get ahead. I turned to him and said, "Do you know that you pushed me?" He said that he had not known and expressed what was no doubt genuine regret. In such situations people act rudely to others without even being aware of what they are doing. I know that with all my consciousness of these things, when I am in an overcrowded place, I also inadvertently become less polite and patient.

Monday, September 27
17 Tishrei, Second Day of Chol Hamoed Sukkot

I went into the corner store today and asked them about their candy gift packages. Although I really did intend to make a purchase, they did not have what I wanted so I left the store. This would not have been so problematic, but for the fact that I know the owner, who helped me, is always super-eager to make a sale and I know that I disappointed him. But of course I do not believe that it would have been right to purchase something I truly did not want to give as a gift. And this whole example now seems trivial.

The truth is that for years I went to this particular store to buy *challah* before Shabbat. I was always given the feeling that no matter how much I purchased, it was never enough – the owner would always ask if I wanted something else. Why am I willing to go through this discomfort? By not reacting to the lack of *derech eretz* on the part of the shopkeeper, I enable his behavior to continue.

Perhaps it is the holiday feeling or perhaps it is the fact that I spend so much time at home, out of contact with people, but I notice that the people around me seem to be somewhat calmer as of late.

Thursday, September 30
20 Tishrei, Fifth Day of Chol Hamoed Sukkot

I did not return the call of the business associate who called to wish me a belated happy holiday. I had called her before Rosh Hashanah and wished her a happy holiday. I will speak to her next week regarding a business matter. Still, it might have been more considerate for me to call her back.

I used to speak with the holy teacher on the telephone every week. Is it right that I do not call him now? I did call on Thursday and we had our usual conversation, which consists of the relating of personal stories and expressions of blessings. I love the calls that come right before Shabbat in which he teaches me some piece of Torah that never fails to set the right spirit for the entrance of Shabbat.

Motzei Shabbat, October 2
22 Tishrei, Isru Chag

The whole business of attending different *shuls* creates many problems. On Friday night, I left *hakafot* early in order to walk Menahem home. He had been hospitalized before the holiday and was at home all of Sukkot. I returned to the *shul* and then left again. Two people saw me leave and told the *gabbai* that I was angry and that is why I had walked out. At *Minchah*, the *gabbai* came over to speak with me. I could not believe that someone had told him that I was angry. I apologized for walking out. Then we had good, enjoyable *hakafot* for *Minchah*.

I am increasingly less involved in doing the kinds of acts of *derech eretz* that help give meaning to life. Is it *derech eretz* to speak of one's own acts? Is it immodest to tell the world what a good person I am trying to be? The flip-side of this is teaching by example.

While I am relating the little "boy scout" type of situations I am involved with each day, the media is telling stories of horrible crimes. I am not simply talking about people who show rudeness or inconsideration, but those who are committing acts of cruelty and evil. Putting a stop to this cruelty and evil is, of course, a far more important subject. But I can only deal with what I am personally involved with. It is possible that the greater politeness and consideration there is in society, the less frequent terrible acts of violence will be.

I waited this morning until Menahem had put on his *tefillin* before interrupting him to ask how he and his wife are doing. To call and visit them more often would have been more ideal, though. I am not sure, however, that they care for this type of attention. I only know that they expect nothing from me and are grateful for any sign of concern that they receive. They are so totally devoted to one another.

I am now beginning to comprehend how some of my old-time gentleman rules, like "ladies first" and opening the door for a woman, are sometimes perceived to be insulting and patronizing. If, for example, I see an elderly, *mesorati* woman entering the *kupat cholim*, I will hold the door open for her, and she will most likely be pleased by my action. A clearly secular, younger woman in the same situation would most likely not be as pleased.

Wednesday, October 6
26 Tishrei

I have been thinking more than once about how I have not offered money to Israel G., the father of six children, of which the four youngest are his own. Yesterday I saw him plodding wearily up the hill, probably after having taught another music lesson. I just believe that had I begun to give them a sum of money on a regular basis, as I had considered doing, it would have created a feeling of dependence in them. After I helped them last time, a subsequent meeting was uncomfortable. Why? Neither knows what the other is thinking, but I think that his seeing me reminds him of his weaknesses. This is not good so I will wait. If he asks me for money, I will certainly give it to him. I pray that he will find a way out of his situation. In any case, it does not seem to me that his situation is completely bad – I saw that his children had new clothes for the holidays. I see in *shul* how much the children love both their parents. I believe that this man and his wife are essentially good people who have fallen on hard times.

Thursday, October 7
27 Tishrei

In the fight against terror or the war against a cruel enemy, *derech eretz* is not the first priority and can sometimes even be out of place.

Friday, October 8
28 Tishrei

We are enjoined by God to be forgiving. I have a friend who I have known for some years and although I consider him my friend, I very often cannot stand speaking or being with him. The reason for this is that he is filled with bitterness and hatred, and spends a lot of time slandering Israel, the Jewish people and also individuals, at times. I do not like such talk and it often leaves me with the feeling that I have transgressed the sin of *lashon harah*. I have often told him that I don't want to hear such talk, but it seems to be an element of who he is. I often save and bring this friend newspapers. Today, instead of saving the week's papers as I ordinarily do, I threw them out. If I ask myself why I did this, I can recall a phone conversation we had this week that made me feel particularly low. I also don't want to give him more "ammunition" for his *lashon harah*. Plus, I remember that when I asked him to save a certain paper for me one time, he did not do it.

I felt bad for throwing the papers out. Why shouldn't I do something that will bring another person a little enjoyment? I think that maybe one of the reasons why I threw the newspapers out was because I simply did not want to reward with pleasure someone who had brought me pain. I now remember a story I read a few days ago in which Rabbi Aryeh Carmel writes of how Rabbi Israel Salanter, the *mussar* master, did just the opposite of what I did. He was especially considerate to someone who had insulted him. I don't know if I am capable of such a level of righteousness.

If this friend is so destructive to my mood, why is he still my friend? Answer: because he can also be interesting and enjoyable to be with, because when I am in a certain critical mood about what is happening here in Israel, I share some of his perceptions. Also, this friend has helped me in a number of practical ways, including the operation of the computer I work on, so I feel indebted to him.

I had yet another moral test this morning. Yigal N., one of the people to whom I regularly give *tzedakah* money on Fridays stopped me and told me that he needed five hundred dollars to buy his son *tefillin*. I spoke to him briefly and offered to give him my old *tefillin*. He said that they must be new. He mentioned Rav Ovadia Yosef, and I asked him why his organization does not help him. He replied that they are in a difficult situation now. I thought to ask Rabbi Halperin about what to do. I also briefly thought about buying the *tefillin* for him. Instead, I gave him most of the cash that I had on me as a contribution towards his buying the *tefillin* himself. I do not know if this was the right course of action. I am sure that he could buy *tefillin* at a cheaper price than the amount that he requested from me.

Sunday, October 10
Rosh Chodesh Cheshvan

I went to see Ruth F. today. She has been on my mind a lot recently. Thanks to her sensitivity, I did not have to stay for a long time. She is a very good woman. I sympathize, thinking of how good a marriage she had, and how lonely it will be for her now. Her daughter is returning to Canada on Wednesday.

Yesterday, I made a special effort to get to the *shiur* of Rav R. and also gave money to his *gabbai* for him, even though he had not given *shiurim* for a month. I did this to help keep the *shiur* going, even though I have sensed for some time now that the *shiur* no longer gives me very much.

Israel is not, by American standards, a violent society, yet it is far more violent than could ever have been dreamed of by its founders. The principal Jewish character trait is *chesed*, loving-kindness. Violence would seem to be in direct contradiction to the way we define our essential nature. How does one explain it then? I don't believe one can attribute crime to the wars as sadly, wars have been an ongoing part of our reality, even before the establishment of the modern state. Perhaps one could point to Westernization and imitation of other societies, as well as immigrant cultures clashing with each other. It is possible to blame it on the breakdown of traditional frameworks of religious belief. I don't know. I do know, however, that this violence must be fought. Education is one answer, but when I hear young people, even children, cursing and speaking in a rude and ugly manner on the bus, I am sure that much of this is a result of the "education" they receive at home.

Yesterday, during the prayer service, someone complained to me about the speed that the *shaliach tsibbur* was davvaning at, and his inability to keep up with him. I agreed with him. I know that he wanted me to say something to the *shaliach tsibbur*, but I remained silent because the *shaliach tsibbur* is far more veteran in the *minyan* than I am. Because no matter what my intention is, I might insult him. Because he is a very nice person. Because I sense that haste is an essential part of his character. To attempt to change him is to impose upon him a burden that he will not be able to sustain for long. I also did not think to tell the *gabbai*, who might have relayed this complaint on. Such a thing should probably be handled in a frank and direct way. Yet, by not dealing with the situation, I feel that I let the person down who expressed his dissatisfaction to me.

Wednesday, October 13
3 Cheshvan

I left the house this morning at ten o'clock and, on the way out, I saw a religious woman with a child looking for an address. I did not merely give her directions – I took her to her desired destination. On my way back home, I was asked by two Americans if there was a laundromat in the area and I also showed them the way. These two small incidents of helping others made me feel as though the whole outing was worthwhile. I discover again and again that I feel no greater satisfaction than when helping others.

Thursday, October 14
4 *Cheshvan*

This morning, I tried to appease the dissatisfied congregant by leading the prayers at a slower pace. At the same time, I did not go so slow as to make the others present impatient.

Friday, October 15
5 *Cheshvan*

I heard a story that disturbed me greatly: a couple who lived in a building, where they knew most of the veteran tenants, moved out without saying a single good-bye to anyone. Sometimes there are situations where there is a sudden break in relations that comes without any warning and where the deserted party is left devastated as a result.

After attending a *shiur*, I went downtown and stopped by to see Yigal, the man who was looking for money for his son's *tefillin* last week. This time I asked him to tell me his story. He told me that he is suffering from leukemia and that the doctors told him some time ago that he only has six months to live. He is the father of three children. He needs 3,000 shekels for the *tefillin* and only has 2,200 shekels. I calculated that I had 5,000 shekels in my account at that moment and wrote him a check for the 800 shekels he needed. It turned out that he had no checking account so I asked him how long he would be sitting there. I then walked to the bank to withdraw the amount of money in cash. I returned directly to him, instead of looking for books as I had planned, and gave him the money. He thanked me but I did not see joy in his eyes. Perhaps he was wistfully comparing himself to someone who can go and get money easily. Perhaps my donation took away some of his satisfaction in making the special effort to buy the *tefillin* for his son independently. But I cannot really consider all of this – he asked me for the money because he needed it. I know that if he collects more money today he will then have the amount I gave him for some other important use. This man is so polite and gentle in his manner to everyone, including those who do not give him money. He just seems to be a very good human being who has fallen on hard times.

Sunday, October 17
7 Cheshvan

I just wrote two letters of a kind I dislike writing. One was to a newspaper correspondent, objecting about an unfair article he wrote about Arabs in Israel. The other was to the editor of a publication who had both misspelled my name and omitted a stanza of a poem that I had written for a recent issue. I do not like to criticize or correct. It is difficult for me to write these letters because I am so sensitive to criticism myself, but we are biblically enjoined to correct our fellow man in such a way that it does not embarrass him (and when there is some possibility of their making a correction).

Even when our good deeds seem to go unnoticed, I believe that the sparks of life are somehow collected and elevated to heaven when we perform a good deed. Conversely, the world seems to spiral into a descent when we do something wrong, lowering our collective spiritual level.

Monday, October 18
8 Cheshvan

The other day at the supermarket, a pretty young woman who worked at the checkout counter told me that her husband had forbidden having an animal (a cat) in their house on halachic grounds. I could see that she felt deprived by not having a cat and was ready to give her ours. Today, I went through her checkout line again and when she saw the cat food I was buying she seemed to look at it wistfully. I could have waited and gone to another checkout line in order to save her the discomfiting reminder, but it might have appeared to be rude.

I still cannot get over the pictures I saw on television of the starving people in Angola. I wonder if there is anything one can do to help, even if it is only to give money to some relief agency.

According to Samuel Huntington in his book, *The Clash of Civilizations and the Remaking of World Order*, there are currently at least twenty-five areas in the world in which civilizations are in violent confrontation with one another. The largest share of these conflicts involve Islamic peoples who have a strong sense of historical grievance and zeal for religious conquest. When I put our conflict with the Arabs – and especially the Palestinians – in this context, it seems unlikely that we are going to have the kind of harmonious peace that would be beneficial for both peoples any time soon. Although Huntington's perspective may be wrong and the conclusion I draw from it about our conflict with the Arabs might therefore also be incorrect, it seems to me that I nonetheless have a duty to share this perspective with others to the best of my ability. Part of *derech eretz* lies in warning our community of any perceived danger. This is so even when the person's influence may seem minor, and when they claim no special prophetic insight.

I believe that the moral weakness of the political "left" here in Israel is a failure to contend with, or even recognize, evil in the Palestinians. The moral weakness of the "right" is to disregard the other side, failing to take into account its humanity.

Yesterday, I went to a lecture that I found offensive. Our forefather Avraham was portrayed as being a nice, simple, yet mixed-up guy searching to "find" himself, while not doing a very good job of it. I raised my hand at the end of the talk, but the time for questions was declared over. I did not wait around to approach the speaker – I wanted the audience, not the teacher (who knows the standard interpretations of the text far better than I do), to hear my remarks. I perceived the correct action to be one in which a public error be corrected publicly. I should add that I would have done this respectfully, without attacking the teacher directly. Polite criticism.

What I saw in the teacher's approach was an effort to undermine the accepted collective tradition and to substitute it with a post-modern, super-individualistic one. In other words, the most overtly non-political lectures can often have the deepest political implications.

After the lecture, I got on a bus and went to sit in the back, where two young men had their feet up on the only free seats. I gestured to one of them to move his feet, demonstratively wiped the seat off with my hand, and sat down. The wiping-off gesture provoked a scream of ridicule from the other wild-looking young man. He was then joined by a cacophony of other screeching hoodlums. I looked around and saw that I was surrounded by a group of ten to twenty young men with brilliantly toned hair and earrings. For the next ten minutes, I was subjected to rude, loud whistling and shouting. They also made a few insulting remarks about religious people but I did not respond. Instead, I engaged in a quiet conversation with the one of them who sat next to me, learning that he is a cook in the army. Later, towards the end of the journey, I recognized a young religious man whose father prays daily in my *shul*, sitting quietly on the other side of the bus. I had thought that my silence was a way of not aggravating the situation, but it seems that I might have set a bad example for this young man with my sheepish, cowardly behavior.

Adolescence can bring on wild behavior, rudeness and vandalism in many teenagers, but one cannot rationalize and argue with a gang. To try and show them the error of their ways would probably provoke even greater rudeness. Perhaps this is one of those situations in which there is seemingly no right way to demonstrate *derech eretz*.

I met Menahem on the way to Tel Aviv this morning. He was in distress – his wife had been rushed to the hospital and the doctors could not decide what to do with her. After returning from Tel Aviv, coming home to rest and clean up, and going to *Minchah*, I went to the hospital to visit Menahem and his wife. The surgical procedure is scheduled for either tomorrow or next Monday. I had intended to stay through the evening, if only to take Menahem home with me in a cab in order to spare him the ride on the bus. However, sensing that staying might place pressure on them, I left on my own. Nonetheless, I feel a bit troubled that I did not take Menahem home as he actually looked weaker than his wife. I pray that they will both have a speedy restoration of health.

I could have pushed myself and gone to the Old City to see the holy teacher, yet I did not. Why? I did not have the money to pay for the lesson, and even though I knew that he would shrug it off, I could not. Secondly, I knew that if I went to his lecture at that late hour, I would fall asleep, despite my best efforts to stay awake. Still, I am troubled that I did not do more for my teacher and friend.

Thursday, October 21
11 *Cheshvan*

I cannot decide what to do about Menahem and Naomi K. I had a *misheberach* said for Naomi in *shul* today. Should I go to the hospital tonight? On the one hand, it seems right to be there, for who knows if Menahem will need help? On the other hand, I sense that they like to be by themselves.

Friday, October 22
12 *Cheshvan*

I ended up going to the hospital last night. I arrived just after they had completed Naomi's procedure. She was conscious and looked well. I also made the extra effort and went to the holy teacher's Hebrew class in the Old City.

This morning, I overcame my tiredness and went to Rabbi Eisen's *shiur*. I also met Yigal, the man to whom I gave money for *tefillin*. Today, there was no word of thank-you for the large sum I had given him on the previous occasion. Instead, there was the information that he still has to buy the *bar mitzvah* suit and other decorations for the event. I also went to see the former dentist and gave him his weekly sum. He is always grateful, sometimes *too* grateful.

Sunday, October 24
14 *Cheshvan*

Sometimes I struggle with the classes that I attend, but I see value in persevering and remaining loyal to one's teachers. Somehow, this "dry spell" will pass. One should not give up at the first sign of trouble.

Last week I wrote a letter of criticism to the teacher of one of the most popular Torah classes I attend, regarding his interpretation of *parashat Lech Lecha*. I felt that his interpretation did an injustice to the whole sense of the portion in question, which deals with the Divine promise to Avraham, bequeathing the land of Israel to his descendants.

There are times when one must speak the truth no matter how much unpleasantness it brings. At times, one has to risk one's relationship with others, even by rebuking them.

Derech eretz is not just about being nice, amenable, easygoing and accommodating. There are considerations which, at times, transcend the protection of people's feelings.

Monday, October 25
15 *Cheshvan*

Last night I was walking home from Har Hatsofim after the Kafka conference when, just as I had crossed over to Lechi Street, I saw behind me on the other side of the street that someone was lying on the ground with another person standing over him. I ran back to see if I could help. The young man on the ground was unconscious, with some blood running from his nose. A young girl also ran towards them with a mobile phone in her hand. Apparently, the young man had been running and dribbling a basketball and had mistakenly run into a protruding wire from a sign, which had been negligently left in an inconspicuous place. He regained consciousness after a short amount of time and was able to stand up. The ambulance was slow in coming so I walked them to the emergency room at Hadassah Hospital in Har Hatsofim. I tried to calm the young man who, although panicked, did not seem to be seriously injured. We arrived at the emergency room and, at my urging, he was seen by a nurse who said that he was unhurt. Afterwards, another nurse and a doctor checked him. While his friend went to get his medical insurance document, I stayed with the youth and spoke with him, calming him down, and learned a bit of his story. When his companion brought the counselor of their group, I went on my way. Both of them thanked me profusely.

A few thoughts following the incident: firstly, this dangerous wire should be removed immediately. I expect that the counselor will inform the proper authorities about this, but perhaps I should call about it in the morning just in case he doesn't. Secondly, I was a bit taken aback by the hysteria of the injured young man who, as it turned out, was finding it difficult to adjust to being so far from home (he was a foreign student). Thirdly, I was disappointed by the slowness of the treatment in the emergency room, as well as by the fatigue, resignation and looks of indifference on the part of the emergency room staff, especially the nurses. My suspicion is that they had been dealing with too many people for too many hours. Lastly, it occurred to me that what *derech eretz* really involves much of the time is simply basic, human decency.

Something else I observed was that there were many more Arabs than Jews awaiting treatment in the emergency room. A young Arab woman, apparently in great pain, entered, although there was something about the way she expressed the pain that made me wonder if she was not exaggerating slightly. Anyway, I thought that the first thing that should have been done for her was to attempt to calm her down, yet no one did. The nurse who finally approached her just seemed to act as though there was nothing urgent about her situation. I actually wanted to help her, but thought that any action on my part would be misinterpreted by the crowd. As it turned out, she had someone with her.

I do not believe it is done with malice or forethought, but I have seen Arabs act with disrespect in public areas, especially hospitals. At the entrance to the emergency room, we had to wade through a crowd of smoking Arab men who seemed to believe that they were on their own private property. Another example is the overflow of large numbers of Arab visitors in wards where many patients need quiet.

Tuesday, October 26
16 Cheshvan

I noticed rude behavior on the part of participants at the Kafka conference. This took the form of loud talking, whispering and exchanging messages during lectures, which displayed a basic lack of consideration and politeness.

I am sometimes also guilty of this offense. Often, I do not really listen when others talk because my mind is elsewhere. Even worse, sometimes I cut the other speaker off because I believe that what I have to say is more important.

Talking in *shul* happens all the time. It is also common at lectures. It is not always easy to avoid talking because if one does not participate in a conversation, one might run the risk of offending the person who initiated the chat. Possible solutions might be to either leave the room or to sit in a place where one cannot be heard.

Wednesday, October 27
17 Cheshvan

I did not obtain some information a neighbor had asked me to find out. I went over to apologize to him but he said that it was all right because he had received the information from another source. I left the *shiur* on Mishnah early this morning, but did so in such a way as not to disrupt the class.

Thursday, October 28
18 Cheshvan

This morning I was standing in line at Amram's grocery when another man, who had arrived after me, went ahead of me in order to give his things to the grocer. He only had one or two items, whereas I had many. I said something to him to indicate that I was in the line before him, but then I let him go ahead of me. I probably should not have said anything. The man, who has lived in the neighborhood for many years, is quiet and unassuming. In his haste, he simply did not notice me. I should have just let it go or, if I genuinely cared that much, I should have insisted on my rightful place ahead of him.

People in Israel tend to be very focused on their goal and, in doing so, ignore any objects that stand in their way. The same can also be said for Israeli drivers, who look straight ahead while driving, completely oblivious to anyone else on the road.

Friday, October 29
19 *Cheshvan*

Last night, I went out with a woman whose number I was given a few months ago. She is a good woman – honest and straightforward. We had a nice talk for an hour and a half, but there will be nothing further between us.

When people ask, "Why not her?", I believe that it is greater *derech eretz* to respond with silence, not elaborating on some possible objection I might have. Even saying that this person is "not the right one" may be too much. The minute one begins to elaborate, one runs the risk of insulting.

The idea of *derech eretz* as silence deserves further attention. When one comes to a mourner's house, for example, one is required to remain silent until spoken to. I think of my own silence in many of the classes I attend. I think that this silence serves to protect myself, preventing me from revealing my ignorance and lowering the level of the discussion. There can therefore be a wisdom and humility in silence, when one realizes that the subject being discussed is well beyond one's own knowledge.

After my *Pirkei Avot* lesson, I went to give *tzedakah* to Yigal. He showed me his unpaid electricity bill and said that he is now without electricity in the house. I was going to go with him to the municipality but then I realized that I had no checks on me. He told me the amount he would need to have the electricity turned back on – five hundred shekels. I went to the bank and, after a long wait, I came back and gave him another four hundred shekels (I had already given him one hundred). He took the money as if it was nothing. Perhaps he was too embarrassed to say thank-you.

The former dentist, who I go to every week to give *tzedakah*, always says thank-you in such a heartfelt way. The fact that I appreciate this so much shows me that there is truth in the criticism that I do good deeds in part to receive gratitude.

There is a great conflict that rages within me: on the one hand, I do not expect gratitude for my acts of kindness, yet on the other hand, when someone does not thank me, I feel resentment.

I was so tired after having gone to the *shiur*, seeing all the people who were asking for money, and going shopping, that when I came home I did not have the mind for anyone. Yet I saw Israel R. sitting alone so I went over to talk with him. He is still waiting for medical treatment. He has both pain in his legs and an eye problem.

I see a great number of poor people, some maimed and lame, when I go to the Geulah and Meah Shearim neighborhoods. There is too much suffering in the world, too much demands *tikkun*, correction.

Monday, November 1
22 Cheshvan

Yesterday, as I was sitting and waiting in the *kupat cholim* with my daughter, a woman came in with two small children. She was prepared to wait in the long line with the rest of us. I sensed, however, that she was actually waiting for a blood-test, which requires waiting in a different line. I told her to open the door to the other room and go in, which she did. She thanked me. A simple, small thing.

It wasn't her gratitude that struck me — what shocked me was the total indifference of the whole waiting room to this woman. Sadly, most people are only concerned about themselves.

Tuesday, November 2
23 *Cheshvan*

I committed the sin of *lashon harah*, which is a violation of *derech eretz*, a short time ago. My friend L. told me that someone who I would not have expected to pray at the Conservative *minyan* was seen praying there. I later mentioned this to someone else. I also told my friend, the holy teacher, about an incident in which I had been involved and, in doing so, I hinted at the questionable behavior of another friend. These are two cases of my opening my mouth when I should have kept it closed.

Wednesday, November 3
24 *Cheshvan*

I think that someone stole my hat this morning. In my mind, I am thinking about how to find the "crook" when there may not be a crook at all. I remember once accusing someone, in my mind, of taking a small *siddur*, which I later found. One has to be so careful to avoid jumping to hasty conclusions regarding personal insults.

Thursday, November 4
25 *Cheshvan*

Although I tried, I did not make it to the memorial service for Rabbi Goren. Had I been more determined, I could have made it. Can one fail in *derech eretz* simply because one is not enterprising enough?

I have been reading some stories about Reb Shlomo Carlebach, of blessed memory. I read about how he always gave to others in whatever way he could. I see how his kind of giving exceeded the parameters of *derech eretz* and was on a different level of righteousness altogether. His love and caring for each human being was profound.

Like most people, I am indifferent to strangers. I think of how Reb Shlomo Carlebach blessed each person he saw, trying to help by exuding love to everyone.

In my reserved, restrained demeanor; my self-containment, my desire not to make a fuss, and reluctance to be obtrusive, I reveal how closed and narrow a person I am. My own *derech eretz* is that of a small-souled person, a person who is good in his own, simple way, yet does not reach that higher level of love and compassion.

I called Ruth F. last night. I felt guilty that I had not seen or spoken to her in a while. We spoke for about fifteen minutes – she sounded really down. I must go and visit her sometime. She is such a good woman and I always enjoy her company. True, her husband was the one who I was really friendly with, but she is suffering now and there really is no simple answer for how to lessen her pain. How I wish there was!

Of all the elderly widows with whom I am friendly, I suppose I like Ruth F. and Anita the most. The most demanding one is Mrs. B. I spoke to her this week – she wanted me to translate her husband's will into Hebrew. I said that I would try, but told her that she should try to find someone more experienced than I for the job. I have distanced myself from her and see her far less frequently as a result. Another widow who I feel that I have neglected is that of a saintly Jew, Mr. Rosen. His wife is an intelligent, good woman. I have not gone to see her recently – the last time I saw her was at the wedding celebration of a fellow congregant's granddaughter. I feel guilty that I have not been to see her. Sometimes I feel that such a visit is too awkward because it brings with it painful reminders of other, better days.

There are two other women, one widowed and one divorced, who I have been friendly with over the years. They are both around my age, and are candidates for re-marriage. One of them in particular is potentially suitable, but I am afraid of insulting the memory of her deceased husband by starting something. Most of all, I am afraid of failing and being disappointed. I am attracted to this woman, yet I do nothing. This seems to be the story of my life – not the sins of *commission*, but the sins of *omission*.

Friday, November 5
26 Cheshvan

The wildest types of characters are generally those in the late-teen age group and perhaps, to a lesser degree, those in their early twenties. Those in this age group contend with the frustration of having physical strength, on the one hand, yet are essentially unsure of their self-identity. It is this group that disturbs people on buses with their noise and rowdiness. It is this group that harasses young women.

The sort of family violence that is now prevalent in Israeli society is beyond anything I could have ever imagined when I first came here. A part of this problem might be attributed to the negative influence of certain aspects of American culture. It might also be a result of other global, Western trends, such as those celebrating new forms of paganism. There are new, non-Jewish populations in Israel that come from areas of the world with high rates of alcoholism and family violence. I would have hoped that the principle of kindness, a distinguishing characteristic of the Jewish people, would have checked such negative tendencies.

I met Yigal this morning. He told me that he will be traveling to Romania next week for a liver transplant. He also told me that Rav Ovadia Yosef had arranged the transplant. However, he still needed money to pay for the transport of blood transfusions that were necessary for the procedure to take place. He has a rare blood type – O minus. I gave him most of the money I had on me, and then went to my *shiur*. Afterwards, I went back to the bank. The teller told me that my account was in minus, which I knew meant that the transaction that I had made the day before had not gone through. I went to the cash machine and proceeded to withdraw the maximum amount that was allowed. I fell short of the full sum that Yigal had requested.

Instead of returning directly to Yigal, I stopped by the former dentist, to whom I give twenty shekels every Friday. For some reason, I could not find the twenty shekel note that I had set aside, although I searched and searched. He told me, "Never mind this week," but instead, I took the fifty shekel note that I had set aside to buy *challah* and other things for Shabbat, and gave it to him. He then took a twenty shekel note and returned it to me. I accepted the change, not only because it was the money I had designated for my Shabbat shopping, but because I saw this good man wanted to give me something in return. I then went to Yigal and gave him seven hundred of the nine hundred shekels he had said that he needed. I told him that I was looking forward to seeing him upon his return. I have a feeling that he is going to make it. I took his mother's name and will have a *misheberach* said for him in *shul*.

Part of me feels that I should have waited with the bank-teller, letting her call the manager to check my account. I would have then been able to withdraw the full amount that Yigal had needed. However I felt that the delay was a sign that this was not the right thing to do. Maybe it shouldn't just be me who does everything for others. The very fact that I returned to him afterwards with most of the money was some kind of encouragement, a sign that he was cared for.

As I was giving *tzedakah* to a character who seemed to be very questionable, I muttered something to myself, imitating his strange accent. I had not noticed that a young girl who was also about to give money to him had overheard me. I could tell by her facial expression that she thought that I had been mocking him. Not only did I fail in the *mitzvah* of giving with the right spirit, I may have also insulted this girl by mocking an accent which might have been of her ethnic group too.

I helped a woman and her two daughters find a bus to the Old City today. After I directed them as to the route to the correct bus-stop, I saw that they might have misunderstood me with regard to the first turn. I ran after them and redirected them.

Sunday, November 7
28 *Cheshvan*

As I was returning home from *shul* on Shabbat, I walked into a building in which water was leaking down from the second floor to the ground floor. Because it was Shabbat, I could not actively help out with the leak.

To my embarrassment, I met the people who are on the house committee and who deal with these problems on the stairs. I really wanted to help, but did not because of Shabbat. This raises the whole question of whether or not one can create a situation in which other Jews might act as "Shabbat *goyim*" (using the service of non-Jews to perform acts which are forbidden to Jews themselves on Shabbat). I believe that I will ask the closest person I have to a rebbe, my holy teacher, about the correct course of action in such a situation.

The rabbi wasn't present at *seudah shlishit*, so the blessing over the bread was recited by one of the regular attendants. His pronunciation is an English imitation of the kabbalistic rabbi he learns with and sounds strange, to say the least. There were three of us, middle-aged men, sitting there who burst out laughing. I tried to contain myself, but continued laughing to myself for a long time afterwards instead.

If there is one thing I hate to do, it is to personally insult someone. This man is a good person – I am really ashamed of myself. Afterwards, I looked at him to see if he showed signs of having noticed us. He gave no outward indication. When I spoke to him afterwards, I made the mistake of maintaining eye-contact with him a little longer than usual.

A woman with whom I had gone out on one date, and had no intention of calling again, phoned me last night to invite me for lunch at her home. I said something about being busy now with some projects. I recall that she said "sometime this week." I responded "not this week," but I clearly meant "not ever."

I hate disappointing people, but I was angry at her for calling me. In my world, the man is the one who initiates such things. Of course that world of etiquette is long dead. I was also angry that she had not understood the negative signals that I had given her during our previous meeting. It had been very nice meeting her but for me, there was no further reason to meet. I thought she had understood that. Perhaps she did, but when a person wants to be with someone, they sometimes cannot see that their feeling are not reciprocated. Having been on the other side of this type of situation, I know that the human capacity to ignore signals in the hope of having one's own way can be great. I am sorry about what happened because she is a nice woman, just not the one for me.

Monday, November 8
29 Cheshvan

This morning, our regular prayer leader for the Torah reading, who tends to make mistakes, had to be corrected more than once. However, the corrections were given in such a loud, insistent tone that he became flustered, lost his rhythm, and made further mistakes. It is true that even when he is corrected in a more gentle tone he continues to make mistakes. Nonetheless, I was repelled by the tone of the person who made the corrections this morning. It revealed a fanaticism, a perfectionist attitude, and a lack of consideration for the reader, as though his mispronunciation of a syllable was the greatest sin in the world. But, of course, a defender of the corrector would say that his perfectionism stemmed from his love for the sanctity of the Torah. In fact, I learned another, more excusable reason for the corrector's harshness: his wife is expecting a child any moment. Clearly, he wanted the reading to be as correct as possible, so as to please God. His own tension was expressed in his strictness in correcting the reader.

Last night I attended a lecture to which my friend Yaakov Fogelman brought me. A young man spoke about various techniques of learning Torah and the truths that can be found in the Gemarah as opposed to Western methods of self-searching. After his first few statements about Western philosophy, I could see that he did not know what he was talking about. He certainly knew more Gemarah than me, which is not saying much. But his patronizing, idiotic generalizations about Western truth and science were so off the mark that I could not help grimacing. He saw my expression and said that he would give me a chance to reply later, but did not. I deliberately did not push the matter because this was the last lecture in a series of six, this one being the first that I had attended, and I did not want to embarrass him. I was going to tell Yaakov about his misperceptions, but I think that the right thing to do is to write the young teacher a personal letter consisting of my corrections.

Instead of trying to publicly contradict the writer of a particular article, column or letter, the right way to correct such a person is through a personal letter containing one's comments. I am trying to practice this more and more.

I just returned from visiting Ruth F. She is such a good person. I feel great sympathy for her. She made me supper, and then we read the article her son had written about his father for the newspaper on the computer. I am now thinking of writing to this son in order to tell him about how his mother is doing, and also to compliment him on his article. I would also like to ask him if her remembers the words of Wordsworth that his father cited to me at our last meeting.

Derech eretz involves meeting one's obligations to others in a deep way and not on a merely formal basis.

Tuesday, November 9
Rosh Chodesh Kislev

There are many times when one does not know with certainty the right way to act. In such cases, one can only do one's best. The holy teacher called me yesterday and I could hear in his voice that something was wrong. I asked him if he was all right and he said, "No, my father just died." I stopped my work and went as quickly as I could to his home in the Old City. I did not know if he would be there or in Har Nof, at his father's house. He was in his home, sitting alone. He thanked me for coming. I asked, perhaps stupidly, but without any real choice of words, if he needed help in any way. He thanked me and said that he wanted to be alone, and then told me the time of the funeral.

I came home and called two people who I thought might want to attend the funeral. It was a small funeral. There were no memorial speeches because it was Rosh Chodesh. We went to the cemetery after the funeral, and then back to the holy teacher's house. I went with another mourner, a kind man from Scotland, to gather together a *minyan*; first to the neighbors and then out on the street. At the holy teacher's insistence, I was the prayer leader for *Minchah*. I did not stay afterwards because I did not feel that it was the right thing to do. I believe very much in the wisdom of our elders who tell us to be silent and speak only when spoken to in a house of mourning. True comfort is given by one's presence.

Yesterday, a taxi driver, who was apologetic about having taken me on a route which was filled with traffic, turned off the meter and said that he would only charge me what it read at that point. I thanked him, but nonetheless gave him what I thought would be the full fare to my house.

One shortcoming apparent in people who look to do good deeds for others is their tendency to feel that they are the only ones who do such things. In fact, there are many other people out there who are considerate and do good for others. This can be seen in so many different ways. I saw it yesterday when I asked people to join the *shivah minyan*: there were those who really considered it and wanted to help and those who did not.

This morning, after prayers, I was corrected for repeating words during the chanting of the *hallel*. The *gabbai* told me that this is an act that is frowned upon by the rabbi. I thanked the *gabbai* for the correction and said that I would not do it again.

I was helping my friend move some things into his basement this morning. When we came to the end of one part of the work, he said, "I do not want to take up your whole morning," and so freed me from waiting with him until the carpenter's arrival. This kind of consideration is characteristic of him and his wife and is what makes so many people want to be their good friends.

Derech eretz requires a special kind of intelligence and intuition, enabling the person to be sensitive to the needs of other people. Many good-hearted and well-intentioned people fail in *derech eretz* because they lack such intuition.

Friday, November 12
3 *Kislev*

I received a letter from Rabbi Greenberg, with the royalty check that I had sent back to him enclosed. He asked me to accept the check for my role in our joint publication. Truthfully, I felt that my work had been worth much less than what he had given me credit for. He is such a good, considerate person. I am so glad I worked on the book with him, if only because it shows something of what he truly is, what he has given to the Jewish people.

I will not go downtown this morning because I need to take my daughter to her tutor. As a result I will miss my *shiur* with Rabbi Eisen, and will also be unable to meet with the former dentist to whom I give *tzedakah* each Friday. Rabbi Eisen has many pupils who attend his *shiur*, so I do not worry so much about this. The former dentist, however, is another matter. In seeing that my daughter gets to her tutor on time, I am putting my family first. Of course, I could always make a special trip downtown later just to give money to the former dentist.

I wrote a proposal for publishing this work, but have not sent it out yet. There is a question of whether or not it is *derech eretz* for me to write and publish about myself. However, I think that it is a legitimate project because such a work may be of real help to others.

My daughter told me about her two Arab co-workers at the pizza-place where she works. She said that they behave in the best possible way and that they have a high standard of perfection in their work. This, of course, is one form of *derech eretz*.

I saw a woman with a small child getting out of a taxi across the street today. As she was taking the baby-stroller out of the trunk of the car, the drivers of the cars who were waiting behind the taxi began to honk their horns furiously. They showed no patience whatsoever for this young woman and her baby. Drivers' impatience and rudeness is a central area for violations of *derech eretz*. Many drivers are not really comfortable or competent in driving and their lack of *derech eretz* is a reflection of their nervousness.

Great wealth and prosperity can make a society understand that material wealth is not all that matters and can lead to an effort to find new areas in which to excel. It can also lead to a conscious decision on the part of many people to be less selfish and more involved in helping others; a kind of democratic noblesse oblige, in which the goal of being a good human being and contributing to one's community becomes central.

Unfortunately, Israel does not have the same kind of prosperity that America has achieved in recent times. We are still at a stage in which a very large share of the population is hungry for greater material comforts. We are also seeing a growing gap between the upper and lower strata of society.

A friend of mine believes that I have this whole thing wrong, that American prosperity has led to even greater hunger and greed for material riches, comforts and distinctions. There is in fact a lot of evidence that suggests that Americans have become far less involved in voluntary work and communal activity (of the kind that deTocqueville saw as the key to America's unique well-being as a society). However, I believe that material abundance does give a certain power of choice, and that one option is to turn away from an exclusive obsession with greedy acquisition and move towards helping others.

Perhaps, though, the real key to this idea lies not only in the economic realm, but in the realm of national security as well. Post Cold-War Americans have a degree of security that perpetually threatened and tense Israelis do not have. They are less pressured by the demands that society makes upon them and can thus seemingly afford to show more consideration to others.

I remember how, during the oil embargo in 1974, Americans turned ugly against one another in gas lines. The fact that Israelis feel pressured in so many different areas of everyday life can account for a share of the *derech eretz* problem which is so manifest here in Israel. For example, I was in a taxi the other day and there was a large traffic jam at the northern exit of the city. Cars began to move on to the shoulder of the road, trying to get ahead of the line, and then forcing themselves back into it. There was no police presence there to keep things in order. Horns blared – there was a sense that everyone there was fighting just to move an inch ahead. Clearly, this was not pleasant at all.

It makes sense that those who have a lot should be more generous about little things than those who have nothing. But what makes sense is, of course, not always the reality, and there is no end of examples that can be brought that prove just the opposite.

One of the things I am trying to do in this journal is to test myself against the ideal of *derech eretz*. In doing this, I am hoping to increase my level of *derech eretz*. One of the dangers in this exercise, however, is becoming a prisoner to routine; and so instead of responding to the real needs of others, there is a risk of imposing one's own agenda of goodness and personal perfection on them. I started out with good intentions, but often, these intention do not necessarily lead to what is best for others. Thus, I have found that it is inappropriate to act like a *derech eretz* robot just in order to live out an ideal.

An acquaintance of mine told me that he finds that Israelis to be so concentrated on the target, the goal, on reaching the destination of their journey when driving on the road, that they lose sight of what is going on all around them. In other words, they do not see the field. This prevents them from reacting properly to all the possible surprises that can come from so many different directions when one is moving forward in a vehicle. *Derech eretz* on the road (and perhaps in other areas of life as well) requires a quality of vision, of perception, that helps people to see things in a broad and comprehensive way. It is all about seeing the full picture.

There is a difference between doing something for someone because you know you are supposed to do it and doing something for someone because you really care about the person. There are times when I feel worn out, times when I cease to care. Yet there are also times when I suddenly surprise myself by demonstrating that I actually do care in a much deeper way than I had thought possible.

Disappointment comes when one who has cared for us turns their attention elsewhere. Here too, it all depends on the way in which this withdrawal of attention is carried out. *Derech eretz* does not mean that one never causes another person pain – sometimes you have to be cruel to be kind. It means considering the other and striving to cause a bare minimum of pain. We are all like children who sometimes need to take the bitter-tasting medicine.

By and large, I know that I am a kind person. But I also know that this is the image of myself that I wish to transmit to others and that this desire can, conceivably, lead to a kind of smug self-righteousness.

When I am on the bus, I sometimes offer my seat to people who then reject my offer. I, in turn, sometimes reject the seat that people offer to me. (Am I that old looking?) Last week, when I saw how much the young man who gave up his seat for me wanted me to take it, I sat in it, even though I only had two stops left.

Monday, November 15
6 Kislev

Yesterday, when I was out in the street trying to get the last two people for a *minyan* at the *shivah* house, I saw a young man in a black suit at the bus-stop. I asked him to come but he said that he was in a hurry to learn. I said something to the effect of, that the one who is occupied with one *mitzvah* is freed from another. He came and, to my surprise, did not rush out when more people came in. He stayed to the end of the davvaning and then gave words of consolation to the mourner.

Yesterday, I wrote a letter to the newspaper complaining about the lack of *derech eretz* displayed by the Palestinian leadership. Arafat's wife accused Israel of poisoning their water and air, leading to Palestinian deaths; a blood-libel. The truth is that, as I wrote, the Palestinians take full advantage of the Israeli health system, a system which was founded and is supported by contributions of Jews and Jews alone. Instead of gratitude, we receive only hatred and evil accusations in return.

This morning on the bus, the bus driver saw a young girl reach the door of the bus, but did not open the door for her and drove on. Rushing and impatience are major sources of incorrect behavior.

If one had more time, space, wealth, and means of attaining what one wanted in life, then he or she would most probably be able to show a greater politeness and consideration towards others. When one is under pressure to earn money, threatened on all sides by debtors, and contending for few resources with many others, then it is naturally more difficult to be generous and polite. Having said this, I seem to be suggesting that Israel will become a model society of goodness when it reaches a high level of material prosperity, which I acknowledge is not necessarily true.

In the book, *Tuesdays with Morrie* (which is based upon conversations between a wise teacher who is dying of multiple sclerosis and a former student, now friend), by Mitch Alboim, the dying teacher teaches his former student the value of being totally present for the person you are with. He points out how often, people do not really listen to one another; they interrupt, pretend to listen, and often have their minds and hearts elsewhere. He indicates that the true way to respect another person is to give one's full attention to that person.

Many people love to pretend that they are the busiest people in the world. They talk with more than one party at a time on their cellular phones, interrupting a conversation and putting the caller on hold. This might be necessary for doctors and certain other types of professionals, but I doubt whether or not it is really necessary for most people.

People forget to turn their phones off even when asked. Phones ring during synagogue services, at lectures and movies. People also use their cellular phones when they walk in the street and on the bus. Do we really need to have signs posted outside places of worship, theater halls and even bathrooms, requesting that people turn off their mobile phones? Most alarmingly, many people use their phones while they drive. The Israeli government recently passed a law imposing a fairly steep fine for doing this. However, as far as I can see, people continue using these phones while they drive, without the benefit of a hands-free microphone speaker. This is because there is little law enforcement; the Israeli police have so many tasks at hand that they ignore many infringements of the law that would probably receive greater attention in other countries.

I am troubled by a letter I sent to a teacher a few weeks ago, criticizing his interpretation of *parashat Lech Lecha*. In his interpretation, he had delegitimized the connection between Avraham's journey in life and our possession of the Promised Land. I indicated in the letter that I hoped to hear certain changes in subsequent classes, but I have not gone to the class in the past couple of weeks. This is wrong of me – if I asked for an emendation, the very least I can do is give the teacher a chance to make it.

When I find something someone says objectionable, I tend to go and speak to the person in private, not wishing to embarrass him or her publicly. Having said this, I believe that sometimes there is a need for public criticism.

All too often, we make the mistake of prejudging people negatively because we feel ourselves to be outside of their group, estranged from them. Then, when we do make a connection with them, we realize how wrong we were in our hasty judgment. I believe in the directive in *Pirkei Avot*, "Judge each one favorably." I also learned this from my parents. The exception to this rule is when a person has *repeatedly* shown that he or she acts incorrectly and that one's negative judgment of them in the past has consistently been justified. In such a case, and only that case, one would be wise to *not* give the benefit of the doubt if a situation lends itself to assuming otherwise. In such a case, the person is assumed to have done the apparent evil, and innocence must be proven. This is certainly not done in the case of judging strangers who are not known, one way or the other.

I have noticed that very often, when people thank me for things that I have done for them, I almost feel offended. I think to myself, "What is there to thank me for – I have only done something that is naturally the right thing to do." This morning, when my holy teacher and his brother asked me to bring the *Sefer Torah* for the *minyan*, I simply went and did it. When I was thanked for doing so, I was somewhat taken aback.

I was very reserved and quiet during the prayers at the *shivah* house. I cannot help but feel inferior in the presence of those who so eloquently express words of comfort and blessing. I feel as though I do not know how to do this adequately.

I met Israel R. on the street today. He told me that his feet and back ache and that he finds it difficult to walk. I was tired and eager to go home but he began to talk and tell me his life story. He was born and raised in Czernowitz, which at that time was under Austrian control. During the war, he was taken to a camp which, at some point, was liberated by the Russian Army. He was then made a soldier in the Russian Army and fought on the western front. When the war ended, he was transported in a train with other soldiers to an unknown destination – what turned out to be Mongolia and beyond. The war against Japan lasted only five days. After the war, he learned that all the Jews of his local community, including almost all of his family, had been rounded up in the synagogue and murdered by the Nazis. He had come back after the war to find no one there so he went to Bucharest, where he happened to meet a Jew he had once known. This man had a factory and he went to work for him. He stayed in Bucharest for forty years, throughout the period of nationalization of the factory. During this time, he corresponded with his one remaining sister who had gone to live in Palestine. In the 1980s she came to Bucharest to see him. Then, in 1990, when he was already in his eighties, he himself came to Israel. He told me that he only wants to speak Hebrew, although his period of study in an *ulpan* did not enable him to do this.

When I heard his story, I felt guilty for not having helped him more. Earlier that day, I had gotten a lift back from the cemetery with a chiropractor. I tried to ask Israel R. if he would agree to let him treat his back, but I am not sure if he understood me. A person of true *chesed* would not have asked, but would rather have simply brought the chiropractor. I wonder, though, if this chiropractor is competent, whether he would be any more effective than the doctors and physiotherapists. I hesitate over this question and meanwhile, nothing is done.

I urged Israel R., however, to walk a little more each day. I also told him that I would accompany him to *shul* on the *yahrtzeit* of his family's destruction. This is the least that I can do for him. Other people (my brother, may his memory be blessed, comes to mind) would have moved mountains to help other people. I, however, am not such a person.

Listening to people who no one else seems to have time for is something else I could have learned better from my brother all those years ago. As a child, he would always sit and listen to the old people in our town.

At the cemetery today, I wanted to go and visit the grave of Rabbi Pearl, my old teacher and friend. However, I did not know exactly where it was and it would have taken a lot of time to find it as it is at the opposite end of the cemetery from where we had the *azkarah*. Also, the man who gave me a ride was in a hurry to get to a *simchah*, a *brit milah*. I considered forgoing the ride and going to my old teacher's grave instead in order to put a stone on it, in his memory. I began to think about him, but I also thought about how tired, hungry and weak I was, and how I had other obligations at home, and so I took the ride. Had I been a *tzaddik*, I would have put everything else aside and gone to the grave in any case, but I am not a *tzaddik*, and did not. I feel guilty; I feel that I have been unappreciative of someone who was both my teacher and a very close friend.

Tuesday, November 16
7 Kislev

Today, I went to the class of the teacher to whom I had sent the critical letter. The class was filled with insight and was truly uplifting. I felt that I was truly learning Torah in it and was thus filled with gratitude. I hope that the teacher saw my presence as a vote of confidence.

I have never, and would never, try to be involved in any kind of intimate relationship with a married woman. Such a thing would be in violation of the biblical sin of adultery. However, it does sometimes happen that I might, in some way, signal to a married woman my interest in or my unwilling attraction to her. I very much try to avoid this and, thank God, it happens very rarely. The problem is when one comes into regular contact with such a woman. I try to be as business-like as possible, striving to act nonchalant and normal. In so doing, I try to convince myself that there is nothing there at all.

My failure to find a new wife is a source of major personal distress. I could always claim that I have not found a new wife because God has not sent me the right person, but the truth is that I thought I would have met her by now. Foolishly, I always thought that I would know immediately when I had met the right one; a person who, in her great kindness, would speak to me in such a way that we would understand one another deeply and be mutually attracted to each other. This, however, has not yet happened. As the years pass, I wonder if it ever will. In fact, I sometimes come close to despair. I also sharply feel the disorder and the sad longing that my single status creates within me. If, with the years, this sadness diminishes, it will not detract from the fact that it is not ideal for me to be alone.

My difficulty of finding a second wife is connected with my idealization of my first marriage and the depth of my disappointment at its ending. I used to believe in sharing hopes and dreams with my wife. Even now, after the failure of my first marriage, I still hope for this kind of "ideal marriage" for myself.

The topic of *derech eretz* within the world of *shidduchim* is complex and generally beyond the scope of my knowledge. I believe that one reason for my slowness in this process is my great reluctance to hurt or disappoint anyone. Invariably, what happens in these meetings is that one side wants to continue and the other does not. So often, I may be already thinking of how to make a proper rejection in the first few moments of a meeting. And here I might add that while it is no pleasure, I have always found it easier to be the rejected one than the one who says no. This is because no matter how nicely a "no" is packaged, if someone wants to be with someone and feels that they are not wanted in return, it can hurt deeply. Therefore, even with all the *derech eretz* and good intentions in the world, even the kindest person can cause pain in such a situation.

Instead of calling the holy teacher to ask if I could be of any help (I wonder if he has cleared out his father's apartment yet), I simply told him that I would be unable to learn with him today. Perhaps it would have been wiser to simply not call at all. I suppose one has to be humble enough to realize that one cannot always know if one is actually helping someone – one just has to keep on trying.

Wednesday, November 17
8 Kislev

Competitive activities demonstrate a lack of *derech eretz* by their very nature since they require a person to defeat, and often humiliate, another person. There are, of course, rules of restraint in competitive activities, in addition to the notion of sportsmanship and fair-play. I remember how, as a child, my one great difficulty with sports was reconciling my great desire to win with my sympathy for anyone who lost. However, if a person plays to lose, choosing to care more about the other side, he ruins the game and betrays his teammates in the process.

We often tell white lies so as not to hurt another person. As a result, we may signal one set of intentions when our underlying intentions are really different. I think specifically of my call yesterday to the holy teacher. I did not want to meet him as I had other, more pressing things to attend to, yet I was anxious not to give the impression that I did not *want* to meet with him, rather that I *could* not. I feel that I showed a lack of consideration by doing this. The holy teacher has other things on his mind right now, such as the painful ordeal of cleaning up his father's house and affairs. If I were even half of a human being, I would have offered to help, and meant it.

There have been many occasions when I have wished that I had a valid excuse not to fulfill an obligation, like being at the office, but because I do not want to lie, I end up meeting the obligation. In synagogue life, there are many *azkarot* and trips to the cemetery that I simply don't like. I attend them only out of a feeling of obligation, a sense that this is what has been commanded of me, what God wants from me.

Two nights ago, I watched *Politika*, the Israeli television debate show. The moderator speaks to thirty or forty people in different studios during the course of the show. What invariably happens is that there is a shouting match between a number of people at once. There are cries to get attention and people get cut off when they try to speak – an absence of civility is inherent in the show's format. Debate, democratic conversation, and even rivalry in opinion and thought can most certainly be expressed in a far more civil way than is evident in this program, which is often cited as a microcosm of how discourse is improperly conducted in Israeli society as a whole.

Thursday, November 18
9 *Kislev*

Last night I went to an interesting presentation by the editor and writer of *The Israel Almanac*, Naftali Greenwood. At the end of the speech, I went over to him to buy a copy of the book. There were few people in the audience and only one other purchase was made. I thought of buying two books just to help the "small man," as my father would say. I asked my friend Yaakov Fogelman if he wanted the book for his store. He said that he would try to negotiate a better price and buy five copies. I then bought only one copy. I felt bad about this later – I passed up a chance to do something good for someone. At the time I could not think of a use for the extra book. I thought about it again this morning and realized how much other friends of mine would have enjoyed it. By not buying the extra copy, I failed at least two people.

I saw Ruth F. walking home yesterday. I like her a lot but I was in a hurry for *shul*, so I did my best not to be seen by her. Is this a violation of *derech eretz?* Must one always greet another person with a friendly face?

This morning I wanted to ask Miller about Mandelbaum, his ailing neighbor and friend. However, when I saw that Miller was late for *shul*, I did not stop him. I think of so many people I have not visited or called, especially among my acquaintances who are elderly and unwell.

Rabbi N. returned yesterday. He began to learn after *Minchah*. I was tired and I thought of running away, but when I asked myself what God would want me to do in such a circumstance, I stayed and learned. I have always felt resentful towards Rabbi N. because he tends to go on and on in his learning, does not think of anyone else's time, and always finishes late. He is also not able to explain himself very well. I also feel that he imposes himself upon people. Even though my criticism is legitimate, the thoughts that I have been having have shown a lack of *derech eretz*. Yesterday I was able to overcome my resentment, but I know that it will return. When it does, I will have to fight it in the same way that I did yesterday.

Friday, November 19
10 *Kislev*

I am in a rush now. It is not proper *derech* eretz to write in haste – it is better to wait and think each entry out carefully in order to share the best that I can offer with the reader. Consideration for the reader is, after all, a first element in the *derech eretz* of the writer.

While I was running my pre-Shabbat errands, a young beggar jumped out in front of me at the entrance of the Israel Center, screaming, "My house has burned down!" I sidestepped him and kept walking. I immediately felt great contrition, but did not turn back. About a year ago, I was confronted by this same young man and I gave him more money than I usually give those who beg in the street. I have seen this person ask for money in other places as well. The question in my mind is, why doesn't this young man do something to change his situation? Perhaps this is not fair. Another thing that aggravates me is his American accent. However, even if you come from the richest country in the world, you can still be very poor. I thought at one point about turning back and speaking to the young man, to find out the truth of his situation, but I did not. I was unsure of whether or not he could be trusted.

I had spent the previous hour giving *tzedakah* to a number of people. I had in fact planned the whole expedition because I wanted to give the former dentist, who I had missed the previous week, more than I usually give him. I feel that I do not take the epidemic of poverty in Israel seriously enough. There are now more beggars on the streets than ever before.

I do not know if Yigal, who went to have a liver transplant in Romania, is still alive. I continue to pray for him. I passed his spot and felt such a strong yearning that he should live. I am wondering if I should make a greater effort to somehow find out how and where he is, and what help I might be able to give him and his family. The more God gives us, the more we are obliged to share our good fortune with others.

Sunday, November 21
12 *Kislev*

I felt badly about the money that I lost on Friday until I realized that I probably dropped it in an area where almost anyone who found it had a greater need for it than me.

My daughter recently showed great *derech eretz*. The owner of the pizza-place opposite the one where she works offered her more money to come and work for him, but she refused. She said that her present boss was the first to give her a job and that he shows much consideration for his workers.

The rabbi of my *shul* loves to learn and places supreme value in it, as does the Torah-learning community as a whole. However, in his learning and delaying prayers as a result, he causes much inconvenience to others, especially to those who have worked during the day, and are eager to go home. In another *shul*, the *gabbai* always makes sure the prayers begin on time, even interrupting the rabbi in order to ensure that it happens. Which is the *derech eretz*?

Is it *derech eretz* to go to my publisher with this journal when I have stopped doing the work I have a contract with him for? I don't know. It is possible that the meeting would help give me the push I need to complete the work I have been contracted to write.

How a person reacts when they are pressured and have a great deal to do is a test of *derech eretz*. I was interrupted from my work frequently this morning, but I did my best to overcome my own impatience. I promised to help a prospective author write a passage for the back of his book. I also arranged a time to go to *shul* with Israel R. next *erev* Shabbat.

I cannot help feeling that deep down, I am inadequate in the area of *derech eretz*. Even when I am doing something worthwhile, I often feel resentment and impatience. I do not have the kind of spontaneous care for and love of others that the great masters of *derech eretz* had. This is because my focus in life is primarily on my writing, which may be my most mistaken judgment of all.

Monday, November 22
13 *Kislev*

At this moment, I could be at a *brit milah* of an acquaintance's grandson. I am not going, however, so that I can make some progress with my work. I am not really close with this family in any way. Moreover, they know many, many people and I doubt my presence will really be missed.

Tuesday, November 23
14 *Kislev*

This morning I have been thrown off balance by many small things that have gone wrong. For instance, I left a telephone message with a wrong number. The problem is that when one works in haste, one often aggravates the situation by making even more mistakes. I now try to calm myself now with these words. I want to call my holy teacher, but I fear that he will sense my impatience.

Last night, Rabbi Rakeffet related the following story about Rav Soloveitchik: a young man who had just been orphaned was a friend of Rabbi Rakeffet at *yeshiva*. He decided to devote his time to learning Torah and not go to college in order to gain a profession. The young Rabbi Rakeffet told the Rav about this friend. The Rav told him to bring the young man to him immediately. He told him, "I am not sure I know what *derech eretz* is, but I am sure you must go to college this year." The young man then said that registration was already closed. The Rav told the young man to go to the registrar and that it would be all right. He then sent Rabbi Rakeffet to the registrar with an instruction from him that the young man be admitted to any class he wanted. This story was told by Rabbi Rakeffet in order to demonstrate that the Rav did not, as many now claim, instruct all of his students to learn Torah exclusively and not work for a living. It was also related to demonstrate the kind of understanding and wisdom that the Rav had in helping his pupils.

I did my best today for David B.'s son at the unveiling of his tombstone. There were only seven adults there. After the reading of the *azkarah*, we stood and spoke about David B. I mentioned his giving of *tzedakah*. He was a truly generous person. His son, daughter-in-law, and two grandchildren (only one of whom he lived to see) were there as well.

It was from my father that I learned the practice of visiting those who seem to have been forgotten or left out in some way. It may sound obvious, but one major obligation in *derech eretz* is keeping in touch with people one cares about. It is about showing them that one has not forgotten them or eradicated them from mind and heart.

Wednesday, November 24
15 *Kislev*

There is an inner violation of *derech eretz* when our thoughts are impure. It is probable that this area does not fall within the traditional scope of *derech eretz*, which concentrates on our relationships with others. I can think of a number of areas in my life in which I somehow sense myself inwardly violating *derech eretz*, though no one knows about it, except for myself and God. I am thinking, first and foremost, of the realm of sexual thoughts and desires. My thoughts centering on financial greed are also questionable. Envy, hatred, spite and jealousy figure into my daily thoughts. When I laugh at people internally, mocking and ridiculing them in my thoughts, I know that I am behaving incorrectly.

Does achieving perfection in *derech eretz* mean one must have a dull, boring personality? I often discourage certain people I know from relating off-color jokes. I may feign amusement at such jokes, but I really dislike them. Hearing these jokes makes me feel doubly wrong – for allowing myself to listen to what I don't enjoy hearing and for being two-faced. How hypocritical should one be in order to avoid offending someone?

The inner anxiety, tension and guilt, which so often constitute my mental state, contradict the ideal of *derech eretz* in some way. This is because one inevitably transmits these feelings to others in one's tone and one's way of responding to them. These feelings send a message of impatience, whether or not I want such a message to be sent.

I must undergo an inner transformation that I somehow do not feel myself capable of. To be a harmonious, calm and open person is something I aspire towards, but I doubt that I will even come close.

Two widows called this morning: Ruth F. called to give me her son's address. The second call was from Mrs. B., who wanted to know where to send an article she had written. In both cases, I was polite and patient, but I could have been more helpful. I could have made an appointment to go and see Ruth F. I could have elaborated more in my response to Mrs. B. There is a value in doing more than what is technically necessary. This is yet another proof that I am not at that higher level of *derech eretz*. I give to others, but not always in a complete way.

How should we react when people are ugly and rude to us? *Pirkei Avot* teaches us to be slow to anger. But what about when we aren't? And when our efforts at understanding, politeness and kindness are treated with contempt, when we are ridiculed, scorned and humiliated? Do we still have to show consideration for others then?

Isn't it *derech eretz* to put people in their place, to be assertive and fight back in self-defense?

In a war for survival, when the enemy is ruthless and cruel, where is *derech eretz?*

Thursday, November 25
16 *Kislev*

I just made two calls to find out how two people are. Menahem was not in *shul* this morning, so I called his home and spoke with his wife. It turns out that he is so worried about her condition that he himself feels weak.

I also spoke with another friend who is suffering from a sore throat, an infection that resulted from a minor operation. I called and asked if I could help him in any way. He, in turn, asked if he could help me. I thoughtlessly told him about a problem I was having with my computer. He was about to come over to help me, but I insisted that he not leave his home. I do not want him to exert himself when he is not feeling well.

The prayer leader at the second *minyan* raced through the prayers this morning. He led the prayers in a flat monotone, as though the words had no meaning. I remarked on this to the *gabbai* and he said that this man is a nervous person, that he will not be leading the prayers for much longer, and that although he had spoken to him about it in the past, there had not been any change. I don't know how correct it was for me to involve the *gabbai*, a third party, in my criticism of the prayer leader. This is especially true when the issue at hand was my dislike of the mannerisms of the person. Nonetheless, I felt that it was my responsibility to articulate my opinion on this matter on behalf of the *tsibbur*. We must remember that we are praying to God and should therefore not simply be racing through the prayers.

Friday, November 26
17 *Kislev*

Yesterday, I called Seymour K. to find out how he was doing. I had not called him to thank him for the invitation that he had sent me for his second son's *bar mitzvah*. He was very glad to hear from me, but I could sense his loneliness. He has a very good wife, but he is immobile and unable to get out. He used to be such an active person, a real doer. I know that it will be difficult, but I am going to arrange a day when I will go and see him.

I am somewhat shaken up. I went down Strauss Street towards King George Street and saw Yigal sitting there. I gave him a blessing upon his return. He said that he had been to the United States and that the liver that was supposed to be transplanted was not suitable for him because of his rare blood type. He asked me if I knew of anyone with an apartment who could take his family in because his landlord had just evicted them for not paying rent. I debated as to whether or not I should pay the rent for them, but I couldn't decide. One reason for my hesitation was that I was sure he had told me that he was going to Romania for the transplant and was not entirely convinced that I could trust his word. He also told me that his landlord was a terrible person. When I excused myself for asking, he told me more details of his story: his former wife is a convert who he had met at university in America. He said that upon learning about his illness, she had returned both to America and to Christianity. He also told me that his oldest son had been killed in a car accident. To this alleged catalogue of woes, I gave no immediate answer. I gave him a sum in *tzedakah* that would probably exceed the amount that he would collect during the entire day, which eased my conscience. It did not solve his problem, though. He and his children will spend Shabbat sleeping in their *shul*. I now have to see if I can get him some real assistance. I thought of two possible people that I could ask for help. He also asked me for my telephone number and so I gave it to him.

Motzei Shabbat, November 27
18 *Kislev*

The first thing that I did this *motzei* Shabbat was to call Reuven C., my social worker friend. He wants to come with me to see about helping Yigal. He can also try to verify his story by speaking with the social worker of the district in which Yigal lives. He knows of emergency funds. He told me that I should have never simply given money to him directly, but should rather have paid a third party involved.

I was troubled throughout Shabbat at the thought of Yigal and his family without a home. I still am troubled to a degree, but less so after speaking to Reuven C., for now I feel that there is a way of possibly finding him more substantial help, and to therefore address his situation more realistically.

Sunday, November 28
19 *Kislev*

If Yigal's story is true and there are therefore three children without shelter, then I am sure that there is a kind person from their *shul* who will take them in. I suppose I should not be so certain in this presumption.

I feel as if God has given me a great test here and that I have somehow failed.

I received a request for a donation from a learning institution in Jerusalem that I occasionally go to and where I have studied in the past. I ordinarily do not give money to this institution on the grounds that: 1) I do not agree with certain policy practices of this institution (although I do believe that it generally achieves more good than bad). 2) It already has the support and sponsorship of a large group of Americans, many of whom are wealthy. I believe that I should save my resources for people and institutions who are more needy. I do not know if I am correct in this attitude.

I have been waiting for Yigal to call for about an hour, but he has not called. Is it time for my imagination to run away with me as it already has? I can't help thinking now of the student who came to Buber who Buber put off, and who then committed suicide. I am very concerned about Yigal. I feel that even though I have been there for him in his more desperate moments, I should not have put him off – he needed help right then and there. Maybe I should call the hospitals and see if he has been admitted. Perhaps it is already too late. Perhaps he became sick from being out in the cold. Perhaps the children got sick from not being in a warm home.

I imagined all this even then. What I probably should have done on Friday was simply make him drop everything, come with me to see the children and the landlord so as to verify his claim and pay the rent.

I called Reuven C. and updated him that Yigal had not called, and told him that he should not wait. He said that he would be at home all night anyway and that I could call him whenever I wished. I believe he sensed the guilt and uncertainty in my tone.

Monday, November 29
20 *Kislev*

Yigal finally called at nine o'clock this morning. He said that he was in Geulah at *Yad L'Achim* and that his children were in a private home in the neighborhood. He said that he had received 1,400 shekels from *Bituach Leumi* and that he needed to pay his landlord an additional 2,200 shekels. He said that he was trying to receive the sum from *Yad L'Achim*. I asked him to call me back in fifteen minutes. I then called Reuven C. He seemed to be distracted and not really interested, but said that he would check Yigal's story out with the social worker whose name I had given him. He also told me not to give Yigal any cash, that if I paid the rent I should pay it directly to the landlord. When Yigal called back, I offered to go with him to help pay the rent. He said that he had received the money from *Yad L'Achim*, and now did not need money for rent, but had no money to live on. He told me that he would be on Strauss Street the next day. I made an appointment to meet him there. I thought about bringing him *tzedakah* money. About fifteen minutes later, he called back again and said that the landlord would not accept the money but wanted three months rent in advance and security guarantees. Yigal said *Yad L'Achim* had found him another family with whom to place his children, in Ramot. He was about to pick his children up from Geulah and take them to this new house. He gave me the address and phone number. I told him that I would meet up with him on Friday. I figured that since he did not pay the rent money he was in no urgent need of cash.

All of this is very confusing. I do not know what is truth and what is not. I do not know how best to help him. The *tzedakah* and welfare organizations can help him in ways that I cannot – the best way that I can help him is to find an organization that can help him. It would make a great difference to me if I knew that his story was by and large true – that he is a single father taking care of three children and that he is suffering from a life-threatening illness. I had initially thought about taking his family in myself. Of course this is impossible – my daughter is at home. I am also reluctant to sacrifice time away from my work. I am just not generous enough. This illustrates how I am a limited person in my ability to give, in my devotion to helping others.

I could go to the address that Yigal gave me and investigate, but I will not. The fact that he gave me the address, phone number and name of the social worker indicates that he is telling the truth. Also, if he was interested in money and only money, he would not have informed me of the latest development, and would have allowed today's meeting to go through as planned.

What is the best thing for this man's children? This is the question the social worker must have considered. As I understand it, she wanted the children to be put in an institution, and there may be no other choice. What is my role in this? To help Yigal hold on to his children when this may not be in their best interests?

The children are being raised as Orthodox, even *charedi* Jews, yet may not even be halachically Jewish. This is another element to be considered. In a way, I am afraid to meet the children, and begin to feel a responsibility towards them. I do not want a life-long involvement. This again reveals my true lack of charity, my falling short of the higher level of *derech eretz*.

Tuesday, November 30
21 *Kislev*

I received a call from a good friend this morning. He has left his wife of thirty years and is living with another woman. I told him the truth, that his betrayal will have negative consequences for his children and grandchildren. I implied that he should be thinking about his family. He asked, in effect, "But what about myself?" In response, I told him that as a responsible, religious person, what he is doing will cause him great inner turmoil. I also told him that he could call me any time. He indicated that he is sure of his decision and is content right now.

I spent a good part of the early morning thinking about Yigal and his problems. Later on in the morning, the holy teacher called me. I told him briefly about the situation with Yigal. He recommended that I withdraw a bit and give myself some time to think clearly. I understand that he is trying to help me and protect me from a situation that he is suspicious of.

I am now wondering whether or not I spoke strongly and candidly enough with my friend who has walked out on his marriage and family. I should have told him that he is doing something wrong and that he will regret it later. Then again, I don't think at this point, and at his age, my friend is someone to be lectured. I hope that he will somehow reconcile with his wife. In fact, it is his wife who needs the consolation and help at this point, but I do not really know her. He is the one I am friendly with.

Twice this year, I gave the kind of expansive, blessing-greetings that my holy teacher gives. Unfortunately, bad news came to these people soon after. I do not believe my greetings were responsible for this, but I also believe that I should be more careful about what I do. What is appropriate for others, for those with the true Carlebach spirit, is not necessarily appropriate for me. I am a more restrained, cautious and fearful type of person.

I have developed the habit of avoiding real work in order to engage in all kinds of learning and reading of other books. This is a truly bad habit – one has a responsibility to oneself to carry out the tasks that must be performed on a daily basis.

My daughter asked the question that I believe is most important in the case of Yigal: what is best for his children? If he is living with a sword at his neck, why didn't he first and foremost search for a home for them?

I was shaken by what I saw last night on *Politika*. The topics up for discussion were the whole unemployment question, the issue of foreign workers, and the problems of crime, drugs and prostitution. There was shouting, accusations, verbal violence and much ugliness.

Another alarming incident was reported yesterday in the paper by Eitan Haber, a journalist. Recently, as he was driving, he saw a blind man about to cross the street at a dangerous crossing. Five or six people were there, yet not one of them tried to stop him. The indifference, the apathy of it all, is shocking. On the other hand, from what I have personally observed, people here are generally careful to help the blind when they need to cross a street or identify a bus as the correct one. I know that I usually take blind people who ask me for assistance to whatever destination they are heading.

It seems to me that many new immigrants from the former Soviet Union do not always seem to display the kind of *derech eretz* demanded by traditional Judaism. Some of them have sealed, expressionless faces, and have no *sever panim yafot*, no warm greeting to each and every one. Perhaps this can be explained by their long-term fear that the person who may be waiting to greet them is a KGB agent.

Wednesday, December 1
22 *Kislev*

I know that my friend's abandonment of his family is none of my business. I do not know what is going on and what has gone on in the past. Nonetheless, knowing a bit about his character, I am certain that he has not made a wise decision. I myself cannot comprehend how a person can toss aside all that they have built in a lifetime and bring so much pain and disorder to the life of the one who has devoted everything of herself to him over the years, not to speak of the damage incurred to the children. I think it is a sign of the times that even such a good person as this friend can stray in this way. I hinted my views to him during our conversation, but did not tell him so directly.

I received a pamphlet from Rabbi Greenberg that contained an excerpt from the book we worked on together. He sent it to me with kind words. He has treated me with such respect and consideration.

I asked Yigal what I could do to help him. At first, there was no answer. I then repeated my question. He said, "Anything. Clothes. Money. Even a kind word." I noticed that he lowered his voice when he said "money" and so I suspect that money is what he really wants. I can give him some money, but how much? And for how long?

I can think of other forms of assistance that he needs: first and foremost, a liver for his transplant – I cannot do that. A supply of his rare blood type – I cannot do that either. An arrangement for his family, for his children to be properly taken care of – I do not know how to do that. I can try, but it is really the responsibility of the local organizations to help him. Reinstalling him back into his old apartment? This may be what he needs most, but I am not sure. What really is the situation with his children? Perhaps there is no choice and I must go and check, see how they are, what they need, and if there is something I can do to help.

It is now around 8:15 in the evening. I just reread this journal, which is something that I have been meaning to do for some time now. I am having a change of heart about whether or not to submit it for publication. Maybe I will just give it to the publisher and ask him what he thinks. My instinct tells me that even though what I have catalogued seems to be of trivial content, some value can be derived from it. I don't know.

I had been thinking of going to Ruth F.'s house tonight to pay her a visit. The holy teacher was also giving a class that I said I might attend. I hope some people showed up. It could be said that by staying home and reading this work instead of visiting Ruth F. or attending the class I was looking out for my own interests, but I felt so tired and weak. I do not believe it would have been the right thing to go out and make myself sick.

This afternoon, I spent a great deal of time writing a response to an article that criticized Israel in a biased light. I now seem to spend more time on letter-writing than I ever have before. I feel that I must try to make some contribution, however small, to the greater Jewish community. The problems we face are so great and so many.

Thursday, December 2
23 *Kislev*

I am considering writing a letter to my unfaithful friend, in which I will tell him that his abandonment of his wife not only destroys his family, but ruins the image of himself as he has portrayed it over the years. He is no longer the "nice guy," or even a decent human being, but is now something else entirely.

I have done nothing about Yigal. I expect to see him tomorrow. I will bring him *tzedakah* money. I do not know what I will do if he asks me for three months rent.

Friday, December 3
24 *Kislev, Erev Chanukah*

I looked for Yigal after Rabbi Eisen's class. I sat and spoke with him. He said that he might have to have an operation on his leg. He told me that the doctors said that he should not continue to sleep in a storeroom. I asked him about his children and what he has done to find them a good home. He said that he has tried – the family that are looking after them are feeding and clothing them. I asked him about himself and he said that he could get a one-room hotel apartment. I gave him all of my *tzedakah* funds so that he could do this. I also told him that I would try to inquire around about a family who could care for his children.

I then went to see the former dentist. I found out that he has one daughter who lives in St. Petersburg with her husband and children. They do not want to come to Israel. He is a warm, appreciative person. I also gave him Chanukah money.

On my way back home, I saw Israel R. He said that he has almost no movement in his legs. He is finished with physiotherapy. I offered him the name of the chiropractor and said that I would pay for his treatment. He asked, "Why should you pay?" He also said that he is not independent as he lives in his niece's house. I told him to ask her and that I would send the chiropractor if she agreed.

Rabbi Eisen taught us this morning that true fulfillment comes from a life of responsibility, strong values and *mitzvot*. This is certainly true for me, but I do not know how to transmit this message to others. Also, I do not consistently follow this path myself.

Motzei Shabbat, December 4
25 *Kislev, First Day of Chanukah*

Yigal called to tell me that he has found an apartment, but needs more money. I told him that I would meet him and his prospective landlord tomorrow. He needs eight hundred shekels more. The feeling of being taken advantage of now prevails. I will try to help him, and then inform him that I wish not to be bothered by him for a while.

I am starting to feel increasingly used and tread upon.

On Friday night, in *shul*, there was a harangue request for money for a worthwhile cause, the providing of Shabbat meals for people in hospitals. Where was the festive spirit appropriate for Chanukah? True, it is a worthy cause, but it certainly was not the right time to *schnor* for it. In any case, I intimated that I would make a contribution.

I wanted to walk past Israel R. Instead, I listened to his story again. I repeated my offer of the chiropractor. Truly helping him, though, is to give him attention and to listen to him. He thanked me so profusely that I was both embarrassed and moved.

I stopped by to see Ruth F. She is such a good and intelligent woman. I enjoyed visiting her. She is now volunteering by teaching English to students at the university. Her son received my letter.

Because I gave all of my *tzedakah* funds to Yigal, I did not have cash to give to Israel G.'s family, to whom I had intended giving. The truth is, I still do not know whether or not I should give them money. I like them a lot and I would like to help them, but I do not know if a few hundred shekels is what they really need. Their financial situation, as far as I understand, is dire. They have four children from their marriage and two older children from the wife's previous marriage. I gave them money once after they asked for a loan. I am still considering giving them money for Chanukah, but am not sure. There is a question of helping them to retain some pride. Is it *derech eretz* to help people when one is not certain if their reaction will be happiness?

One of the factors that is prompting me to help Yigal is a certain guilt. I have more money than I need for myself. I know of others who have less than what they need. I therefore give from what I have so that they too can have. But is this enough? And what happens when I am not certain if it really helps?

Sunday, December 5
26 Kislev, Second Day of Chanukah

Writing this work makes me more zealous, and perhaps more rigid, in the area of *derech eretz*. The knowledge that my actions are being observed, so to speak, causes me to be on my best behavior.

I try to banish thoughts that Yigal acts in an unappreciative manner from my mind. He calls at all times, not thinking that he may be interrupting, asks for more money immediately after I have given him money, and does not even say thank-you. I have excused him not only because of his illness and problems, but because he comes from another kind of world. But is this right? Is his behavior acceptable? A person has the right to save themselves. If I sense that Yigal's demands are upsetting me too much, infringing too much on my peace of mind (as they already have), then I might stop helping him. I will help him today, and in so doing will hopefully free myself of him for a while. But my gut feeling is that this feat will not be so simple. I will probably end up devoting more time to him than I would really like. This might constitute a violation of my true self.

My thoughts are along the following lines: "You have been given so much. How can you not give to and help others who have been given so much less?" It was this attitude that resulted in a rift with my childhood friend – I let him know that I might be able to help him and he found the opportunity. I gave him what he asked for and he did not return the sum within the agreed upon time. I waited for a long time, but then he stopped answering my phone calls, even after I intended to forget about the loan. The conclusion that I have come to is not that one should not give, but that one should give wisely.

I think that Yigal expects to meet me and receive cash in hand as he has on previous occasions. Instead, he is going to meet someone who is going to accompany him to his prospective landlord and pay the additional money that he needs in order to rent an apartment directly to him.

Helping others often puts me in contact with the sick, the disturbed, the poor and the dependent – ailments that I myself most fear.

Monday, December 6
27 Kislev, Third Day of Chanukah

I went to meet Yigal yesterday. He was on time. I said that I was ready to go with him to meet his landlord and give him a check for the additional amount of money. Yigal said that the landlord had told him that he could not meet today because of a funeral he had to go to. I told Yigal that I would be ready to meet with him at any day at any time, and would provide a check then. I told him that I would not give him cash on the spot. He said that he would see if he could get a donation from a *gemach* fund, and then would not need my help. I inquired about his health. He said that he has cancer of the liver and that he also needs two kidney transplants. I asked him about his children. He said they were on trips with the family that they are staying with. He showed me a vial with the medicine with which he is injected. He said that he has to pay for each injection. I asked about medical health funds and he said that he does not receive any assistance.

As the day wore on, I felt more and more guilty that I had not just given him cash. Perhaps he is lying, but he is obviously in great need, and is certainly sick. Nonetheless I felt that giving him cash again at that point would not have been right and would have constituted a kind of blackmailing.

I waited for Yigal's call in the evening, ready to meet with his landlord and help him. When he called he told me that he had received a donation from a *gemach*, that he now had the money to pay for the apartment, and that he was to meet with the prospective landlord tomorrow. I just listened. I thought of offering future aid, but did not.

In the evening, a person to whom I owe so much and a true *ba'al chesed*, Kadish W., called. We had not spoken for a long time. We spoke about his teaching. I told him the story of Yigal. He advised me that I should distance myself from him. I got the impression that he felt that I was being taken advantage of. He knows a great deal about cancer since he nursed both his parents through their final years with the disease. I told him that Yigal had said that he had cancer of the liver. Kadish told me that there is little chance of survival with such a cancer, and that a person suffering from it would not be able to walk around freely.

My two spiritual mentors have both indicated that I should distance myself from Yigal, yet I cannot bear the thought of someone dying with no one to help him. I want to help if I can.

When there is no spirit in prayers and there is no one singing, I try to raise my voice and sing louder. How I miss the times when prayer was conducted with ardent fervor and strength! All too often, I hear that my voice is the only one singing. What has happened to us?

Tuesday, December 7
28 Kislev, Fourth Day of Chanukah

Last night I went to the funeral of Rav Zimmer's father. He was ninety-four years old when he passed away. I do not remember having heard a more dignified, beautiful appreciation of a son for his father. This is a family that is originally from Frankfurt and so were no doubt influenced by Rav Hirsch's approach of "Torah and *derech eretz*." Rav Zimmer spoke of his father's appreciation for the aesthetic side of Judaism, his love and preservation of the *nusach* of his own community, his *torat adam* in showing respect to each and every human being, his adopting the middle way, Rambam's approach, in not going to extremes, his love for and dedication to his family, and his willingness to give and sacrifice everything for his son.

I know that Rav Zimmer is a person of great *derech eretz* and I expected the funeral would be conducted in such a manner, yet I was still deeply moved by it. He is the kind of righteous person who restores one's faith in the special ethical quality of the Jewish people.

I was in a rush this morning when I met Israel R. Nonetheless, I could not pass by without saying a few words. He was sitting outside on a bench near his house. I spoke with him. He repeated the story of what happened to his family, how in one day they were all murdered by the Nazis. I can see that the loss of his family has shaped and formed his existence. Nothing will ever change this reality. Even if he had succeeded in building a family of his own, the nightmare of his past would still lurk in the background. I will listen to his story again and again for as long as I have to.

There are so many people out there who suffer incredible pain, a brokenness that can never be completely healed. I sometimes wish that I could just run away from it all. How much can a person give and how much can they take? One alleged reason for the Kotzker Rebbe's final years being spent in silence is that he was overwhelmed by the suffering and problems of his *chassidim*. This depth of feeling and compassion challenges the classical image of a correct person, steeped in *derech eretz*. The extent of human suffering would seem to demand that anyone with a true heart would go beyond the boundaries of conventionally acceptable behavior in order to help others. They would give so much of themselves that they would lose all sense of their own private well-being. Only that this is not the Jewish ideal. I think that this idea is demonstrated by the fact that a person is prohibited from giving more than twenty percent of his income to charity, and also supports the notion that one has to put one's own life before the life of another in a case where it is only possible to save one life.

Wednesday, December 8
29 Kislev, Fifth Day of Chanukah

On the way back from the post office, I heard that the widow of my teacher, Rabbi Pearl, had a stroke. It happened on the same day as her husband's *yahrtzeit*. I tried to call a few people to find out how she was. I will go to the hospital to visit her. Aside from being a true *eshet chayil* to Rabbi Pearl, she is a good, modest person for whom I have great affection.

Last night, after Rabbi Wein's lecture, I took a ride home with Hannah R. and her friend. Hannah kept us waiting, though, because she was talking to a woman who seemed very disturbed. Later she said that she wondered if she had done the right thing by agreeing to listen to the woman, who claimed that she had no one to talk to. I was surprised at how confused Hannah R. was – she is a woman of great experience; a mother of four and a grandmother of over twenty. She said that she was thinking of a story in which a person had refused to help another person and then the disturbed person committed suicide. I told her the Buber story, which is a similar scenario. I also told her about my recent attempt to help someone which had then become very problematic. I told her that I was confident that she would know how to be kind, yet draw the line.

I made a *shivah* visit to the Zimmer Family. On the way out, Rav Zimmer thanked me for coming. I said something like, "Israel would be blessed by having more people like your father and yourself." I probably should not have said that. I expect that Rav Zimmer is the kind of man who is embarrassed by such talk.

After the *shivah* visit, I abandoned my plans to go to the bookstores and took the bus across town to see Anita instead. She had a mild stroke and has problems with her left arm and leg but her mind, thank God, is perfectly lucid. Her daughter, three of her grandchildren, and her oldest son were there. I had a good talk with them all. I feel that having a sympathetic non-family member there was good for them.

Yigal called again and told me that he rented an apartment not in Beit Yisrael, but rather in another *charedi* district. He asked me if I knew of someone who could help him buy a refrigerator and a hot-plate for Shabbat. I said that I didn't. By answering him in this negative manner, I feel that I had somehow come to accept the advice of my friends and let him find help from others now. On the one hand, I am sorry about this, but my suspicion is that Yigal has lied to me (which does not, however, mean that he is not in need). I also find that his insistent telephone calls and demands show a certain lack of consideration on his part. But then again, I have never found myself in a position where I have been as desperate, so I am in no position to judge him

I reluctantly sat down next to Rav A. on the bus today. I somehow knew there would be a request of some kind and I was not in the mood to give to him. He began talking about Rambam and the tipping of the scales with each deed we do. Was this a hint for me to give him *tzedakah*? He told me that the Tax Authority says that he owes fifty thousand shekels. He also has other debts. He has three married children and five others who are not married yet. I did not offer anything. This had nothing to do with my bitter experience of paying my childhood friend's taxes and not speaking to him ever since. Rather, it was because of the feeling I had that it is not for me to bail out all those who get themselves into trouble.

I would still like to give money to one family from the neighborhood for Chanukah. But again, as they have not asked, I wonder if I should.

In the hospital, Anita was in a room with four other people, all of them Arabs. One was a girl who lay silently by herself. Another was an old woman whose family made tremendous noise and jumped around, showing no consideration for the other patients. Again, the *derech eretz* conflicts which arise from two clashing cultures.

Thursday, December 9
Rosh Chodesh Tevet, Sixth Day of Chanukah

I cannot help dwelling on the irony that the renewal of Israel's negotiations with Syria falls out on Chanukah. These talks are predicated on Israel's conceding the Golan Heights and Chanukah is about our war against the Hellenistic Syrian-Greek culture. There seems to be an obliviousness to the religious sensitivities of the holiday.

My holy teacher says that Rambam teaches that those who beg in the streets should only be given small sums of money. Perhaps there is an assumption here about the character of those who beg in the streets, or what they will do with the money.

Smoking in hospitals, even in designated areas (where the smoke nonetheless travels to other places), seems to signify a true lack of *derech eretz*. It seems to me that public-health officials who tolerate such a policy are truly negligent in their duties. This smoking occurs at Hadassah Hospital in Har Hatsofim and in Hadassah in Ein Kerem as well. I think that I will write to the directors of these hospitals in order to protest.

Friday, December 10
Rosh Chodesh Tevet Bet, Seventh Day of Chanukah

I visited Anita again yesterday. I happened to take the no. 9 bus back home, which stops at the hospital. If not for that, I probably would not have visited her. I brought her apple juice, which she was running out of. I do not think she particularly needed my visit in other respects.

The *gabbai* who has been away this week returned. I was sure that he would want to take the *amud*, as I know that he enjoys doing so and had not led prayers the entire week he had been absent. It was my turn, however, as I usually lead the prayers on Fridays. In my mind, I had already accused him of taking away an honor that was mine. He did not do so, of course – I davvaned. My thoughts created unnecessary ugliness.

When acting as a *shaliach tsibbur*, one should not go so fast as to show contempt for the prayers. Likewise, one must not go so slow as to place a burden on the public. The answer is the middle way.

The prevalent mentality here of "you must fight for everything" usually means that one ends up battling needlessly for things that are ultimately of very little importance. Does the fact that Israelis have had to fight for their survival so many times in their short history create a readiness to fight over every little thing?

Sunday, December 12
3 Tevet

We are told that the people of Israel are to be a "light unto the nations," but in actual fact, we have much we could learn from others. At times, we seem to act in contradiction to our own paradigm.

What I just read in Rabbi Wagschall's book seems to make complete sense: a guest may not take the liberty of inviting an additional guest to the host's home. I must instruct my son about this lesson with regard to the invitation he recently received from his cousins, who are themselves guests in this case.

Is it *derech eretz* to send a group of people to settle land, build communities, invest years of their life in a place and have them raise their children there, only to then suddenly tell them that they must, for the good of the public, move? Can this be justified even in light of the fact that it is being done to achieve peace? Is it naive to expect the government to behave with consideration? I think not. I think that almost any action can be judged in terms of whether or not it is in accord with the ideals of *derech eretz*. There is a right and wrong way of doing things, no matter if we are talking about an individual, a group or a government.

The recent change in the electoral system here, which enables people to have one vote for the Prime Minister and another for the party of their choice, has aggravated one of the most pressing problems in Israel today – tribalism. It encourages what we see more and more lately, whole communities fighting for their own narrow interests without considering the effects of their actions on the whole nation. This could be the Sephardi *charedi* tribe of Shas, the Russian tribe of new immigrants, the Ashkenazi *charedim*, the ruling, elite tribe of secular Ashkenazim, or even the Arab tribe. Focusing solely on one's own group's needs indicates a failure in *derech eretz* towards all the other people living here, towards the state of Israel, and towards the well-being of the Jewish people as a whole.

Derech eretz is about cooperation amongst communities as well as individuals.

There has to be a balance between protecting one's own interests as an individual and showing concern for the community as a whole. It is not a question of perfunctory, robotic actions. Selfishness and contempt have become increasingly evident in Israeli politics in recent years. We are witnessing a further distancing from the ideals of the *chalutzim*, the original pioneers, who promoted a sense of communal responsibility.

Monday, December 13
4 *Tevet*

Back to my own petty decisions: what is the right thing to do? Should I go to the demonstration in support of keeping the Golan even though I am not certain which way I will ultimately vote, despite the fact that deep down, I support the fight to retain it, or should I go to the poetry reading, which I was not invited to. Or maybe I should go to the Torah class, where I will probably learn something of significance.

I just called Menahem and learned that he has a cold. I feared much worse. I feel an added responsibility towards him and his wife as they do not have the support of so many people, especially since they left the Conservative synagogue.

I feel guilty about not having been in contact with the Goren family. I said I would call the daughter and have not reached her yet. I tried twice, and was relieved when there was no answer. I should try again this week.

Tuesday, December 14
5 *Tevet*

I went to the poetry reading in the end. I looked at the magazine from which they were reading and saw that my piece had not been included. I spoke briefly to a couple of people I know and left. I then went to the *shiur* on *parashat Vayigash*, which I enjoyed and learned a lot from. Was it correct of me to leave the poetry reading in the middle? I don't know – I just didn't want to be a spectator at a show that I knew I would not enjoy. I did not do this out of spite – even if my piece had been chosen to appear in the magazine, I would not have read my own work aloud.

I seem to have forgotten Yigal. Sitting outside yesterday at a vegetarian restaurant on Jaffa Street, I was bothered twice for money by a man in his twenties who is a regular feature around the area. I have, on occasion, given him small amounts of money, but I generally refuse him because he is rude and comes up to each person, putting his hand in his or her face. He seems strong and healthy – and he looks like a villain.

I could have refused him in a nicer way but, feeling guilty for not giving, I was rude to him in return. All this makes me ashamed. I will probably give him *tzedakah* the next time he asks me, even though I don't like him.

I must work on learning how to say "no." I hate saying no to anything, not just when it comes to requests for money.

Thursday, December 16
7 *Tevet*

My visit to Anita seemed to improve her mood. Strangely, what helped was not my presence so much as the newspaper I brought her. I tried to visit her again yesterday but came at the wrong time, and could not get in. I will try to go today.

I no longer attend the *shiurim* of Rabbi R. I nonetheless gave one of the *gabbaim* money for him this morning. I did this because I learned from Rabbi R. for many years and because I do not want the *shiur* to be stopped due to lack of funds. It would be a shame for those who enjoy it to lose it.

Last night I spent the evening watching a movie. Why do I feel guilty about this and consider it a violation of *derech eretz*? Because there were people I could have called instead. I chose to amuse myself at the expense of possibly giving something to others. And, as is often the case, I ended up not enjoying myself, but having a lingering feeling of guilt over time wasted on what turned out to be pretty shallow stuff.

The current Prime Minister of Israel acts with *derech eretz* in many ways. I think of how, before going to meet with the Syrian Foreign Minister, he sat for a few hours with the leaders of the Golan community. He could only have expected to hear painful criticism and objections from them. I feel that he will choose the course of action that he deems correct, but will do his best to help them at the same time, not simply abandoning them during this tense time. He also seems to me to be a person who keeps his promises, who has long-term goals and works hard to achieve them. I recognize these good qualities in him even though I do not agree with some of the fundamental principles behind his policies.

One reason that I did not rush to the Golan demonstration is because I am not absolutely sure that I am opposed to the agreement that may be agreed upon with Syria. Although it is probable that I will not agree with it, I won't really know until it is fully formulated. I didn't want to be at the demonstration on false pretences, being part of a group which is so adamantly opposed to any possible agreement.

I just received a copy of a major review written on the book by Rabbi Greenberg and myself. There were some very kind words about my role in the book, and also a very sympathetic approach to the work and life of Rabbi Greenberg. And yet I believe that the review fell short. It related to the personality of Rabbi Greenberg without objectively addressing the hard contents, the philosophy of the work.

My continued avoidance of the Goren work is a major failing in *derech eretz*. I should perhaps call the publisher and tell him that I have given up, although that would not strictly be true. I don't know why I can't persist with it.

I did not feel like running downtown this morning. I wanted to read and study *The Religious Thought of Hasidism*, by Norman Lamm. Still, I ran downtown after taking my daughter to her lesson in order to help Rabbi Eisen, Yigal and the former dentist. I was rewarded for my zeal by a profound lesson that Rabbi Eisen taught: the reward for a *mitzvah* is the *mitzvah* itself, as performing kind deeds is the ultimate gift in life.

I went to see Yigal the *shiur*. I intended to give him a smaller amount of money than I usually do, a symbolic gesture that I had not forgotten him and did not blame him for having lied (which it seems that he did). He was not there. I wonder if he has become very sick. I will call the hospitals to check if he is there.

I then went to see the former dentist. I caught him at a moment when he was deep in thought. He looked despondent. When he turned and saw me, his face lit up. I had planned to give him a certain sum of money and did. He was, as always, too grateful. I should have given him a larger sum, a larger bill. It was as if an opportunity presented itself in that moment and I did not grab it. I will try to make amends next week. It hurt me to see him look so distraught.

I believe that I am getting carried away with the cats. First there is the one my daughter brought into the house when it had been abandoned and was about to die. Then there is another one that follows me when I walk home, to whom I give food. Now there is a third cat; small, grey and blind in one eye, who sits at the front of our house, crying for food. I usually do give it some. I think I am correct in giving food to the cats, but I think that caring for animals should be the job of those who have a natural affinity for, and closeness with, them.

In his shiur, Rabbi Eisen distinguished between a *tzaddik*, who does all he is supposed to do according to the law, and a *chassid*, who lives *lifnim meshurat hadin* and therefore senses what the right thing to do is in any given situation.

Sunday, December 19
10 *Tevet*

I arrived in *shul* early this morning, at 5:30 A.M. We had difficulty forming a *minyan* for the early part of the prayers. Had I not been there, I would have been guilty of foisting the responsibility of completing a *minyan* onto others.

I just called Hadassah Hospital in Ein Kerem to see if Yigal is there. To my relief, they said that there was no one there by his name. I am certain that if he were sick, he would be in that hospital because it is the one where he is generally treated.

I just wrote another note of correction to a teacher of mine. I do not believe that I will send it. Perhaps the proper thing to do in this case is to wait until the end of class and then make my comments face-to-face.

I am still shaken up by something I saw today. I was on the hill above Bar Kokhba Street and had just finished reading the newspaper. It is an isolated place and few people are there at that time of day. I began to walk towards the hill that leads to the *shul* on Hagannah Street. As I walked, I saw a young man with an excited yet shameful expression on his face. I am almost certain that he was an Arab. I saw that he was looking in the direction of the center of the hill, where there is a small playground. I followed his gaze and could not believe what I saw: there, lying on the hill, was a couple doing what a couple should only do in private. I was confused and kept walking. I did not want to see the sight that was before me. Should I have interfered? I do not know. Was it a man with his girlfriend? Was the Arab a passerby who was fascinated by the scene, or was he acting as some kind of lookout? As I walked away, I yelled out, "What is this?" They seemed to pay no attention – I continued walking.

In retrospect, I probably should have done something. What if it was a rape? But there was no sign of struggle. They were in a public place, out in the open. She did not show any signs of resistance. Should I have interrupted them and risked the man's anger? Should I have interrupted them and broken their private moment of love? Should I have interrupted them on the grounds that a family with children might soon venture by? I don't know. I feel that I should not interfere in other people's private business. I was shocked, ashamed and angry afterwards.

Perhaps the right thing to do would have been to approach them and ask the girl if she was all right. That would have broken the whole thing up. I should have done this. Had I had the answer to a question that was going through my mind, it would probably have determined my behavior: had I known that she was a Jew and he an Arab, I would have most likely interfered. But even so, what if it was with her consent?

Monday, December 20
11 *Tevet*

Reading the statistics on poverty and unemployment in Israel, I feel a certain guilt about being one of the more fortunate ones and not doing more for others. Rambam teaches us that the greatest *tzedakah* is to help a person find a way of gaining independence through their own work. I do not help people in this way.

Having "more" does not yield much in terms of additional security and well-being. Even though I give about twenty to twenty-five percent of my income to *tzedakah*, I doubt that my contributions could support entire families. I did make an offer to provide a monthly subsidy to one family I like. Instead, they accepted a one-time gift, a relatively small amount. I doubt if the help that I can offer them can redeem them from the financial straits that they find themselves in.

Is it *derech eretz* that I have never asked who it is that receives the money that I give everyday to the shul's *tzedakah* fund? I have always hoped and believed that it is for the families of the *shul* who have a large number of children, but are low on financial resources. I sometimes suspect, however, that the money goes to *yeshivot*. This bothers me because I want needy families to be the recipients.

The truth is that knowing about the poor in Israel and seeing them daily deprives me of my peace of mind. How can I be wholly happy if so many others are not? One reason I distance myself from one particular friend is because he shows such contempt and lack of sympathy for those who have not succeeded in the commercial world.

The events of recent years in Israel; the amassing of considerable wealth in the upper-income stratums and the development of the high-tech economy, which cannot compensate for the work lost in the more traditional industries, means greater inequality in income in Israel than has ever been seen before. I do not know how, or if, this should be corrected. I wonder if a society and economy based more on traditional concepts of Jewish economic and social justice would be a better one.

When the rich unions can paralyze the country at will, when the gap in earnings between electric company workers and doctors is so great, it is clear that there is something inherently wrong with the economic system here. Unfortunately, I do not know enough about such subjects to speak of them with real authority and insight.

Tuesday, December 21
12 *Tevet*

There are issues of *derech eretz* in the realm of food. For example, we are told that one should not gorge down one's food or eat in a sloppy manner. Above all, we are commanded that one should always make a blessing before and after eating. I sometimes drink or eat a snack in the street as I am walking, but I never feel quite right about it. Nor do I feel comfortable eating on public buses. On long bus journeys, I feel uneasy by the thought that other passengers might be made thirsty by watching me drink.

In Israel, people do eat in the street as they walk, and eat on buses as well. Although it is never condemned or commented on, I nonetheless think that it is probably better not to eat in this manner.

I am quite ashamed of my appearance. I often look disheveled, certainly not at my best. This is a problem that I have had for most of my life. I have made some improvement, but I am still far from appearing as I should. Yet in the world we live in today, in which appearances are so diverse, I guess I am just another ordinary person in the crowd.

I myself am offended by the way some people dress and look, even with my attempts to be broad-minded in my outlook. What is most objectionable to me is when I see people in Israel with tattoos, or any other kind of marking that deforms the body. This is a violation of a Jewish religious prohibition. We believe that the marring of the body is a desecration of God's creation.

The non-kosher pizzeria that opened in my neighborhood serves many people on Shabbat. Being the "free and democratic" country that Israel is, it is impossible to do anything about this. I think that both those who make a profit from selling it, as well as those who eat it, display contempt for Jewish tradition and contempt for generations of Jews who risked and, in some cases, sacrificed their lives to keep *kashrut*. I find it doubly offensive when it is done in the land of Israel, and especially in Jerusalem.

There seem to be an increasing number of extremists in both the secular camp and the *charedi* camp. Society has moved away from the center, the middle path, which Rambam sees as the true way for the righteous Jew. The loss of the centrist approach is synonymous with a loss of common sense. This extremism is weakening the Jewish people and Israel.

The truth is that the large immigration from the Soviet Union, and the large influx of foreign workers, has changed the public face of Israel. The "stranger in our midst," unfortunately, no longer only refers to the Arabs. This new reality has changed my attitude. Whereas once I would have had a more sympathetic, kindly approach to the person I could safely assume was a fellow Jew, now I am more distant and cautious. There are now faces in society which resemble more those of traditional anti-Semitic oppressors than of the Jewish oppressed. This affects the way one acts. It is one thing to be polite, but another to feel real sympathy with a member of one's own community.

Wednesday, December 22
13 *Tevet*

Yesterday, I did not push myself, as I should have, to visit Anita on her last night in the hospital. This raises the question of how much one is required to sacrifice in order to act with true *derech eretz*. Lately, I have preferred being by myself to giving time to others. I have so much reading to do and the pile just seems to grow. I feel guilty when I do not make certain visits to those people who I know enjoy my company. Perhaps one reason why I did not force myself to make yet another hospital visit is the impression that I receive that I have overdone things. I saw this from Anita's expression of surprise the last time I visited and brought yet more drinks and cookies.

I am to meet the publisher today about this work. I do not know what to expect. I believe in the importance of the subject, but I am not sure that I have done the topic justice in writing about it in this way. It seems to me that, even now, I should be learning more about the various concepts of *derech eretz*. It also seems wrong that we will be discussing this work while I am neglecting the work on Rabbi Goren, for which we have a contract. What is holding me back from progressing with the biography?

Thursday, December 23
14 *Tevet*

The publisher spoke about this work with understanding and intelligence yesterday. He saw aspects of it that I did not. We are to meet again. I have the sense that with such a perceptive person working on it, the result will be worthwhile.

I am often tired when I attend the holy teacher's classes, yet I fight my weariness and go. I always try to let him set the time that is best for him. I feel that he is busier and, as it is he who is teaching me and has given me so much over the years, I want to be as accommodating as I can.

I feel bad that I do not attend Rabbi R.'s classes anymore. True, I do give a monthly sum for him (I do this so that the class will not be stopped and so that others will not lose out), but I do not go myself. Why? For many years, his classes gave me something, and usually there was at least one teaching that I could take home with me that I would be fortified by. But the classes have become painfully boring to me. This is not only because I have heard most of the stories told in them before – I get tired of sitting in silence when I do not agree with much of what is said. His is the *charedi* party line: the *yeshiva* students are the true soldiers in Israel and those who oppose them are innocent babes at best, or, at worst, absolute evil-doers.

I tend to be extremely loyal to people who have been good to me in the past. This loyalty reflects my belief that people are not to be used as a means to an end, to be discarded after use. Each individual should be considered as a person of value and should therefore be helped in whatever way possible.

I was waiting for a bus yesterday and was about to board one when I saw Rav A. sitting in the front seat, where he could not be avoided. I instinctively stepped back. I do not know if he saw me but if he did, he could have been insulted by my actions.

After hearing Rav A.'s story about owing money to the Tax Authority, my first thought was to distance myself from him. However, I thought about it again, and resolved that I will give him some assistance – but I was not ready to do so yesterday.

Last night, I attended a forum on Reb Nachman at the Van Leer Institute and noticed how many people walked in and out of the room, without considering whether or not they were disrupting the speaker. These are supposed to be cultured, intelligent people.

This evening, as I was carrying my laundry home, I saw an old Russian acquaintance, Mrs. T., looking as if her world had come to an end. I greeted her and asked her how she was. She told me her story: her husband had been violently cursing at her and she had to go out for a walk. I listened to her. I saw how upset she was and sympathized with her, and tried to strengthen her. At the end of our conversation, I told her what a good woman she is, which I could see made her feel a bit better.

Domestic violence is another phenomenon which, years ago, people would never have dreamed possible in a Jewish state. At first, I thought that there were only isolated instances of this type of thing, but I have since learned that I am wrong. It is possible to isolate supporting factors: an immigrant society, people uprooted from their traditions, tension created by the changed perception of male-female roles in the modern world. But whatever the reasons, there are no justifications.

There is a real virtue in giving a person one's full attention. I sometimes feel that I don't have the strength to do so, but I nevertheless force myself to. It seems like wherever I go, I meet people who tell me their stories. Yesterday, my friend from *shul* who used to be a scientific photographer told me about his problems. Just now, I spoke with my old teacher's widow, who has so many problems that she could only tell me a few of them in the fifteen minutes we spoke.

I went to Yigal's usual spot again today – he was not there. I continued on my way and met the former dentist from Russia. I made up for last week and gave him a sum that was larger than usual. I would not have to give him anything and he would still be kind. He asked me what he could do for me. I told him to keep his spirits up.

Rabbi Eisen reminded me of something that I tend to shunt aside: the Jewish ideal to be married. A man alone is incomplete. Deep down, I feel like a complete failure for not living up to this ideal. I have known and believed this for years, and yet have not been able to affect any change.

Sunday, December 26
17 *Tevet*

Yesterday, I met Israel G. and three of his small children on my way back from *shul*. He told me that he and his wife have separated. I urged him to go to marriage counseling and offered to pay for it. I told him that they must think of the children. I asked him who initiated the separation. He said that it was a mutual agreement. He also said that there had been things that he had wanted to do and had not had the time for. I did not tell him what I thought, that he was being selfish and should put his children's well-being before his own. This is the family that I wanted to give *tzedakah* to before Chanukah. I feel so badly about their separation. I will call a mediation agency for them, although I doubt that anything will come of it.

Tuesday, December 28
19 *Tevet*

I just did something that I rarely do: I did not answer the doorbell. This is because for some time now, the woman who delivers the mail rings the bell at this early hour. There are ways for her to deliver the mail without disturbing people in this way and I think that she acts without consideration by doing so. One possible alternative is to get her a key to the building. I should tell her that she disturbs and ask her about this possibility. Sometimes one has to be honest and straightforward so as not to encourage a lack of consideration on the part of other people.

I listen to the news less frequently these days. This is because the budget debates, with the politicians' endless claims and accusations, do not really interest me. They certainly do not lift my spirits. The fact that religious parties are involved in threats, accusations, demands and greedy assertions troubles me. However unfortunately, a political party is a sectarian interest, a group intent on putting its own interests before the well-being of society as a whole.

A person with *derech eretz* is someone who negotiates in good faith, who keeps his word, who does not act behind the backs of others, who knows how to listen and to keep what he has heard to himself – a person who is honest with those he deals with.

Wednesday, December 29
20 *Tevet*

I still have not seen Israel G. and his wife, who are separated. I really want to give them the marriage counselor's phone number.

To be happy for the success of another, especially a friend, is a good quality. Envy and begrudging others' good fortune is a negative quality. My question is, why do Israelis say of themselves that they do not like to *mifargen*, to be complimentary towards one another on their successes? Maybe the source of this narrowness, envy and resentment is the background of physical poverty that is so prevalent here.

Thursday, December 30
21 *Tevet*

I finally called Ruth F. yesterday. I felt guilty at the thought of having abandoned her. We spoke briefly – she sounded well. She said that she would invite me along with someone else for dinner. I said that I would be happy to come. She called me today and we agreed upon the day and the time. It is hard to know what to do after one's friend passes away – how friendly one should be with the spouse. I know that in some cases this scenario led to me being more friendly with the widow, but usually the frequency of my visits diminishes with time. I have still not visited Mrs. B. Her pessimism, bitterness, total immersion in her own health problems and prying questions make visits increasingly difficult.

Sunday, January 2, 2000
24 *Tevet*

I called Israel G. and gave him the telephone number of the marriage counselor this morning. I told him that I would pay for any counseling. I also told him what I had told the counselor: that he and his wife are two admirable people who face certain difficulties and who can and should be helped. I gave Israel G. my number again and asked him to let me know what happened.

I went to give the former dentist his money on Friday. He seemed more desperate somehow. He said, "I now come and beg on weekdays too. I was afraid to do so because I feared that I might become a burden to the public." I have decided to increase the amount I give him each week.

Yigal was not in his usual place again. I fear that something has happened to him. If that is the case, I am guilty. I know that he probably lied, I know that I did try to help him, but I also know that I did not help him with total conviction, as one would help a family member. I did not discard the advice of others and follow my own instinct which said, "He may be a liar, but he is truly sick and needs more help." I tested him with the check I wanted to give directly to the landlord, and he was found wanting. However, I could have interpreted his response in a less rational and more compassionate way. Maybe what he needed first and foremost was the knowledge that someone cared for him, against all the odds. And I did not do that.

I visited Anita on Shabbat. It was a brief visit. I sense that she has aged due to the incident. I cut my visit short when a couple entered, the husband of which I somehow do not feel comfortable being around. I did my duty, though I can honestly say it was without much desire.

My father, may his soul rest in peace, also visited a number of people to whom no one in the world paid much attention. There was Joe Bedell, the blind, old featherweight boxer who lived in a shack by the river. There was also Freeman Neilsen, the lonely Dane, a craftsman and widower, his paralyzed son, and also Rosoff, the tailor.

On Shabbat, I sat with Israel R. and talked with him about the weather, the Six Day War and the history of the neighborhood. I felt guilty because on Friday, in my haste, I had forgotten to buy him a newspaper (which he did not expect of me, but I thought he would enjoy).

There are certain people who spread an air of gloom about them with their very presence. They make other people feel low with their negative vibes. This reaction can also stem from one's own instinctive dislike of the person and discomfort with one's own negative feelings. I notice that I have this feeling sometimes with some public figures who preach ideas that I believe are damaging. I also feel uneasy around gossipers.

I just discovered that I gave Israel G. a telephone number with one digit wrong. I called him and learned that he is taking his father to the hospital for an operation today. I wished him success and asked him to please be in touch with me and let me know what is going on. I do not want to help just for the sake of helping, but rather to have the desired result – to bring this family back together again, under a new and improved circumstances.

Monday, January 3
25 *Tevet*

At the supper last night at Ruth F.'s, I was polite and quiet. I could have brought her a gift and stayed longer than I did. I was content to let the other guests dominate the conversation.

Tuesday, January 4
26 *Tevet*

I was the *shaliach tsibbur* this morning in *shul*. I heard one of the *gabbaim* praying loudly near me. I chose to ignore his cue, which was for me to pray at his pace. I was the prayer leader and I would set the pace. After the prayers, when we were learning, he reprimanded me for being three minutes early for *shmoneh esreh* and causing a delay as a result. I did not answer him. He later apologized to me, not for the correction, but for reprimanding me in public. I accepted his apology for the public reprimand, agreed with him that I should have gone slower, and smiled at him.

I have been rereading this journal. Much of it has to do with giving *tzedakah* and little to do with the work I do.

I do not believe that I behaved correctly yesterday with regard to the woman I went out with on Thursday. I could have called her and wished her a good Shabbat, but I did not. I could have called her and asked her out for this week, but I did not. I instead told her that I would call her in the coming week. She was offended at first, but then said, "When you are ready." I appreciated her making it easy for me.

I read in the *Talmudic Encyclopedia* that it is not proper *derech eretz* to shout when one talks because it is rude and animal-like.

I will go on writing this work even if I decide not to publish it. I feel the subject is so important, and that I have so much to learn, that it is the right thing to do.

Wednesday, January 5
27 *Tevet*

At Leiberman's request, I accompanied Dov home from *shul* this morning. There was a strong wind and I was afraid that he might fall.
Leiberman is an especially considerate, quiet and caring person. His presence cheers and helps others.

I do not have a warm, outgoing and joyful approach to each and every person that I meet. I am much more reserved in my greetings – a quiet smile is usually the best I can offer. I believe it would be wrong, and equally impossible, for me to adopt the kind of happy approach that some of the Carlebach disciples have mastered.

I believe that my pride all too often gets in the way of my *derech eretz*. How? I become discouraged by not being able to do more, make any great influence, and so I despair at the small efforts and changes that I can make. It is true, though, that *derech eretz*, I believe, involves a kind of humility by which one understands one's own limited power, yet wishes to do what one can to help in any case.

I did not visit Mrs. B. I should go and see her.

Thursday, January 6
28 *Tevet*

This morning, I looked for Dov in order to walk with him to *shul*. The wind was not as strong as it was yesterday. I saw him walking at his own pace and I did not interfere. But when the davvaning was over, I did not think to wait to accompany him home. The rain was too strong.

I finally got around to visiting Mrs. B. She seems well. She has a fighting spirit. She maintains the *tzedakah* fund that we once ran together. She showed me a letter of thanks she received from a student for whom she bought school supplies. By doing this, she also showed me the way she publicizes whatever good she does. Though I do not like this in general, I see a certain advantage to this type of thing from an educational perspective.

Yesterday, I helped Phil Chernofsky set up the room for an Israel Center lecture, but then I was so tired that I did not stay until the end, so I did not help him put everything back at the close of the evening. I generally like to help, but I feel a special debt of gratitude to Phil from whom I, and much of the English speaking population in Israel, have learned so much Torah.

Sunday, January 9
2 Shevat

I received a call from Israel G. on Friday. His landlord is threatening to cut off his electricity and water if he does not pay his rent money. I asked him how much it was – close to five thousand shekels. He said that he is expecting a check this week and would pay me back in a few days. I told him that I did not have that sum of money in my account now. He said that the landlord was very insistent. I told him that I would give him a check. It is a long story, but in the end I met he and his wife and gave them the check.

As I sit here writing, I am worried about whether or not my check will clear. I will probably go downtown later this morning or tomorrow to make sure that the money to cover the check is in my account.

One of the reasons I did not hesitate to give them money was my guilt over Yigal, who I did not see again on Friday. However, the main reason for my generosity is that I believe that this is a good family that simply does not have enough money to make it. The real help this family needs is someone who can help them solve their financial problems. I just tried calling the marriage counselor I had previously contacted on their behalf in order to ask him if he is the right person to give financial advice.

On Friday, I received a call informing me that Anita had suffered another, more serious, stroke. I spoke with her daughter. *Hashem yirachem*. If it is anything like what happened with Ma, then the daughter is really going to have the most difficult kind of burden. The daughter said that she prefers no visitors now. I had thought that my presence might help. I know that this was wishful thinking.

I make it a rule to always call people back as soon as possible. Often, I do this reluctantly. *Derech eretz* often means one must do not what one wants to do, but rather what one knows is right.

Monday, January 10
3 Shevat

I called two hospitals this morning. There is no sign of Yigal and no information about Anita. I must either call her daughter or go and visit. I think that I will wait until later in the morning and call her daughter.

I am not sure whether or not to publish this journal under another name. Would that be *derech eretz*? It seems to me that the real question (and the one I have not answered myself) is whether or not I really believe in this journal, and believe it can help anyone but myself.

The woman to whom I had paid the rent for the G. family called. Apparently, I had mistakenly written the previous year on the check. I told her that I would correct the check or give her a new one. I even gave her three options as to where to meet. She said that she would decide on this and call me back. It is important to be good-natured with everyone. This is true even though I did harbor a certain bad feeling towards these landlords, who threatened a family with young children.

I called Anita's daughter to find out how Anita is doing. There has been some improvement today – she is sitting up. Unfortunately, I know how it often goes, two steps forward, three steps back. I pray that she will have a full recovery.

Tuesday, January 11
4 Shevat

I just returned from the bank in Ramat Eshkol, where I deposited the new check for Israel G. I also withdrew money from my account to make sure that he would get the difference today. I learned there that, to my disappointment, he and his wife are already divorced. (I had been working to try and prevent the divorce). However, they are still, in effect, common law husband and wife. The divorce enabled her to get government aid which would otherwise have not been available.

When he paid me back, Israel G. thanked me for my help and said that there are not many people like me. The fact that he paid me back so promptly means that I will probably pay the rent again if asked. However, the whole situation with the divorce was misunderstood by me, and now I feel my wisest move is to stay away from any further involvement. They could have told me before I loaned them the money that they were already divorced.

Wednesday, January 12
5 *Shevat*

On a trip to Tel Aviv today, I found people to be very polite. The bus driver, to whom I gave a large bill, informed me that I was going in the wrong direction. He insisted on returning all my money, even after he had to break the large bill. A woman at a bakery answered very politely when I somewhat rudely asked her about a *kashrut* certificate. She showed no sign of annoyance at my making a small purchase with a large bill. The people I asked for directions were uniformly polite.

I found the address of the people whose flowers we mistakenly received. I walked down to their apartment, bringing both the flowers and some mail which had also been addressed to them.

Thursday, January 13
6 *Shevat*

To my regret, I am now certain that the woman with whom I have gone out twice is not right for me. It is very hard to be sensitive in these situations, not wanting the breaking-off of the relationship to come across as a personal rejection. How to convey the message as delicately as possible is a difficult question. I am saddened by having to do this and must think of the most proper way.

Last night I saw some American Jewish teenagers, loud and drunk, breaking bottles on the street downtown. I went over and asked them to stop. They sneered at me and I walked away. They stopped for a while. They did not break bottles as before, but rather scraped a broken bottle along the ground. I did not have the energy to deal with them.

Monday, January 17
10 *Shevat*

My friend Dov is in hospital. I do not know if it is wise to go there. I believe that the right thing to do is to wait for word from one of the other *gabbaim* who will visit him. I must also call Anita's daughter to find out how her mother is doing.

There are countless small decisions one must make as to what the right way to act is. *Derech eretz*, as I understand it, is synonymous with doing the will of God – one goal and one concept.

I feel a quiet joy and contentment now, which is rather rare for me. It is an appropriate mood for self-introspection.

This morning I saw Dov's wife at the bus-stop and made the mistake of asking her how he is doing. She answered a nervous, positive answer. I understood: she herself had just come from her house and he had been alone all night in the hospital, so she did not know how he was and was worried. I should have been more sensitive.

I visited Dov yesterday. He has, besides a heart condition, a painful skin condition which involves terrible redness and itching. The ward was crowded and hot.

I also visited Anita. She was in better shape than I thought she would be in. She recognized me and spoke coherently. I was her first visitor outside of the immediate family. Her eldest son is here until Wednesday. I thought of offering to help her daughter by spending one day a week with her, but I don't know if the daughter would want this. I am also not sure if I could do it.

According to the *Talmudic Encyclopedia*, it is not proper *derech eretz* to interrupt others when they talk, to be quick to respond, to answer in a clumsy way, or, even worse, to be deceitful or speak about something from a position of ignorance.

Last night on the bus, there was a group of rowdy young girls with a young man. They spoke not only rudely, but in a vile manner. I did what I hate to do and intervened, reminding them that they were in a public place. They did not stop talking, but did change the content and tone of their conversation.

Tuesday, January 18
11 *Shevat*

I tried to minimize the pain in telling T. that I did not want a relationship with her. She reacted in the wisest way, assuring me that she did not have any great expectations. She responded to my consideration with consideration of her own.

Wednesday, January 19
12 *Shevat*

There was no *minyan* at first this morning. I saw Rav Zimmer put his coat on and thought that he was going to the *shul* next door to request two others to come and help us complete the *minyan*. I gestured to him to stay and went out instead. I was only able to bring one person. However, when I saw him getting ready to leave to go to the other *minyan*, I went out again and brought another person. He thanked me after the davvaning for doing this.

I brought a book review that I had written to Alec Israel, the editor. It turns out that I brought the wrong version on disk and the correct version typed. He was patient and considerate and reworked the whole thing into his computer. He is always especially considerate. I was troubled to learn that he has a serious medical condition requiring dialysis.

Thursday, January 20
13 *Shevat*

I just called to see how Dov is. He still has the flu and now his wife has it too. I offered to bring them whatever provisions they might need. They said that they will call if they need me. They are people I have great feeling for. They are true pioneering Israelis, modest, hardworking and quietly religious. He fought in the War of Independence. He is often my teacher in halachic lore on our frequent walks home from *shul* together. Of all of the *gabbaim* in *shul*, he is my favorite.

There are times when it is *derech eretz* to offer help which will probably not be taken, simply because the offer itself is a sign of caring and might serve to help the person as a result. In this case, however, I hoped that they would not refuse. I want to help them in any way that I can. I worry about Dov's fever. I asked them whether or not a doctor had visited. The answer was no. I thought to have Bob, my doctor friend, visit. But I did not want to interfere to this degree.

Anita's son returned home, leaving her daughter as the sole caretaker. Against this background is a school-strike and so the daughter's four small children are at home. I just spoke with her. They have moved her mother to Herzog Hospital in Givat Shaul. I foolishly expressed my disappointment at this decision. It's just that the last person I regularly visited there deteriorated quickly. The daughter said that her mother was only having short visits, as she tires easily.

In my naiveté, I sometimes kid myself that my presence will be that little bit of critical help that is crucial to an ill person's recovery. This is not simply innocence, it is also probably arrogance. Yet one should not abandon a person who has been good to him or her – one has to fight to help them. This supports Rambam's idea of the balanced scales in which any deed, however small, can tip the balance. I learned this attitude from my mother, who taught it to us children when my father was sick. After all these years, I realize that it is that childhood lesson that compels me to try to help when others might give up.

There is a famous Gemarah about Yehuda HaNasi who was punished for being cruel to a mouse by being struck ill. He only recovered from his sickness upon an act of kindness towards another animal. I have never felt particularly close with animals, but since my daughter saved a kitten and brought it into our house, my appreciation of them has changed. I do not believe in going overboard, but I think that it's necessary to be considerate of animals' feelings. All creatures, great and small, are God's creations and should therefore be treated with kindness.

I will try to see Anita today, although the hospital is far away and I am pressed for time. I may also call Dov again.

Last night, after learning and the *Tu B'Shvat* party at *shul*, I was eager to go home. Instead, I went with the *gabbai* to make *seudah shlishit* purchases and carried the heavy bottles back to the *shul* for him.

For the second week in a row, the former dentist who stands at the corner of Jaffa and King George streets was not there. Yigal was also not at his usual place. I so deeply regret now the last conversation we had.

As I was buying a newspaper in a store in Ramat Eshkol, I stood next to a man berating the girl working there for turning to help someone else while he was being waited on. I immediately recognized the man as a well-known artist. I doubt that he remembers me, as it has been over twenty years since we last spoke. I took no chances and left the store unobserved. I thought it might be embarrassing for him to be seen in a dispute of this kind, but I was wrong. He went on and on berating the girl. If I had not known him, I would have intervened to put a stop to it. He was obviously expressing frustration at something else that was troubling him. What it was, I do not know, but I think that bullying subordinates is particularly contemptible behavior.

Rav Zimmer, who is obligated to say *kaddish* for the year after his father's passing, leads the davvaning every morning now. He does not have a great voice, but he prays with such deep concentration and at such an appropriate pace that he has improved the whole shul's davvaning. The prayers are not rushed, as they often were before – every word is enunciated clearly. This is another case where a person's doing the right thing influences others positively.

I did not make it to visit Anita. I feel somewhat guilty. I had thought to go, but somehow it didn't work out. I will hopefully go next week.

I will not call the G. family because they have my phone number – they know how to find me.

Sunday, January 23
16 *Shevat*

The rains we have had and the subsequent clear, cold air seem to improve the quality of life here. Everything seems cleaner and more fresh. What does this have to do with *derech eretz*? There is a relationship between the environment, the atmosphere in which we live, and the way we conduct our lives. When we are blessed with rain and the weather seems to be following a natural pattern, it is somehow easier for us to behave properly towards others. When the world makes us feel better, we can be better people.

We, as human beings, have a responsibility to preserve our environment, the natural world, and act as protectors of the animal world. This responsibility raises the question of the water crisis, the polluted streams, the polluted air in the major cities, the waste, the problem of too many cars on the roads, and the protection of natural habitats here in Israel.

I fear that my contribution to the preservation of the environment – picking up garbage off the streets and making sure that the garbage bins are closed (especially in the summer) – is minimal.

I called Dov to see if he and his wife needed any help. He is somewhat better, although they are both still weak. I repeated my offer for them to call me if they need assistance.

One should not help other people if it is at one's own expense. Yesterday, I agreed to meet with and help correct the work of Dr. Barkan, the father of a friend of my daughter's. In the end, he had to cancel, which I understood. But then, in rescheduling the appointment, I completely forgot about my own schedule and scheduled the meeting at a time that was inconvenient for me.

I expected to find Anita alone in the rehabilitation center, but there were three people with her. Before I had a chance to sit down, I was asked by one man to wind up his *tefillin*, which I did. Then, another wheelchair-bound patient asked me to help him put his *tefillin* on, which I also did. As I was doing this, yet another group of people came in to see Anita. I did not particularly enjoy being with the whole group, but I sat (or rather stood) politely, spoke briefly with Anita, and left. I had asked her if she was able to read and she said that it was too hard for her. My newspaper gift remained in my bag.

I stayed home tonight because I wanted to help Dr. Barkan with his paper. It also gave me the chance to have a very good chat with my son. This is an example of a good action that brought an immediate reward.

Tuesday, January 25
18 *Shevat*

I reviewed Dr. Barkan's work last night. I hope my comments will be of help to him. He is a person who has served as a doctor in the army for many years, often under dangerous conditions. He has also gone on various humanitarian missions in many places, the last of which was during the earthquake in Turkey. He is one of those people who performs the holy task of bettering the name of Israel in the world.

Yesterday in *shul*, I silenced a friend when he began to talk to me after I finished the *shmoneh esreh*. I did not want to disturb others who were still praying. I know that he is a person who talks with and listens to many people, but there are times when, in his constant questioning and chatter, he can ruin a learning session or simply irritate the person giving it. He fails to realize that there is a proper time and place for everything.

Wednesday, January 26
19 *Shevat*

Another incident occurred with the woman who delivers the mail: she rang the bell again and when no one answered, she immediately rang it again. I decided a while ago to stop answering, but today I went down anyway. Downstairs, I saw her yelling and being yelled at by a young man from the building. He told her that her ringing was disruptive and that she should not continue to do it. She tried to answer him but could not speak. She made angry, hostile sounds instead. Apparently, she is disabled. In any case, I tried to stop the argument. I think that he was so angry that he was ready to throw something at her. I was more surprised by him than by her, though she did not behave correctly either. However, two wrongs do not make a right. In the future, I will try to answer the door for her immediately, so as to prevent disturbance to other people. I now understand why she never answered when I asked who it was through the intercom – she cannot speak.

Thursday, January 27
20 *Shevat*

Yesterday, I had a long talk with my former wife, mostly about the children, and also about her work. An amicable relationship between a former husband and wife is one of the real tests of *derech eretz*. I think that my resolution early on not to speak negatively about her was helpful. It is so crucial to cooperate with one another for the good of the children, not to try to score points against each other or to deny each other's identity. It means maintaining a human face, even if it entails suppressing certain negative feelings. But this is only possible if there is a basic level of decency on both sides and one is able to overcome his or her hurt for the sake of the greater good. Nonetheless, there have been times of tension and also resentment for me. There is also the anger and frustration that I harbor that such a good marriage (my definition) had to come to an end

I also owe a debt of gratitude to my children, who did not turn against me during the divorce.

Sunday, January 30
23 *Shevat*

Two *shiurim* I attended recently were ruined by participants who, not satisfied with the teacher's answer to their questions, continued to obstinately insist on their own line of thought. A questioner can often offer a new element to the learning, but in this case, both the questioners proved to be disruptive and broke the rhythm of the teacher's train of thought. I know three people who persistently act in this way and who end up talking more in a *shiur* than the teacher does, to the dismay of everyone present except themselves.

Even a small thank-you can make us feel that our actions are worthwhile. My daughter's boyfriend said thank-you for our Shabbat hospitality. I appreciated this greatly.

Monday, January 31
24 *Shevat*

I debated about whether or not to go to the funeral of Alex Berlyne, who gave me my first writing opportunity at The Jerusalem Post. The truth is that I was interested in going in order to see the crowd, which is not the right reason for going to a funeral. I was not very close with him and he knew many, many people. Nonetheless, I will simply go and pay my respects. I will not take a place in the *beit hesped*. I will stand outside.

I went to Alex Berlyne's funeral. It was the right thing to do. I stood at the back. I started walking to the cemetery until I was offered a ride by someone I vaguely recognized. His name came to me later. This same person gave me a ride back. I think that he was as relieved as I to simply sit in silence and not start with stories of "where do I know you from."

It often happens that we underestimate certain people, think less of them, only to later see them in a different light and realize that they are better people than we had previously thought and that we have been mistaken. I believe that this idea is the premise behind *Pirkei Avot*'s injunction to initially judge everyone in a favorable way.

I went to see Anita after the funeral. She was sitting and looking at a book, trying to read. She told me that they are going to move her home next week and that her daughter is trying to find someone to be with her. I told her that I had an appropriate person in mind. I believe it is far too premature to send her home, though. She needs a lot more physical therapy. We had a nice talk – I know that she enjoys my company.

As I was about to leave the hospital, I saw a young man near the food machines. He asked me for five shekels. I recognized him – he is the son of my former neighbors. He is severely mentally retarded. I spoke with him and tried to give him the coin. He repeated certain phrases over and over again. Now I realize, so many years later, why there was always such disorder in this family's house. *Hashem yirachem*.

I could not interrupt the davvaning in *shul* today, but I should have requested that a *refuah shlemah* be recited for the soldiers who were injured in Lebanon yesterday. I do not know if one recites an *ilui neshamah* for those killed but not yet buried.

Sunday, February 6
Rosh Chodesh Adar I

On Friday, I spoke with S., a visiting professor who a friend introduced me to a year ago. She is here now for a short period of time. We agreed to meet today, on Sunday. Then she called me on Friday afternoon, asking if she could come for dinner on Shabbat. As she is not religious, I knew that her coming would involve her having to violate the Shabbat, but I invited her in any case. She was a Jewish woman with no place to go for Shabbat dinner – I thought it right to say yes. The truth is that I have wished for a long time to be more active in having people over for Shabbat meals. I have always been reluctant to invite guests because of my poor cooking skills, but this year we have had more guests than in the past. I hope to continue with this.

Monday, February 7
Rosh Chodesh Adar I Bet

A soldier named Yedidya Gefen, may his soul rest in peace, was killed yesterday in Lebanon. Four other soldiers were seriously injured. I pray for their full recovery. I also pray for the family of the young man who was killed. But what should I pray for? That they will know no more sorrow? That they should have blessings from their other children? That they should have the strength to go on?

I received a call from Israel G. in which he requested another loan for rent. I said yes. Only later did I realize that the money he requested was not for the apartment in which his former wife and children live, but for his own separate apartment. Had I known that, I would not have agreed. However, since I had already told him I would, I gave it to him. Another reason I did so is that he repaid the previous loan promptly and without my having to ask him to do so.

Tuesday, February 8
2 Adar I

I was surprised by the politeness of the young soldiers at the museum the other day. They did not take advantage of their overwhelming presence by disrupting others and were not noisy. There are many realms of society in which there has been great improvement in *derech eretz* over recent years. For example, phone operators are more polite, as are postal clerks. There is no smoking on the buses. Also, there are many more restaurants where the personnel have been trained to treat the customer with respect.

Thursday, February 9
3 *Adar I*

I went with Judy Brown and some friends of hers to the memorial service for her late husband, Bob. What a good person he was, and what a pleasure to be with! His widow is also an especially warm and kind person. All of the people there, most of who I no longer see, were extremely warm to me.

Is this the end of my friendship with S.? I sense that she might be deliberately distancing herself from me, but I am not sure. She said, "If I stayed here, I am not sure that we would continue to be friends because I would join a Palestinians' Rights Organization." These words angered and insulted me. Did this outburst demonstrate a lack of *derech eretz* towards me or was it simply an honest expression of her true feelings? Was it a tactic to alienate me? In any case, I will not call her or see her again. I feel bad about this and would have liked it if we could have parted on friendly terms.

Thursday, February 10
4 *Adar I*

I spoke to my sister-in-law last night and learned that my Uncle Larry had died at the age of eighty-five earlier on in the week. He had not lived a real life for the past four and half years or so. I called my cousin, another nephew of Uncle Larry's, whom I speak to very rarely, and thanked him for caring for him. He seemed embarrassed to be thanked. I do not know him well, but my sister told me that he is a mensch.

S. called me and invited me to dinner with her and a woman who is supposedly anxious to meet me because she has read one of my books. I know that this is a peace offering on her part and so I will not refuse, even though I am still angry over her political stance. I will, however, do my best to avoid discussing any politically contentious issues. The truth is, I believe that any meeting will run smoothly because it is now clear to both of us that there can be nothing romantic between us. Her rudeness came, I believe, in part out of the tension of wanting, yet not wanting, a relationship to develop between us – as well as a fear of rejection.

Friday, February 11
5 *Adar I*

Rabbi Eisen, in his lecture on the biblical commandment of respecting one's parents, pointed out that there are certain situations (for instance, when a parent orders a child to violate Halachah) where a child should not obey his parents. However, he said that even when a child does not obey his parents, it must be done in a way as not to dishonor them.

I think that Rabbi Eisen's teaching can be applied to other situations in life where we do not go along with what another person wants. However, there should always be an element of ensuring that one does not humiliate or insult the person in the process.

I went out for lunch with S. It was enjoyable. There was no talk about the rude outburst. After lunch, we walked together in the direction of town. We said our good-byes on friendly terms.

Today I went to the *yahrtzeit* service for Mr. Rosen at the cemetery. He was a Jew who greeted everyone with a welcoming countenance and his family has followed in his righteous footsteps. The service was conducted in a respectful and tasteful way.

I have just returned from visiting my favorite *gabbai*, Dov. This is the first time since he has been out of hospital that I was able to do so. I do not know if I should have told him about the *azkarah* I attended. I tried to fill him in on what is going on in the *shul*, trying to entertain him to the best of my ability. I pray to God that he will make it back to *shul*. I told him that I would meet him and walk with him everyday when he decides that he is ready to return.

Sunday, February 13
7 Adar I

I had a polite conversation with an Arab taxi-driver last night. When he picked me up he was listening to a Hebrew-language radio station. He also spoke in Hebrew, though with mistakes and a strong accent. He told me that he works primarily in the Jewish neighborhoods because the roads are better and there is less bargaining over the price of the fare. He is working as a taxi-driver to earn enough money to build his own house.

Last night, I went to a concert of a choir singing *Psalms*. There was something so pleasant about the woman who hosted the evening and directed the choir. I really enjoyed the experience. It was an evening dedicated to the appreciation of the pleasant and the beautiful – *darchei noam*.

On Friday, I went to give money to the former dentist from Russia. When I passed his spot, my thoughts turned to Yigal. I wonder if he is still alive. I pray that he is.

Israel G. called me on Friday to apologize for not being in touch with me about paying back the loan. He has not received his checks from work yet. I told him that I was not worried about it. I again reiterated to him that I would like to help *all* of his family.

I saw Rob B. this morning. I had been angry at him because of his involvement with groups which ostensibly support "peace," but which can certainly be seen as favoring the Palestinian cause. I had thought that I would say something critical to him, but I saw how tired he looked. Also, he is a well-meaning person with good intentions. I could not bring myself to be critical. Was this *derech eretz* on my part or just cowardice?

I have not called or visited Ruth F. for some time. I have also not seen my old friend Israel R. Perhaps I made a mistake in not encouraging Dov to try and walk to *shul*.

I did not call the woman who I went out with once, even though I told her that I would. I do not really want to call her. Is it better to pretend that there is interest when there is none in order to protect someone's feelings?

I also have not called my publisher, Tzvi Mauer, to let him know whether or not I intend to move forward with this manuscript. I have also not spoken to my nephews (whose business is in trouble) or my niece (who I believe is about to intermarry). Why don't I speak with my niece and urge her to break off her connection with the person she is involved with? I think one reason is because I know that such an intervention will not have the desired effect and will only alienate her from me even further. Another reason is that she is thirty years old and obviously at an age where she is anxious to settle down. A third reason is that she herself is the product of an intermarriage (and conversion) and might be insulted by my objections as a result. A fourth reason is my fear that I will succeed in influencing her and she will break off her engagement, and then she might never get married. On the other hand, it may be that even if she intermarries and has children, that she will one day decide to raise them as Jewish.

Wednesday, February 16
10 *Adar I*

I just read what the *Talmudic Encyclopedia* has to say on the subject of *derech eretz*. It stresses the importance of the "middle way" in one's *middot* – trying to strike a balance between the extremes of indifference and anger, between a person failing to react at all and becoming agitated. Other extremes mentioned are those who are miserly and those who do not draw the line and are excessively generous. Also, those who are totally absorbed in the sensual and those who lead a life of abstinence.

The *Talmudic Encyclopedia* also gives guidance as to how one should criticize: one should first utter positive words of praise and then make the criticism. This shows that the criticism is not coming from hostility.

I just called my holy teacher, who was very tired yesterday, to find out how he is feeling. By calling him, I took the risk of possibly disturbing him or, conversely, of being a source of encouragement to him. I believe that I succeeded in being the latter.

Thursday, February 17
11 *Adar I*

Tzvi Mauer, my publisher, called. I have not progressed with the Goren work, so I scheduled a meeting for next week in the hope that it will move the matter forward.

The problem is that the decision over whether or not to publish this work is a decision of whether or not I believe it will truly serve God. Perhaps I should put this issue in perspective and regard this work as an effort, the best I can do, and not be overly anxious about whether or not it will really change anything or anyone. Perhaps in this sense *derech eretz* can also be connected with the concept of *hishtadlut*, of making the maximum effort. We should not expect perfection, but must simply do our best. I now feel more complete with going ahead with this work.

I just returned from handing in a piece of work, a book review. I spoke to the editor about the review. I then inquired about his medical condition and offered the help of my friend, Dr. Bob. I first asked him if he was satisfied with the medical treatment he was receiving because I didn't want my offer to come across as if I was trading the name of my friend in return for his printing my review. I just want to help and I do believe that Dr. Bob is really capable of helping. Besides being an expert in his field, he is a very caring and intelligent human being.

It is hard to draw the line between helping and interfering. There is no black and white answer to this dilemma. I think now of people who I have tried to help in a significant way, such as Yigal. I do not know what happened to him. I still think about him and regret turning him down the last time he called. I did not help him in a substantial way. I think about Israel G., whose divorce I wanted to prevent. I was no help there. Now he owes me money and has not fulfilled his promise to pay me back. I think of my efforts to help Israel R. overcome his foot problem. He would hear nothing about my offer of chiropractic help. And, most recently, I visited someone

I most wanted to help, Dov. Instead of encouraging him to start walking, I simply went along with his theory that he himself must feel ready first. What he said sounded reasonable, until I learned from someone else that in such a situation the person is never "ready" and must push themselves even when they do not feel up to it.

Friday, February 18
12 *Adar I*

I am considering calling the worried parents of my son's traveling companion back. It is too early though, so I should wait until I return from my errands at around eleven o'clock. I hope to calm them somewhat by telling them that my son said that he would not call during the first days of the trip. In any case, their call brought to the surface a subconscious fear deep inside me. By worrying about my children, I reveal a lack of trust in God and a lack of trust in them. It undermines confidence all round.

I often find that my impatience and sense of inner urgency (even when it is to do my duty) make me act in a rash, impetuous manner. For instance, as I sit here now, I very much want to call the boy's parents, to fulfill my duty, and get it over with. My strong emotions of guilt and a pricked conscience often lead me to act with undue haste. I am aware of this weakness and try to work on it. I do not, however, think that I am very successful.

Last night, I tried to show loyalty to the group of writers I belong to by attending one of the member's reading. The last time I went to a reading, I left in the middle. This time, I tried to make up for my previous rudeness and do my duty. But the truth is that I felt myself living a lie since I doubt that what was read is really of much interest to anyone except to the person who wrote it. It is like telling the bride that she is beautiful, whether she is or is not – *shalom* before *emet*.

Sunday, February 20
14 *Adar I*

I did not call Dr. Bob last night about my concern for Dov. I spoke with Dov's wife on Friday, and detected a hint of desperation in her voice. I pray that he will have a *refuah shlemah*. His condition has deteriorated, yet I am reluctant to interfere. He does have children who are aware of what is going on.

I am going to meet S. in Tel Aviv today. I am disturbed by the haste in which I decided to go. It is, of course, *derech eretz* to be a good host, to want to help her come closer to her Jewishness, but my *yetzer harah* is also involved here in my ambiguity about our relationship. At some point, I feel that I succumbed to the temptation of spending time with her.

I saw Israel G. at *seudah shlishit* yesterday. Of course, we did not mention the debt on Shabbat. His four small children were with him. They love him so much. I can see that he is a good person and I really want to help him. I think that I will forget about the debt, although I know that this will not really help him very much. I thought about the possibility of speaking to him about his whole financial situation and seeing if there is some way of providing him with more substantial help.
Later on, I waited beside Mr. S. who, having come from abroad, was saying *kiddush levanah* alone. I waited by him so that he would have someone to say "*Shalom aleichem, aleichem shalom*" to. Israel G. walked by and said, "This week," indicating that he intends to pay me back soon. If he does, this will increase my desire to speak with him and hopefully find some way of helping him more substantially.

Monday, February 21
15 *Adar I*

Yesterday, at a restaurant, my companion was ready to yell at the waitress for her inability to put the credit card through the machine. I mediated and calmed the situation. The truth is that people become easily infuriated for all kinds of petty reasons which could be avoided by a moment's patience and clarification. *Pirkei Avot* teaches us the virtue of being "slow to anger."

Yesterday, I experienced the *derech eretz* of respecting and honoring the local custom when I davvaned *Minchah* in the Old Jaffa Market. People tend to respect you when you honor their customs and ways.

I have decided not to call Dov's house again. Had I been able to get in touch with Dr. Bob, I would have called to ask if they wanted him to pay a visit. I spoke to the other *gabbai* this morning and learned that Dov has not improved and is very weak. I think it best not to disturb him, as I have nothing real to contribute.

I witnessed a traffic accident today. I was standing and waiting to cross the main road at the Ramat Eshkol intersection. At the traffic light, an old van driven wildly swerved, tried to stop, and then crashed into the car in front of him. The driver in the front car was holding his shoulder and could not move. He was a middle-aged Arab man. The driver of the van was a young Arab man, who got out of the car to inspect the damage. I tried to call for help. A man in a *kippah* called an ambulance. Many cars honked, as the traffic was stopped. I could have waited and given my account of the events in the police report, but I left when I saw that the injured person was being looked after. Both of the vehicles were clearly not in good mechanical shape. The young man was driving so wildly. Why is there no police supervision in such a crowded area? By being present, the police can deter recklessness and, in so doing, increase the level of *derech eretz* on the roads.

Tuesday, February 22
16 *Adar I*

Yesterday, during the lesson given by Aviva Zornberg, I gave my full concentration to learning from her. I did not allow myself to become distracted by a crossword puzzle. My quality of learning was obviously enhanced as a result of my increased effort.

Unfortunately, I am all too often guilty of being easily distracted. My daughter sometimes says that I am in another world when she is talking to me and that I don't really listen to her. She is right, of course – my behavior is insulting to any person who notices it.

The *Talmudic Encyclopedia* teaches us that a sage is not to walk with a proud, upright posture and an outstretched neck. I wonder if this relates not only to showing proper humility before God, but also to our relationships with other nations. I think it is odd that Jews, who are living in their own independent state, should walk with a poor posture, stooped downwards, while the Arabs walk with a proud, upright gait. I wonder if there is not something about our posture that makes us vulnerable and open to hostility from other nations.

Wednesday, February 23
17 *Adar I*

Rabbi Avraham Twerski points out that we often insult others by not acknowledging the gratitude that they express. I feel that I am guilty of this and must work to correct it.

Neither S. nor I said anything to insult each other when we met in Tel Aviv. There was an atmosphere of politeness and friendliness the whole time that we spent together. Yet when I discovered that she had the time and could have arranged for us to meet again and did not, I felt disappointed and rejected. She was not willing to make any special effort or sacrifice for me. She does not seem to be the sort of giving and kind person that I would like to marry. Perhaps true *derech eretz* is to bear the hurt quietly, shouldering the insult and carrying on with life.

Thursday, February 24
18 *Adar I*

It was a nice surprise yesterday when Dov showed up for *Minchah*. The father-in-law of our rabbi made an especially beautiful blessing for his recovery before the *shiur*. After the *shiur*, I walked Dov home. I had heard that his wife has trouble sometimes moving him around the house. I told her that I am home most of the time and that she can call me anytime for help as I live only a few minutes away. Both Dov and his wife are so reluctant to demand anything of anyone. They are anxious not to burden others. The special beauty of their being satisfied with their lot often moves me.

I am supposed to have a meeting with my publisher today. I have not come through for him on the Goren work, though I have not given up. I have had ideas for other works that I could do with my old publisher, but I believe that it would not be ethical to turn my attention to them. At some point I must make a real effort with the Goren work. Then, if I still cannot do it, I will simply tell the publisher so. I must prepare for our meeting. To come unprepared is to show disrespect.

I am considering whether or not to call S. this morning to say good-bye. The truth is that I enjoy being around her, but I will not call. In another situation, were there not romantic issues involved, I would have no trouble in putting my pride aside. But there are other factors at play in our relationship. If my feelings for her are not reciprocated, I will just accept my disappointment, act cordially towards her in the future, and carry on.

I am glad that the meeting with my publisher was cancelled yesterday. It was scheduled to be at the same time as the funeral of the singer, Ofra Haza, may her soul rest in peace.

Rabbi Eisen spoke today about the necessity of having Torah knowledge, which is the blueprint for living a life of *derech eretz*.

Friday, February 25
19 Adar I

I was on my way to my regular Friday lesson when I saw that a car was stuck on the road. Instead of getting out to help, the driver behind him simply honked his horn. I went over and pushed the car, moving it over to the side. The driver then managed to restart it. I then got on a bus. There was a large bottleneck of traffic at the gas station in the center of Ramat Eshkol. One policeman passed by on a motorbike and did nothing. I got off the bus and began directing two cars that were obstructing the way. The driver of the first car, an elderly lady who did not know how to back up, tried to follow my instructions. Eventually, with the aid of another car who let this elderly lady go ahead of him, the bottleneck opened up.

I have met a few of the people who have been on my mind lately in the past week: I met Israel R. outside. He still cannot walk, yet he still refuses my offer for a chiropractor. I met Ruth F. at Anita's house last week. I did not, however, meet Yigal, and I still wonder whether or not he is alive.

Wouldn't it have been proper *derech eretz* for S. to call and thank me for my hospitality and wish me well, regardless of her feelings about our relationship? I now realize that I may have been completely rude when I last spoke to her, for she was sick at the time. I can only empathize with her sickness now because I myself have had the same kind of flu for the past few days. It knocked me out. I did not even show her any sympathy.

I just spoke with a friend who has just returned from America. I called him even though I knew that there would inevitably be *lashon harah* spoken against Israel, as this is his main theme: America is good, Israel is bad. Maybe I should tell him that it is wrong to speak in this way, but the Gemarah teaches us that we should not chide or correct a person if they are not open to correction. Maybe I should just break off contact with him altogether. On the other hand, he has been a friend of mine for a long time and he is not directly hurting anyone by his remarks. At one time I thought that his real problem has nothing to do with what he complains about, but really stems from his lack of satisfaction with his work. I tried to make certain recommendations to him as a result but nothing helped. Perhaps he would simply be better off if he were in America. I have no doubt that my friend is right when he says that life in America is much more pleasurable and relaxing than life in Israel. I am sure that the material quality of life is much higher there. But Israel is the only place where the Jewish people can fulfill our covenant with God.

Monday, February 28
22 Adar I

There is *derech eretz* in the way that some people are conscientious and thorough in their work, doing their job in the best way possible. I think of my dentist Dr. R., whose great care, precision and patience never fail to impress me.

Tuesday, February 29
23 Adar I

The newspapers this morning reported that the Health Minister is to issue a decree banning smoking in Israeli hospitals. This will truly be an important step in making Israel a better place to live. The present system of designated areas for smoking has not been effective in keeping the air fresh and clean. I have often been dismayed at how a smoke-filled environment was permitted when the public consists of so many sick people.

Wednesday, March 1
24 Adar I

Yesterday I went to the wedding of Efraim H., the son of the local rabbi. He is a Lubavitcher *chassid*. I know the young man – he is a particularly considerate person, both humble and learned. I pray that he and his new wife will have a life of joy and well-being. At the wedding, I thought of my daughter, who entered into the army yesterday. It hurts me to think that there is a whole segment of the Jewish people who is freed from the fundamental responsibility of protecting their country. I do not believe that the *charedi* world acts with *derech eretz* with regard to their collective responsibility to the Jewish people. They argue otherwise. Still, I believe that *derech eretz* involves caring for the whole of the Jewish people and the whole world at large, each and every one of God's creations. They maintain that they are doing precisely what God demands of them by sitting and learning Torah all the time, and that it is for others to do other tasks. I would accept this claim, except that it seems to me that the most difficult and dangerous tasks are those that those closest to God should take upon themselves because God demands the most from those who are closest to Him.

Yesterday, I gave Chaim M. a check for the fund that his family is setting up for the recruitment drive for bone-marrow donors. He told me that they need to add 8,000 donors to the list. They have been through the existing lists and no donor has been found for his three-year-old grandchild. I pray for miraculous divine help, that somehow a way will be found to her full recovery.

Thursday, March 2
25 *Adar I*

I spoke with my publisher yesterday. I told him that I am going to try again, but that I will probably tell him in a couple of months that I was not able to do the Goren work. He was not angry or disappointed and instead offered his help to keep the work going. I greatly appreciate his patience and understanding. He also helped me with regard to the proposed volume based on this journal. I had thought to include other works as well, but he rightly said that it would distract from the main purpose of the journal. I am now thinking of other ways of making this volume one that will truly be of help to people. One feature I have thought of is a list of practical suggestions for improving *derech eretz* in Israel at the end of the book. I also want to provide a forum by which people can send in their reactions and suggestions.

I just prepared the check and card for the son of Rabbi H. and his new wife. Of all of the rabbi's sons, I know and like him the best.

I have not heard from Israel G. regarding the loan for the rent. He is a good person and I do not want to call him, but the first of the month is coming and he will soon have two more rents to pay. I am not worried about the money he owes me, which I have already given up on in my mind. I simply do not want this person to find himself in a desperate situation. Perhaps I should call him.

Friday, March 3
26 Adar I

Today I went to give the former dentist from Russia the usual amount of money I give him each Friday. As always, he thanked me profusely. He then asked me for my telephone number. I did not want to oblige him, but I gave it to him anyway. Again, I find myself in a situation where I give much more than others would and thus think that the recipients are content with this. But my giving does not solve their real needs and they take my excessive generosity as a sign that I can solve all of their problems.

Sunday, March 5
28 Adar I

Last week, I gave up going to a favorite lesson in order to go and support a friend who was giving a lecture on his work for the first time. I learned a lot from the lecture and am not sorry that I went. The problem is that I felt a certain anger during and after the lecture because it was really a prescription for a messianic age to come. I believe that the reason it angered me is because I am tired of the same old formulas that promise future, all-encompassing perfection when I see so much suffering all around me. I am angry at what I regard to be simplistic answers, when life itself is filled with so many challenges, difficulties, and twists and turns.

This Friday night, the whole *shul* began talking when it came time to sing the concluding song, *Yigdal*. I know that there are shuls where it is not the custom to sing *Yigdal*. Nonetheless, we are enjoined to honor the customs of the place we are in. Why do people come to *shul* if they do not pray, if they find no joy in the prayers? If they only seem to want to talk until the service is over? The *shaliach tsibbur* should, especially on festive occasions, do his maximum to involve the congregation, to help bring them to a higher level of feeling. I see so many people around me who seem to have no consciousness of this and are only intent on going on their own "trip." The *shaliach tsibbur* should be praying for the congregation, both as the one addressing God on their behalf and as the one moving them to pray in such a way as to bring them closer to God. For many years I have prayed in places where I sense the focus is wrong, yet because I am conscious of my place, I do not say anything.

Rabbi Emanuel Feldman makes an important point with regard to the feminist struggle within Orthodoxy. He points out that a Jew is not taught to think of his own rights and privileges, but rather of his duties in serving God. This means that personal joy, fulfillment and happiness are not the main priority and justification for everything. He sees much of the actions of the feminist movement as immodest and in contradiction with traditional teaching. Yet all the time, I see and feel the second class status of the women in the *shul* I go to. I do not know what could be changed to rectify the situation.

Monday, March 6
29 Adar I, Yom Kippur Katan

Although I do not know M.R. that well and no longer have anything to gain practically from our relationship (he was fired from his post at the newspaper), I will try to help him and arrange for him to meet with Dr. Bob. In Buber's language, to relate to a person as a "you" and not an "it." More simply put, one should not drop a person just because one no longer has anything to gain from him practically.

I have not visited a number of people because of my cough. I should try to call and ask them how they are. On the other hand, I feel that people want more from me than I can practically give. On Shabbat, I saw Israel R. outside. I sat and talked with him, even though I was on my way home from *shul* and a long walk. I sat with him for a few minutes. I sensed that he wanted more than my sympathy and listening could give. He wanted "real help," a cure for his ailing back and feet. I gave him what I could, which was not enough.

Tuesday, March 7
Rosh Chodesh Adar II

Professor E. read the Torah this morning. He is a model of *derech eretz* in all that he does. He reads the Torah with precision and without error. He does not speak much, but always answers in a polite manner when people speak to him. He knows a tremendous amount and does not show his knowledge off. He is modest and speaks in a gentle and pleasant way to everyone. He does everything in the best way possible. He is the kind of person who should serve as model for us all.

My decision not to go to the holy teacher's lesson today because of the cold and the rain is perhaps justifiable considering how sick I have been. But the decision not to go to Rabbi Isaacs' *shiur* is less justifiable because he lives much closer to me. I suppose that I was being selfish, but I do not see the point in attending a *shiur* when I am unable to give my full attention to it.

Wednesday, March 8
Rosh Chodesh Adar II Bet

God is a giver. Walking in God's way means giving to others.

There are times when I feel myself weary of giving, tired of the increasing demands made of me. My holy teacher has told me that one of the reasons for the early deaths of some of the greatest masters were the endless demands made upon them from their followers. They gave and gave until they could not give anymore.

On the other hand, giving adds to our own sense of meaning, our own sense of worth. This is so clear to me. Even giving food to the little blind cat that hangs around our front door is a manifestation of this. Today I began the day by feeding the cats. I then gave the *gabbai* money for the weekly *shiur*, gave *tzedakah* for *Rosh Chodesh*, and gave my last copy of my book of interviews to one of the interviewees who asked for an additional copy. There is a way of seeing those who ask, those who make demands, not as *nudniks*, but as those who provide opportunities for us to act in a positive way. There is a way of seeing these people as partners with us in this holy task.

It occurs to me that this work, the topic of which is *derech eretz*, does not contain very many thoughts on situations related to earning one's own living. "Torah and *derech eretz*" means combining Torah study with working for a living. In terms of earning my own living, I am a great failure. Against my own will, effort and ideal, I have not succeeded. Of course, it might be said that my guilt helps make me more virtuous, more ready to give to and share with others than the average person.

I spoke with my friend Yaakov Fogelman today. As usual, we exchanged information and helped each other out. He is always trying to help. He is also always trying to teach Torah, and perhaps offends some by coming on too strong. Yet his manner is so mild and pleasant that I doubt many remain offended for long. His wife and he also exemplify the *mitzvah* of *hachnasat orchim* and always have many guests at their Shabbat table.

I think that what Rambam says about adopting one *mitzvah* and devoting oneself to it, doing it thoroughly and earning one's share in the World to Come in this way, applies equally to behaving with *derech eretz*. We tend to choose certain *mitzvot* and focus on them rather than act upon all equally. Instead, we need to focus on the ideal of being a city upon a hill, a light unto the nations, of establishing a society in which everyone acts with *derech eretz*.

There are certain characteristics that are stereotypically associated with being an Israeli that go against the ideal of *derech eretz*. For example, arrogance, aggressiveness, a know-it-all self-confidence and rudeness. Some say that these characteristics were inculcated within us because the pioneers of Israel felt it would counteract the weakness of the Jewish Diaspora. But haven't we come to a time of mature strength, where no such negative compensatory behavior is required?

The police in Israel do not act with *derech eretz* in many situations. Perhaps this is not surprising given the kind of tasks they have to do and the kind of people and situations they have to deal with. Nonetheless, I think of the way they charged the crowd with horses when we demonstrated against the Oslo accords. I remember seeing one policeman kicking a woman who had fallen down. The police have also been known to leak confidential interrogations to the press the day after they conduct them. Instead of protecting the rights of citizens, they violate them. They abuse their position of power and act corruptly. This is not to say that there are not numerous beneficial police actions.

I cannot bear the gossiping and slanderous reports of the media, with their half-truths and besmirching of names. They also do not respect privacy in medical matters, and create a generally ugly atmosphere in the country. Their only aim is to be sensationalist, to make quick profits, and show little concern for the potential victims of their scoops as a result. My guess is that this trend in the media comes at a time when there is less serious investigative reporting. In a world where everyone seeks instant gratification, no one wants to take the time or effort to do real work. The "me, me, me" mentality lowers the capacity for the kind of dedication which is required if the best work is to be done.

Thursday, March 9
2 Adar II

Rabbi Mordechai Gafni spoke last night about the importance of knowing how to receive (*kabbalah*). He reminded me of what happened on Sunday – someone from the shul offered me a ride and because I wanted to walk, I refused it. I immediately felt badly because I sensed that this person had really wanted to help me. This incident suggests that there are times when we should accept favors even if we do not really want to. The problem is that I love my independence too much – I simply do not like to rely on other people. This is partly so because I am a person who, for years, has just wanted to be left alone and not be bothered, so that I can do my work.

When riding the bus, many people appear to be resentful when someone comes to sit next to them. They are too conscious of having their own space encroached upon.

I did not show any annoyance this morning when a young man who was sitting in my row in *shul* blocked my access to the door. I restrained myself from correcting him and later shook his hand after his *aliyah* to the Torah. I also spoke a few words of friendly greeting to him afterwards. He is not another one of those people who do not know what to do with themselves, like I had originally thought. He is a mathematics student at the university.

Friday, March 10
3 *Adar II*

There is *derech eretz* involved in giving others credit for what we have learned from them. He who brings forth a piece of Torah in the name of the one who originally said it brings redemption to the world. Yesterday I began to read Rabbi Telushkin's book on Jewish values, which I hope will be of help to me in this writing. He does a number of things with his book that are very helpful to the reader: he organizes his teachings and essays day by day, he has a complete list of themes and avoids the kind of repetition I am frequently guilty of. He also brings a wide variety of stories and anecdotes. He incorporates such sources as the Gemarah and *midrashim* into his teachings, making them relevant for today. I will try to learn from his work and look out for important themes in *derech eretz* that I may have missed. But I also know that each one of us can only do what he is capable of. I cannot really hope to emulate such a superior work.

Sunday, March 12
5 *Adar II*

I left two events early yesterday. One was on Shabbat, a "cultural" program in which the speaker began to malign *charedim*. I did not want to hear this kind of *lashon harah* on Shabbat. Then, on *motzei* Shabbat, I left a party of a friend's sister early. I found it difficult to stand idle through all the small talk, and was somewhat disturbed at my being present at a celebration which honored a person who teaches one of the new spirituality heresies. Perhaps it would have been wiser not to have come in the first place. My rudeness, however unintentional, was evident in my leaving early. I did so in the politest way possible, but am still certain that I left a slightly bad feeling in any case.

During a visit to sick friend, I had a warm conversation with four very good women I know. I was saddened by the realization that three of them are widows of very good friends of mine. All of them are kind, warm people who enjoyed long and happy marriages.

I was reminded yesterday of what I knew deep down and what I suppressed, that the first quality that I should be looking for in a wife is kindness. If there is no kindness then there is no basis for mutual love and respect. I believe that I made a serious mistake in my relationship with S. when I hinted my interest to her and, in doing so, perhaps fostered in her an unrealistic hope for "us."

Those schoolchildren who use vile language, mock other ethnic groups and demonstrate defiance and anger when rebuked by their elders have a problem which clearly stems from a lack of proper education in their homes. They have probably been hearing abusive language and seeing rude behavior all their lives. This does not mean that they should not be confronted and corrected, it only means that their problem is more complex than any response, however justified, can address.

I have been debating with myself as to whether or not it was right to give such an unusually large gift to the son of the rabbi. The rabbi came over to me the other day and thanked me warmly. This made me feel that I had done the right thing. The other night, as I was returning home, I saw the young couple walking together. It also gave me the feeling that I had done the right thing.

Last week, I wrote a letter to my beloved teacher and friend, Rabbi Greenberg, who just accepted a new position of great prestige. Instead of congratulating him, I expressed my regret that the new position would take him away from his writing, which I believe he should be doing more of. I was wrong to give my opinion on the matter, even though I expressed my views politely. He has the many burdens of a new job and I added to his burden by reminding him that he is neglecting his other work.

I wonder if I do enough to honor my parents' memory. I write of them, think of them and pray for them, but I have not given any great gift in their name. I have always felt that the best thing that I can do for them is to help their children and grandchildren to the best of my ability.

Monday, March 13
6 Adar II

Israeli Jews have *derech eretz* dilemmas that Jews in the Diaspora simply do not face. We have neighbors who are often hostile and who threaten us with violence. The repeated incidents of violence (this morning, another taxi-driver was probably kidnapped by Arabs) lead to feelings of anger, bitterness and a desire for revenge – feelings that I do not want to have.

The dilemma of how to maintain our strength while preserving our humanity is one that we are faced with all the time in Israel. The danger is, of course, going to extremes in either direction. I think of how our soldiers were killed and injured because we would not fire back at terrorists who targeted the houses of civilians. The survival of one's own people comes before all other considerations. Obviously, though, one should do everything possible to avoid injury to non-combatants.

Acting with *derech eretz* is clearly much more difficult and challenging when one is dealing with threats and enemies than when one is dealing with friendly people who wish you well. Maintaining a positive mood is also easier when there are not constant interruptions in the form of violence from one's neighbors.

I have not seen my holy teacher in over two weeks. I have the feeling that his health has deteriorated in the last month or so. I will do my best to learn with him this week. I must also make a point of questioning him about the doctor he is seeing. He has decided to go against the doctor's recommendation of an operation. I wonder if I should have urged him more strongly to consider the possibility of having the operation.

The editor from the newspaper with whom I had a good relationship has been fired. I do not know if it is right to contact his successor. Is this a betrayal of him? Or is my reaction just nonsensical over-loyalty?

In his book, Rabbi Telushkin makes the important point that whenever we talk about a third party, even if it is to praise them, there is the danger of *lashon harah* because praise can often create bad feelings and resentment.

One of the most frequent complaints Israelis make about themselves is that they do not know how to compliment and praise each other. Although it is true that there are times when praise is not warranted, it can nonetheless be fitting and even necessary, as a sign of encouragement or an expression of appreciation and gratitude. On the other hand, the type of empty, exaggerated praise that is often abundant in "polite" social settings is inappropriate.

My doctor has real *derech eretz*. When he examines a patient, he never allows himself to be rushed. He does his job thoroughly, giving each patient all of his attention.

Tuesday, March 14
7 Adar II

Just as I was entering the *shul*, I heard footsteps about twenty feet behind me. This is a large enough distance so that one would ordinarily open and close the door without waiting for the person behind him. However, I make a habit of waiting anyway and, when I did, I saw that one of the infrequent synagogue attendees who I remember being loud and drunk was behind me. As I stood, holding the door open for him, he gave me a warm smile and a handshake.

On Shabbat, at the end of *seudah shlishit*, I helped the main *gabbai* by bringing the water for the washing of the hands at the end of the meal to the far end of the table. This Shabbat, I placed the water before a person who I sometimes suspect of a certain arrogance. He did not take the water, nor did he pass it on to the next person. He simply left it there and went and washed his hands by the faucet. I was a little insulted by this, but simply picked up the little basin and passed it on to someone else. This is just a petty incident, but is nonetheless a reminder that a true lack of *derech eretz* is a failure to consider others, even in minor ways.

The definition of the Jewish hero as being one who overcomes his own inner evil impulses does not take into account the Israeli Jews of today. There are other types of heroes who have risked their lives and lost them, or have sustained terrible physical and psychological injuries as a result of war. In this sense, courage is essential to true *derech eretz* in Israel. Those who say it is the students in the *yeshivot* who risk their lives for Israel by sitting and learning all day, or those who say that every individual has the right to do all they can to be exempt from army service (as certain famed Israeli "artists" have done), violate true *derech eretz* in the deepest way. For what can be greater *derech eretz* than giving of oneself to help keep the Jewish community, the Jewish people in Israel, alive?

Wednesday, March 15
8 Adar II

I just wrote a letter to the managing editor of The Jerusalem Post requesting that they reinstate Alec Israel. I believe that this is the right thing to do, rather than to rush to establish a relationship with the new book editor.

I called my holy teacher and spoke with his wife about his situation. I was afraid that he had abandoned the doctors completely. He just called me back. He is under their supervision. He told me that the effects of the radiation can last for two years and that this is part of his hesitancy.

My holy teacher sounded much better this morning when he gave me a Torah lesson on the phone. He told me a story about his teacher, Reb Shlomo Carlebach: he was once going through his things when he came across a phone number that he had once been given. He did not know who it belonged to, but he called anyway. It was a woman who, at the moment she received the call, was about to commit suicide. The call saved her life.

I just received a call from a woman who said that she is caring for the family of her sister, who was killed in a traffic accident. I remember her from previous years. I wrote out a check for her and wished her a happy Purim. She sounded very discouraged.

How must God feel when we constantly ask Him for more and more? But we cannot compare ourselves to God and try to imagine how we would feel in such a predicament. The truth is that there are many people who are in great need and are too ashamed to ask for anyone's help.

I now realize that the two university students who asked to see the rabbi are probably looking for a place to eat for Shabbat dinner. We do not have communal meals in our *shul*. I will ask one person whose family I know usually takes guests to host them.

Thursday, March 16
9 Adar II

Two people helped me yesterday: an engineer friend came over and showed me how to execute some operations on the computer that I needed to know and another good acquaintance who runs an internet office helped me send an e-mail to my son and then told me to give the payment to *tzedakah*.

The doctors are striking today. I met Menahem, who had a couple of his check-ups cancelled as a result. There is something terribly wrong with an economy in which there are so many strikes that bring real harm to so many people. The people who suffer most from the strikes are those who need medical attention. I know that doctors are overworked and underpaid, but being a doctor is a calling. In my opinion, it is simply not right of them to cause human misery by striking. It is not right to risk loss of life by delaying treatments, which include important operations. If there is a fundamental flaw in the structure of the Israeli economy, it is that the government is over-involved in it. The selling of government companies is one way of trying to correct this. But something should also be done about the stranglehold the large, prosperous unions have on the economy and, in fact, the whole way the labor market is organized in Israel. Clearly many of the measures that were introduced in order to protect workers have ended up pulling down the economy as a whole. I myself do not know enough to provide all the answers but, like most other citizens, I sense and feel the problem all the time.

Sunday, March 19
12 *Adar II*

In these pages I have deliberately written little about the relationship in my life which is most important to me, my relationship with my children. With reference to my children, I try to live by what I believe to be the Jewish rule in relationships, that those closest to a person come first for him. But one does not really need to "try" when it comes to this – it comes naturally. I write this passage in connection with my concern, and even guilt, over my daughter's returning to the army today. I could have had her exempted by claiming that she is religious. However, I did not want to do so because she did not urge me to. I had and have the sense (perhaps naively) that if she somehow does go through it in the right way and performs a real service, her contribution will be of real help to her. Perhaps I am a fool in thinking this. Rabbi Telushkin writes that what really matters in Judaism is educating one's children to help them become decent people, and not necessarily brilliant worldly successes. Perhaps I am dreaming, but I believe that my children are primarily kind and considerate people.

I know what it is to feel the imprisonment of being in the army. I know what it is to long for it to be over, to only want to get out. I am therefore pained now at thinking of what my daughter might be going through.

My friend C. is a very good person. He is also well learned and highly intelligent. He is more open than I am; he shows greater *sever panim yafot* to Arabs and, my guess is, to non-Jews in general. I have mixed feelings about this openness. On the one hand, I believe it is admirable and correct, and I wish I were more generous in this way. On the other hand, I sometimes feel that this openness is a kind of collusion and even has hints of subservience and betrayal. Yesterday, we fell out over the Supreme Court's ruling that a Jewish settlement cannot exclude Arabs from coming to live in it. He spoke in favor of the decision in a way that left me without an answer, so I changed the subject to the question of the loyalty and general intent of the Palestinians within Israel.

Last night, I could have made a special effort to go to the Old City for the *kiddush levanah* prayer led by my holy teacher, but I felt so tired that I did not go.

Monday, March 20
13 *Adar II, Ta'anit Esther*

All deeds of kindness lose their meaning when I find myself unable to help my own family. I pray that there are kind, considerate people in the army who are helping my daughter now. I realize anew the gift of my own freedom. I am not subject to the whims of cruel people in my everyday life. I am not in an environment where people want to avenge themselves against me for what they imagine others have done to them. I do not face the test of *derech eretz* in the hostile environment of a prison, or against a background of great deprivation and struggle.

I feel guilty that I am always asking God for things. I suppose that my kind deeds, meant to help others, are my small way of showing gratitude to God for all done for me.

I just went over and brought my friend B. a book. How good it was to see a friendly face! There are certain kinds of people who lift our spirits when we speak with them. Just by being themselves, they bring goodness to the world.

I saw Israel R. outside for the first time in a long time. He looks the same, but says that his feet are worse. He asked me about my children and I told him about my daughter being in the army and my son's traveling. Though I attempt to follow my mother's rule of trying to speak as little as possible about my children, I could see no reason not to reply. I might even have been looking to share my feelings with someone else.

Rav Ovadia Yosef did it again with a series of curses against Yossi Sarid, calling him Haman and Amalek. Didn't anyone ever tell him about *lashon harah*? As a political act, his comments might fire up his followers, but it certainly does little good to the Jewish world as a whole. It is sad that we have come to this and that his army of "yes-men" conform to whatever he says and does. I would have preferred him to have criticized Sarid factually and fairly.

Tuesday, March 21
14 Adar II, Purim

On Purim, we must first take care of our families (*seudat mitzvah*), then our friends (*mishloach manot*), and finally, our communities (*matanot l'evyonim*). These are the three *mitzvot*, three responsibilities, that one must meet if one is to perform God's will on Purim. The three *mitzvot* mentioned above and, of course, hearing the Megillah.

Wednesday, March 22
15 Adar II, Shushan Purim

I made a special effort yesterday afternoon, and went to the Old City in order to bring my holy teacher *matanot l'evyonim*, which he will distribute to the long list of people to whom he gives *tzedakah*.

Thursday, March 23
16 Adar II

It is an important principle of *derech eretz* to be truthful. This means knowing the difference between what one wishes to be true and what is really the truth.

I gave *mishloach manot* yesterday without any real thought or preparation as to what the people who received them would want. I did it for myself and not for them. This is not proper *derech eretz*.

It is important to speak with those people who no one else seems to care for.
This morning I spoke with a person who hangs out at the *shul*. I understand that he has a speech impediment. He is a harmless, quiet, religious person. He is so alone, but never complains. Today we talked for more time than ever before. He has a smile of innocence and openness. I know how it is when you are alone, and suddenly someone listens to you and makes you feel that you are a human being again.

Sunday, March 26
19 Adar II

My lack of success and limited influence in the world makes it difficult for me to criticize, to effectively contend with, those who I consider to be the defamers of Israel, the enemies from within – the media. Although I write letters to the newspapers at times, they appear irregularly, and are shorter and less effective than the regular columns of the self-haters. I wonder now if it would be correct for me to specifically name those who write for the Hebrew daily *Ha'aretz* and who consistently undermine Israel's position. There is a broader question, though, of how to act with *derech eretz* while attempting to protect oneself. I think that a prime example of this is Israel's military policy of purity of arms and self-restraint, which often comes at the price of increasing the danger to our soldiers.

The degree of *lashon harah*, self-hatred, distortion of the truth and sympathy with evildoers that flows from the media and the academic world is, for me, one of the most disappointing and difficult things about life in Israel. It goes beyond a simple lack of *derech eretz* – it indicates a level of evil and wickedness. Yet even my saying this is, in a way, a violation of *derech eretz*, as it throws a negative light on Israel.

On Shabbat, I spoke with someone who just came back from New York. He came back with glowing reports. He told me how wonderful it felt to be in a place where one can walk about freely, without stumbling on a border. Now this person did not mean to say *lashon harah* by comparing "golden" America with a less glowing Israel, but he did. When contradicted, he later admitted that Israel is where a Jew who wants to live most completely as a Jew should be.

How can I make this work more interesting, more helpful and more enjoyable to the reader? How can I truly give the reader something of value? What changes should be made to this work? Perhaps I should create structured chapters, perhaps a re-organization in terms of themes? Perhaps I should consider more fully other kinds of *derech eretz* issues, those that I do not ordinarily face?

Monday, March 27
20 *Adar II*

President Clinton's talks with Assad yesterday failed to bring about a renewal of negotiations between Syria and Israel. In one sense, I am relieved as I believe that giving up the Golan may greatly endanger Israel. On the other hand, I am not rejoicing as some people I know are, because I understand that a possible consequence of this is another major outbreak of violence. I believe that this kind of moderate, balanced reaction on my part is the correct way, in *derech eretz* terms. Rambam speaks about us not going too wild with joy, or sinking too deeply into despair, but rather maintaining a balanced stance.

Is there such a thing as existing in a situation that lacks *derech eretz*? I am thinking of the fact that I do not have a wife. An adult Jew is required to be married. I have had sufficient time to find a new wife. I maintain, though, that I have not yet found the kind, understanding, compatible wife that I am seeking. Have I been too choosy and am thus a failure? I find myself in a situation that I never wanted to be in. I was happy being married and shared many joyous years with my wife. Now this is no longer my reality. But the test comes not when life is mapped out according to our exact specifications, but when times are hard, when things do not go according to plan. This is when our wisdom, courage and faith in God are put to the ultimate test.

It is sad to witness those who in the eyes of the secular Israeli public represent the Jewish religion act crudely, selfishly, narrowmindedly and with only their own self-interest at the heart of all their decisions. I would like to see all of Israel moving closer to performing the will of God, the service of God, not out of any collective compulsion or dictate, but rather out of free will and choice. I would like to see people turning to the Jewish tradition because of its richness in spiritual treasures. I would like to see a mutual respect amongst Jews, based on tolerance and understanding of their differing degrees and intensity of religious practice. I would like to see a society where respect and consideration are shown to each and every individual. This, I believe, is central to what God wants from us.

I am aware that there are countless tests and challenges in *derech eretz* that, luckily, I do not face. I think of the poor in our society. I think of the disabled. I think of those whose loved ones are fatally ill. The only option left for me is to do all I can to alleviate their suffering.

If the Jewish principle of *gemilut chassadim*, of doing deeds of kindness, of walking humbly before God, were at the very heart of our being, we would be a better society. As I see it, even those people who ardently champion a just cause can still act with a meanness and spread bad-will when they are quick to find evil in their opponent, thus defeating the whole point of their exercise.

There is no question that the concept of being a Chosen People may be distorted or wrongly interpreted and could have adverse effects: instead of being humble before God, it might engender arrogance toward others.

I saw an instance of public arrogance the other day; people standing in line to receive tickets for the decisive basketball game of the season were pushing, shoving and fighting with each other. The police pushed them back and horses trampled on some of them. Perhaps it is senseless to speak of *derech eretz* with regard to such an event. The way I see it, the lack of *derech eretz* is in being so obsessively attached to a basketball game and fighting to take from others what they so desperately want as a result. Societies that place so much emphasis on competitive sports, on winning competitions and, by doing so, defeating other people, lack *derech eretz*. Also flawed are those societies that value competition in business, on getting ahead of others in the marketplace. The greed of acquisition has a certain ugliness about it. And yet, paradoxically, it is these societies that are able to relieve human misery with their inventions and technological progress. Would a world that is based on the ideals of *derech eretz*, standing in contrast to the values of a modern capitalistic society, be more calm and stable, yet, on the flip side, more primitive and backward? Even those people whose lives are fueled by competitive drive and a hunger for material success contribute to the world, perhaps in ways that those who live a life of *derech eretz* cannot. If we assess the character traits of the greatest inventors and scientists throughout history, many of them were less than perfect in their conduct.

However, when we look at Rambam and Rashi, who were both deeply steeped in Jewish tradition and committed to family and communal obligations, yet were also phenomenal scientists and innovators, it is clear that great creative work does not necessarily have to contradict the principles of *derech eretz*.

I myself have not been tempted to arrogance, as I have had no great success or recognition in my work. It has not really been a challenge for me to be modest. In truth, the temptation lies in the inclination to go overboard in diminished self-esteem, or, conversely, to act in a martyred fashion because one's greatness has been unjustly ignored. It is important to know that while I may not be everything, I also am not nothing.

I am considering not putting my name on this work – out of modesty and also because I am afraid that petitioners will come knocking at my door. On the other hand, this anonymity can be seen as an evasion of responsibility. I should have the courage to stand by my convictions and stand behind my work and be recognized for it. I tend to be over-critical of myself. Perhaps this is an attempt to ward off potential criticism from others.

I just went downstairs to get the mail and saw Israel R. sitting on a bench. Seeing how uncomfortable he looked, I went over and spoke with him. His back aches. I asked him about the treatment. He says that his niece is too busy to take him. I again mentioned the option of having the chiropractor come to see him. But the moment I said this, I realized that I would have to speak with his niece and arrange this with her. She does not seem to be a particularly sympathetic character, but perhaps I should persist and speak with her nonetheless. Still, I am reluctant to interfere. What if I exacerbate the situation?

This morning Dov returned to *shul* for *Shacharit* for the first time. I pray that he will become stronger. I had thought that Ruth F. might be angry with me for not visiting more often. I saw her on Shabbat. Of course, she was not. Her son is coming in two weeks and then there will be the unveiling for Mel's tombstone. I had heard that Ruth F. cannot bear being in their apartment anymore and wants to move. I will speak with her and her son and help them, if they want, go through Mel's things, which is always a painful process.

Tuesday, March 28
21 Adar II

I was thinking about this work last night and came to the conclusion that if I don't publish it, there is absolutely no chance of it achieving anything constructive. Even if I am not assured of its value to others, it can do no harm to try. Nothing ventured, nothing gained. No matter how unknown my work may be, no matter how little I have done with it, it still is my work. To publish it is going the distance with who I am. And if I do not make it available to others, then it cannot possibly help others and help Israel, so better to *try* to help than to do nothing at all.

I was on a crowded bus when a young man sprawled his leg across the seat next to me. I asked him to put his foot down. He complied at first, but when my back was turned, he put it back up. The bus became more crowded. I got up from my seat and gave it to a girl who was standing nearby and motioned to the rude man that I wanted to sit where his leg was. He moved it and I sat down. I began to speak in a mild way about respect for others in public spaces. He asked me a strange question, if I was a Jew. In response to my affirmative answer, he appeared to be uncomfortable and moved away to another seat.

I could have congratulated myself for not allowing this rude individual to feel that he can physically intimidate others, but I didn't feel joy. Instead, I felt anger at having to be involved with such things – it is beneath my dignity. I was also infuriated by the passivity of the other passengers, including one hefty looking man who, upon seeing that the rude person was an Arab, would not, perhaps out of fear or repulsion, sit next to him.

The Jewish stress on modesty, humility and walking humbly before God are the foundations of my faith. Yet I see that there are some situations where humility is synonymous with timidity and cowardice. There are situations when wrongdoing must be actively challenged and resisted.

Derech eretz is not simply watching out for number one. It is looking out for the well-being of others, especially those who are weak and unable to protect themselves. This idea is at the heart of the Jewish tradition.

How can one act with *derech eretz* when other people consistently do not? I would contend that this is the central moral question involved in our relationship with the Arabs. They so often interpret acts of kindness by us as signs of weakness. And they, in turn, try to use physical violence or threats as a way to dominate public spaces.

Wednesday, March 29
22 Adar II

Some good news. Three potential bone-marrow donors have been identified for Chaim M.'s granddaughter. I pray that one of them will be a true match.

Thursday, March 30
23 Adar II

One of the fundamental meanings of *derech eretz* is to work for a livelihood. For many years, I have striven to work as a writer, but it is not the main source of my income. In this sense, I am certainly no embodiment of someone who combines Torah and *derech eretz* and I feel that this is a deficiency in me. It could be said that it is easy for me to act with *derech eretz*, as I do not have the same preoccupations as others who must earn a livelihood.

Why do I place so much importance on the ideal of honesty in my heart and mind? Why is it so important for me to be honest about myself in this work, even if the truth is often unpleasant and embarrassing? I think that the answer is that I learned integrity from my parents and the value of this work seems to be based on this lesson. My father, may his soul rest in peace, used to say that the most important thing a person can have is a good name. So I believe that it is my duty to be honest in this work, and so retain my good name, in order that it can have some value. At the same time, one must be careful not to defame oneself or to be self-accusatory.

On the way to the Israel Center Torathon, I met Larry B.'s wife carrying heavy packages. I helped her carry them and walked her home. We started talking and I apologized for leaving her party early. She is a kind and warm woman.

Rabbi Lopes Cardozo taught us last night that while it is not clear if a Jew has an obligation from the Torah to work for a living, it is clear that a Jew (and here he follows Rav Soloveitchik) has an obligation to build the world, to be a partner in the creation with God. This idea has been central to my life for many years and it is at the heart of the way I see my own writing, my own work. I connect the effort at creation with the duty of serving God.

Acting with *derech eretz* may be seen as a way of building the world, bringing it closer to the form God wants it to have. Building a world of greater human relationships is no less "building" than is the invention of a new technological device.

Last night, I was listening to a *shiur* at the Israel Center when I saw two women working on folding the *Torah Tidbits* sheets. I went over and asked them if I could join them. I helped them for a while and because I did so, stayed to hear Rabbi Lopes Cardozo's *shiur*, which really helped me. As is often true, doing the right thing, even in a small way, helps the "doer" also.

Sunday, April 2
26 Adar II

There are times when one must put family duties before any kind of public obligation. On Shabbat I stayed to talk with my daughter instead of going to make my usual *bikkur cholim* visits. I also missed the morning *shiur* today in order to make sure I saw her off to the army.

I made an appointment with a health expert last week. I scheduled the appointment without taking into consideration the *shiurim* that I have on that day. I will try to change the date but since I already made the appointment, I will not cancel. It is important to realize that one must try to stay as healthy as possible in order to be able to serve God with strength.

Yesterday, I saw Israel R. sitting alone in discomfort. I went over to talk to him. I realize that his niece, with whom he lives, has stopped caring for him. She is not taking him to the doctor. I am wondering whether or not I should try to do this for him. Perhaps next time we meet I will tell him to have his niece make an appointment and that I will take him, if she agrees.

My holy teacher has to have a colostomy. He had hoped to avoid it. He delayed and delayed. But now the cancer is coming near to the bone. He said that the operation will be in two months. I wonder why it takes so long. I have urged him to have this treatment all along, but perhaps not as forcibly as I should have. I pray to God that he will have a *refuah shlemah*, a complete recovery.

I have already declined two *seder* invitations. I feel like I am sinning when I say no. With one refusal, there was a certain lack of *derech eretz* on my part. Instead of saying "thank-you but no thanks," I waited until he asked me if we were coming instead of giving him a definitive answer.

In changing the date of my appointment with the health expert, I let him down as well. I also declined an invitation from friends to go to the movies last night. It might seem petty, but saying no makes me feel guilty and selfish. If one does have to say no, it is best to do so in such a clear way that the other party has no false expectations and is saved the anguish of waiting and indecision.

Serving God with *derech eretz* is essentially serving the name of God by working to enhance His name and reputation among the other nations of the world. Each Jew, in his encounters with non-Jews, has a responsibility to act in a way that does not disgrace the name of God. Ideally, one must act in such a way in order to inspire love of God in all people.

Monday, April 3
27 Adar II

I heard a report on the news this morning that the Israeli government intends to shift their priorities away from external affairs and concentrate more on social and economic problems. There is a sense that these issues have been thus far neglected by the current government. However, also expected this morning is an announcement about the beginning of construction of the trans-Israel highway. This is a project that many believe will do much more harm than good and will seriously jeopardize the environment. I myself do not know enough about it to make a fair judgment.

The Zionist enterprise, the Jewish return to the land, is predicated upon the ideal of bringing new life to the land. It is based on the idea of making barren land fertile, of enriching our environment, not polluting it. However, economic development in Israel comes at a cost to the environment. Modernization, which has brought industry and, perhaps above all, the automobile, also means that the quality of our air and water has deteriorated. There is, I believe, a need for a stewardship over the land, based on *derech eretz*. We should not see the land as our own private possession, but as something that has been given to us by God in good faith. It is our task to develop the land in accordance with God's love of creation. An individual cannot define and determine collective *derech eretz* on his own. Rather, the individual has the responsibility to make a contribution in whatever way he or she can towards the collective *derech eretz*. One way, of course, is by setting an example in all that we do. Another is using democratic means of persuasion to introduce government policies that contribute to a higher quality of life.

Today I heard a wonderful piece of news: a suitable bone-marrow donor has been found for Chaim M.'s granddaughter. I had been praying, but inwardly did not have much hope because I thought it was a long shot. I was deeply moved by the good news. I was also sobered by it. Perhaps I should be more optimistic than I am. This means trusting in God's mercy more.

Tuesday, April 4
28 *Adar II*

Last night, I attended an evening of tribute to the poet Yehuda Amichai, who is very ill. The organizers did not have the sense, the *derech eretz*, to realize that they needed a room three times the size than they had reserved. I arrived early and sat in the middle of a row towards the back of the room. My decision was not based on *derech eretz*. I knew that the place would be crowded and that if I sat at the end of a row, I would have to give up my seat for an elderly person. In wanting to see and hear the tribute, I put my own self-interest first. The tribute itself was conducted, by and large, with *derech eretz*. The readings and the brief interludes of words were tastefully delivered and powerfully presented. There was an atmosphere of animation and concentration. I believe that the people in the hall understood that they were privileged to be part of such a bittersweet farewell to a great poet.

I received a call from Ruth F.'s daughter. The unveiling for Mel's tombstone will be on Friday. I will go over to the house early.

I spoke with my holy teacher. I learned that he has a CAT scan tonight and it is now unclear when the operation will be. I told him the truth, that with the exception of my family, he is the person who has had the greatest influence on me. He taught me the way of greeting each and everyone with *simchah*, with joy. I do not always do this, but I understand its importance and am better at it than I was before. I pray to God with all my heart for his complete recovery.

Wednesday, April 5
29 *Adar II*

I become angry when I hear of those within Israel who are bent on destroying the Jewish state. People in the media and the academic elite constantly work in opposition to Israel. Is my anger justified? Should I allow these people to dominate my thoughts? I feel guilty for not doing more, for not being a success, so that I might have more of an influence in helping Israel. I write letters and try to be active, but I am more than aware of how inconsequential my contribution is. I have recently adopted a new tactic that may enable me to do more for Israel. Instead of writing my letters directly to the media, I will write to those who I think have greater clout than I do and are more well-known and ask them to express my opinions on my behalf. What I really care about is the cause and the well-being of Israel, not signing my name at the bottom of a letter.

Thursday, April 6
Rosh Chodesh Nissan

I went to visit my holy teacher last night. He had to cut our lesson short again. I pray for the operation's success and his full recovery. I cannot banish the guilty feeling that I should have been more persistent in urging him to have medical treatment earlier. Sometimes one should carry on in one's attempt to convince someone of something if it is for their own benefit. My problem is that I am too caught up with minding my own business. I am reminded of my late brother's situation – I should have also pressed him to have medical treatment.

I met my good friend Mrs. C. yesterday. She is going to America for Pesach to be with her daughter and grandchildren. The daughter's husband just left her. I listened to her and told her Phil Chernofsky's story about a middle-aged son who still asks the four questions to his father on Pesach as a way of demonstrating that a child, no matter how old, always needs his parents. Empathetic listening is a central element in *derech eretz*.

I cannot help feeling that all my efforts are futile, that so much is not dependent on me. Nonetheless, I must try to do the best I can which, to my sorrow, is usually not good enough. I strongly believe in helping to create and shape the world for good. I find, though, that so much of my time is devoted to helping care for those whose lives are coming to an end. I love the world of children, of young people, yet find myself increasingly in the company of the old. The sad fact is that many of my good deeds are done simply because I perceive them to be necessary, therefore I feel compelled to do them even if I do not feel great joy in performing them. I often wish that I could do more for young people. I pray for the day that God will grant me grandchildren so that I can hopefully be a help to them.

Sunday, April 9
4 *Nissan*

I went to Mel's unveiling on Friday morning. They chose the verse in which God commands Avraham to rise up and walk through the land for the tombstone. This verse is truly appropriate for Mel, a man who loved to explore the land. The memorial service was conducted with the dignity and taste that characterizes the F. family. It was another case in which I went somewhere to help someone and instead felt helped by them.

I have just returned from an *azkarah* at Har Hazeitim, the Mount of Olives. The person who organized it, M., is a very caring and responsible person. He remembers dates of *azkarot* for others. He is one of those Jews who is always trying to help other people.

I feel that it has been a lack of *derech eretz* on my part not to have written more in this work about many people who are continually doing good for others. I think of certain *gabbaim* I know. I think also of certain friends I have; my holy teacher, who tries to lift the spirits of each person he meets, my good friend C. and his wife, who are always looking to help others. I think of another friend, Yaakov Fogelman, who is always trying to mediate between people and help them make better worlds for themselves, especially in learning Torah. While teaching Torah, Rabbi Eisen is gentle and considerate in his manner. Rav Yoni Berlin is always kind and intelligent in his words.

I have begun asking people about problems in *derech eretz* in Israel that most bother them. Frank M., who was born and raised in Canada, but who has lived here for many years, told me that there is only one area of life that truly disturbs him – the cars on the road. He says that he knows people who are ordinarily polite and considerate, but who, when they get into a car, undergo a complete transformation in character. Also, people arrive here from countries that do not have a culture of driving and so simply do not know how to manage on the roads. He said that it will take years for such a culture to develop.

I blame the Arabs and their leaders for not behaving properly in public areas; in the hospital, the market and even the bank. But I wonder if I am using their behavior as a pretext to hide the real reason for my discomfort and even anger at them: that they are dominating our districts with their growing numbers, something that I see as undermining the Jewish character of Israel. True *derech eretz* would probably be to curb my predisposed resentment towards them and judge them favorably, even greet them with a friendly countenance. The problem with seeing them as neighbors is that there is a real lack of communication between us.

Monday, April 10
5 *Nissan*

Last night, at the *yom iyyun* on Pesach at Heichal Shlomo, almost everyone walked out before the final lecture began. It was late but I decided to stay on, partly because I did not want to selfishly leave before the end.

I am struck again by how little *derech eretz* the media here displays. With their slanderous reports and innuendos, their rush to provide a headline while disregarding the damage done to those who stand in their path, they are guilty of much. They rarely admit to mistakes or take full responsibility for their actions. They exploit the misfortunes of others to forward their own interests. Even when their reports are accurate, they still show an insensitivity bordering on cruelty in the way they pursue and hound individuals and their families at a time when it is most difficult for them. Isn't everything I have just said, though, slander in itself? I think I should clarify that I am not condemning all the media, but am pointing out what appears to me to be a common trend. I would even go so far as to say that there is not a month that goes by here without some new instance of media insensitivity, of their testing the boundaries of decency and respect.

I visited Ruth F.'s son, as I said I would. We had an enjoyable two and a half-hour talk. We talked a bit about his mother's current situation and how she can be helped. In one sense, there is no way to alleviate her loss. However, through involvement in other activities, she can perhaps be helped over time. As it is, she now tutors the blind at the university and is also involved in other volunteer work.

God gives and gives and gives. Meanwhile, we ask for more and more and more.

Tuesday, April 11
6 Nissan

The phrase that appears in the first blessing of the *shmoneh esreh*, "for God's name's sake with love" seems to me to define the ideal goal of this work and is its test: if the work does not serve God with love, then it should not be published. But if it does somehow serve God, even if only in the slightest way, then it is a worthwhile project.

How can we, as insignificant mortals, add to the Name of the Eternal? The answer is that God has commanded us to sanctify the world by treating other human beings with love. God has commanded us to treat each person as created *b'tselem Elokim*, in God's holy image. When we do this, when we act as God has commanded, when we lovingly obey the teachings of the One and Only One, then we do sanctify God's Name.

The name of God is also connected with the name of Israel. How all Jews act to each aother is important for the Name of God in the world. It is as if we are entrusted with the honor of God. With each good deed that we do, we have the potential to add to His honor; likewise with each evil deed we commit, we have the potential to diminish it.

I just received a call from the holy teacher. Good news: the results of his check-up show that there has been no expansion of the growth. The operation for its removal does not have to be rushed. He called because he knew that I would be waiting to hear the news. Not only did he give me the good news, he also taught me a Torah lesson on the phone.

Friday, April 14
9 Nissan

Last night I went to the W. family's house. He is a teacher-friend of mine who, at the lowest moment of my life, helped me maintain my sense of self-worth and made me feel that my life had some meaning. As a token of gratitude, I bring them something every Pesach to help them. Last night our talk was shorter than usual because he was on a long distance phone call with a student. I was happy to see how well his children have grown. We spoke about his work conditions. I was disturbed to learn how little this person of such great knowledge and goodness earns for the long hours he puts in. I was also deeply moved by the warmth with which his family greeted me, and by their gratitude for my gift. I wonder if I will be able to continue helping them in the years ahead when they will have great expenses like marrying off their children.

On the long bus ride home last night, not one person got up for an elderly woman who was having difficulty standing.

I gave the former dentist from Russia a Pesach gift this morning. The man is alone in Israel. Whose *seder* table will he sit at?

The weeks prior to Pesach are a major time for giving to others. What is so startling is how sums that seem small and insignificant to some are vital for others. This has always been true, but it is perhaps more true now in Israel than it has ever been before. A certain sum I gave one night to one person was treated as if it were nothing and a smaller sum I gave to another family another night was received as if it were of tremendous value and importance.

As this work is intended primarily for those who live in Israel, it should have been written in Hebrew. I realized this but I took the easy way out. My guess is that it will only affect a few people as a result because I do not expect a translation to follow.

Sunday, April 16
11 *Nissan*

As I was walking home from *shul* on Shabbat, I saw Israel R. sitting alone outside and went over to speak with him. I listened again to the story of the destruction of his family. It pained me, as it always does, to hear it again. He wanted me to sit longer, but I had another visit to make. I feel so confused and hopeless in my efforts to cheer a few people up because they never really seem consoled as a result.

Ruth F. told me how much her son enjoyed my visit. She knows how to make a person feel appreciated. Nonetheless, I detect a hint of depression in her tone now that she is without her husband.

In the week leading up to Pesach, the laundromat will not take laundry because they are so busy. They are stopping a service at a time when they are most needed. I believe that it is not at all foolish to speak of *derech eretz* with regard to a business. In fact, one of the major improvements in life in Israel in recent years is that certain companies have learned how to show respect to their customers.

When writing, it is *derech eretz* to stick to the subject. But what is the subject?

Today I read a report that Prime Minister Barak has told President Clinton that he is willing to cede seventy to eighty percent of Judea and Samaria to a Palestinian state. I read this and felt a sudden meaninglessness in what I am writing about here. How is it possible to go on politely, making small points, noting details of small encounters in everyday life, when large chunks of our land are about to be given away? Wouldn't it be more worthwhile to devote myself to the struggle against what I believe is a concession that will weaken and endanger Israel? When our people's life is at stake, how can we go on with our daily business? Isn't that a lack of *derech eretz*? The protests and demonstrations that I have attended and the letters I have written over the years seem like an inadequate contribution. The situation makes me want to cry. We must not accept our own powerlessness, we must make every effort to protect Israel, even though we ultimately acknowledge how limited we are as human beings. But *derech eretz* is all about striving to make an effort to change our reality. I feel such frustration when I see the dreams and ideals of building Israel quashed every day.

A certain subsidized channel on television ignores information that does not conform to their own view of the political reality. They shamelessly promote the Oslo accords and do not stop undermining the previous government. I also see how they downplay stories that they do not want to focus on. In sum, they do not report in a fair and objective manner. What is most frustrating is the sense that the Arabs are taking advantage of us – the more we concede and give, the more they want. Meanwhile, they give nothing back in return. Appeasement seems only to have increased their appetites.

Monday, April 17
12 *Nissan*

At the same time that the Tal report was released, its purpose being to help solve the *charedi* problem with regard to army service, my daughter began her army service. The Tal report effectually frees the *charedim* of any responsibility to the army. It is a political ploy, though it does have the positive feature of encouraging the *charedim* to enter the work arena. Is it *derech eretz* for the group that claims to be the most God-fearing to sit back and let other Jews do their work and take responsibility for them? Why have I never expressed my opinion on their evasion of responsibility by refraining from doing army service to my *charedi* friends? Because I knew it would not change anything? In fact, I did try once, and all it did was sour my relationship with a teacher-friend of mine to whom I feel indebted.

The contradiction between "the ideal" and "the real" in *derech eretz* should spur me on to greater action and effort in *tikkun olam*, correcting the situation. I do try at times, but realistically, of course, I am limited in what I can do. The contradictions are so deep and so many that there is no doubt that they will always exist. And so, there remains the question of living with the frustration of failures and inadequacies. I think that I have failed in my own inner attitude – instead of being calm and having an ultimate trust in God, I feel anger, frustration and anxiety. Instead of experiencing a perpetual joy of closeness with God, there is an inner sense of despair at the wrongs of the world and my insignificant role in changing them.

Tuesday, April 18
13 *Nissan*

I was given hope yesterday in my meeting with my publisher, Tzvi Mauer. The fact that he gives this work such thought not only means that I am not so alone in it, but also that he believes in its value and even has a sense of its potential. I am grateful to him for this and hope he that will not be disappointed by my work.

I will go to the Old City for a lesson with the holy teacher today and collect the *shemurah matzah* that he has for me. I had wanted to go to my lesson in Ramat Eshkol, but will not be able to do both.

If someone were to ask what most deeply concerns me at this moment, I would say that it is the situation with the Palestinians. On the one hand, I do not want us to concede vital territory that will endanger us even more. On the other hand, I know that a stalemate may bring violence on their part and then our own violent reaction. I am concerned not only by the political implications, but also about my children and the young people who are their friends who are in the army.

The Arabs know that we are weak and vulnerable with regard to loss of life and concentrate on that weakness, using it as one of their major weapons. This perhaps explains why they, who are so much weaker than us, constantly threaten us, while we do not threaten them. True *derech eretz* means acquiring the courage and willingness to take risks. It means a readiness, if necessary, to engage in confrontation.

While I am writing about *derech eretz*, a non-Jewish state is about to be declared in parts of historical Israel. This may lead to a terrible war. At the least, it will most likely lead to a higher level of conflict than we have at present. I could attempt to prophesy here, but I am hardly qualified. I am deeply concerned. I feel that we made a great mistake in arming people who were our worst enemies and who committed cruel acts of terror. In effect, we rewarded those who had wronged us.

Wednesday, April 19
14 *Nissan, Erev Pesach*

Yesterday, after my holy teacher gave me a box of *shemurah matzah*, I went to *davvan Maariv* in French Hill. I thought of giving the *shemurah matzah* to my friend Lou R. and his wife, who are having a big family *seder* with all of their children and grandchildren. Lou was in *shul* this evening to sell his *chametz*. I asked him if he had *shemurah matzah* and when he said that he did not, I offered him mine. On the one hand, I know I did the right thing as he is having a big *seder* in which all the *matzah* will be used and we are only having a small one in which it will not. On the other hand, the *matzah* was a gift for me. I do not feel right about this. Perhaps the fact that the holy teacher also gave me an Ishbitz Haggadah that I will use for the *seder* will help to mitigate this guilt.

I rushed out this morning to buy packaged *shemurah matzah*, which is far from being of the same quality as the *matzah* I was given.

Derech eretz in giving and receiving gifts is very much a part of the Pesach festivities. There are, as far as I know, no halachic obligations to do so, but guests who come to the *seder* often bring gifts. Gifts from family members also play a central role. There are many issues of *derech eretz* with regard to giving gifts. A gift can be seen as a token of one's appreciation of another person. The danger is, of course, that people use gifts to try and buy other people's affection. However, I find that I often simply want to bring happiness to other people. The thing that I value and enjoy most are books. I give books most frequently as gifts and I myself appreciate being given them.

There are times when the abundance of gifts that God showers upon us every day is overwhelming. There is a desire to show gratitude. The way to show gratitude is to share with others the gifts that God gives us. This does not only apply to gifts in the literal sense, but also help that is of real value.

Tuesday, April 27
22 Nissan, Isru Chag

Pesach has come and gone. I did not work on this journal during the holiday. I believe that I followed the Halachah in refraining from doing so. I also did not want to take advantage of the holiday time for my own purposes.

I just came back from the hospital, where I visited Naomi. I listened to her and her husband tell the story of their medical problems, which have worsened at the time of the doctors' strike. They have been through so much in recent years and both of them are not well, to say the least. I offered help, but, as Menahem said, there is no way to help. Perhaps sitting there, providing a sympathetic ear was help.

I have been reading Oliver Sacks' work in which he tells the stories of those suffering from the most severe kinds of neurological disorders. Helping those who are most isolated in their suffering, most entrenched in their own private pain (those who suffer, for example, from autism, sleeping sickness, epilepsy and Parkinson's) seems to me the most sacred type of work. I wonder if I could have, throughout my life, done more to help those who are plagued with these illnesses. I do not know if I would have been capable of it. In any case, the kinds of problems that I am used to encountering seem almost child's play next to the struggles to help such patients.

In one of his books, Sacks tells the stories of those patients who regained consciousness from the sleeping sickness through the use of a drug named L-Dopa and then went through remarkable transformations, although with negative side-effects. After reading about this, an insight I had was connected with what my mother often said about my father's suffering: "He cannot help it, he's sick." There are, it seems, situations where one's whole life is wasted in sleep, where the sufferer does not have any control.

How frightening is the thought that a human being can be subject to the vagaries of their own mental chemistry without being able to overcome it! The religious question inherent in such a reality cries out to God, "Where is the freedom and justice in this?"

My respect for those who confront painful and even terrible realities and attempt to transform them is infinitely greater than my understanding for those who simply wish to deny that such realities exist. This is one problem I have with a certain kind of passive religious attitude. I believe that God wants us to be involved in *tikkun olam*, in transforming the world for the better, and not in simply ignoring the evil that surrounds us.

During Pesach, I did not make any special efforts to see if I could be of help to others. I tried to be in the mode of quiet joy, to be cheerful wherever I was and to raise the level of joy in the singing of prayers. *Derech eretz* also means knowing how to rejoice when it is appropriate.

The older I get, the more I need this type of quiet joy. On *Chol Hamoed* I went to the classical concert, Etnachta, instead of going to the Carlebach celebration that took place later on that night. How is this connected with *derech eretz?* We need to know ourselves and be honest with ourselves and not simply go where the crowd leads us.

What happens when the helper needs to give the help far more than the one helped needs the help? I don't really think this truly describes the two incidents that took place during *Chol Hamoed*, but it does touch upon something real: I went to see Ruth F., who received four phone calls while I was there. I had thought that she might be alone over the holiday. I saw Israel R. shuffling to *shul* for the first time in months. I offered to walk with him but he said that he could manage alone. And so, in both cases, the do-gooder was left without good deeds to do.

I think that the joy I feel when I am really helping someone is the purest joy of all. There is a certain kind of completeness about it. It does not leave me with the feeling of greed that I often have after other accomplishments, like writing.

I believe that the real source of my desire to help others is the context in which I was raised, where all the members of my family, led by my mother, were always trying to help my father. The list of those who I would like to help but have not is long. Among them are my nephews and nieces and my sister-in-law. The people who I feel most guilty about are Yigal and my Aunt Lakie, who I have not spoken to in a long time, and is so unwell.

Feeling guilty for not helping enough is not constructive. It is wrong to cause oneself pain. A Jew is not supposed to hurt anyone, including himself.

Today I received another invitation to the banquet that will raise funds to help search for the missing soldiers. I myself am deeply conflicted over the whole issue. What could be more noble than doing everything possible to redeem our lost ones, our missing soldiers? Yet our desire to help is taken advantage of by the enemy and is exploited as a sign of weakness. When helping demands that our time and emotional energy is consumed by fruitless blackmailing, is it really wise to do so? Also, when it seems that there is almost no doubt that all but one or possibly two of the missing soldiers are no longer alive? And yet it is precisely our irrational refusal to give up in the face of despair that is so noble and humane.

Friday, April 28
23 Nissan

Jews are forbidden to cause unnecessary pain to animals. We are supposed to be kind to all of God's creatures. I myself do not feel any affinity for animals, but thanks to my daughter, who does have a special liking for them, I have become more sensitive in this area. I have been feeding a partially blind kitten, now cat, on a regular basis for some time. During the worst bouts of cold weather, when it was small and frail, we sheltered it. Now I see that it is gone, most likely removed by neighbors who were tired of cats prowling around the entrance to the building. I recall the passage at the end of the book of *Yonah* where God rebukes the prophet and refers to the investment in caring for and elevating the people. The blind cat, which had no power of speech and no human feeling, no power to communicate in higher ways, still moves me by its absence. I do not believe I feel this way simply because I am a lonely person. Rather, there is a feeling of loss when we are no longer in contact with someone who we have invested time in and have taken care of. I think now of Yigal too. Any living creature on this earth is of value. Why would God put creations into the world if they weren't important? *Derech eretz* is hating cruelty in all of its manifestations, including cruelty towards animals.

The cruelty that the Jewish people have endured throughout our history has made us into a kind and compassionate people. This traces back to our suffering in Egypt and the endless biblical injunctions not to oppress strangers. This quality is also what has made us equally loved and hated by many. The ultimate test of life in Israel lies in our ability to be both strong and compassionate, just and kind. The danger in having power is brutalization. The danger in completely denying resistance to evil is that one invites disaster. The balance that is required is knowing how and when to be forceful and how and when to be yielding. We are faced with tests of this sort everyday.

Again, I sense that my own biggest failing in *derech eretz* is with regard to the Arabs. Why? It is not that I am cruel. On a one-to-one level, I always find myself treating Arabs as I would fellow Jews. Today, an old Arab woman asked for help and I tried to give it to her. Unfortunately, I could not read the Arabic directions she had written down. However, I know that despite all my education (from my parents, from the Jewish tradition and from the American world in which I grew up), I harbor what I can only call "bad feelings"(perhaps "prejudice" is truly an adequate term here) towards them. Most often, when I make a great effort to try and treat the Arabs with the same kind of sympathy of mind and heart that I would have for any human being, I find myself confronted with some incident that summons up frustration, resentment and anger inside me, like an act of violence or terror. It could also be some political action that challenges Jewish sovereignty in Israel or some piece of propaganda that I believe has distorted who we are. It could be many different kinds of actions that come to mind and the result is that I find myself filled with anger again and again.

Do I feel this way because the Arabs are threatening to take our land away from us? Is it because they are our enemies? I believe that this is a big part of it. Were all the Arabs living in Africa, I would not at all be offended by them. I might even objectively note their achievements and special qualities. I do not believe that my "bad feelings" towards Arabs injures anyone except for myself. It makes me feel ugly, small and sinful. Is this the right way to think about those who are created in the image of God, my fellow human beings? With regard to these feelings, there is an inner war going on inside of me, a lack of harmony within. I do not like the kind of person I become when I feel resentful of them, wishing that they would live somewhere else.

Now it might be said that if I was truly wise and imbued with *derech eretz*, I would be kind and welcoming to all Arabs. I would be sympathetic and humane, and not resentful. If I could open up a place for them in my heart and mind, I would also benefit. I do not resent them having their own neighborhoods and villages when there are fences between us. My resentment stems from us having to co-exist in the same space, especially when we have prior right of ownership (of course, I recognize that they are resentful of our being in a land that they regard as exclusively their own). The problem is that there are certain places, Jerusalem and Har Habayit especially, that have significant meaning to both Jews and Arabs, and that both nations consider to be exclusively theirs. Is it *derech eretz* then to share the space, to learn to tolerate the presence of others, while at the same time not letting oneself be forced out? The problem is that the Arabs do not show tolerance or understanding of our claim. Today, a Jew is not permitted to pray on the holiest Jewish site, the Temple Mount, because Muslims insist on their own exclusive right to the area. Their failure to recognize the rights of others is not something unique to our conflict with them. It is almost a worldwide phenomenon, as evidenced by the many wars Islamic forces are engaged in around the globe. When I see that we have a population that is demographically much "older" than theirs, I fear that they are going to take our future away from us.

I am at a certain stage of life where I desire the joy of having small children or grandchildren around me. I pray for the day when there will be a presence of young children in the family. Somehow I envisage happier times in connection with children – symbols of hope and joy.

I feel most ashamed when I see Arab children. They are, after all, children, and have the innocence of childhood as well. Thus when I am somehow disturbed by their presence (and the thought that they are the future that our Jewish children will have to contend with), I am ashamed. I am also angered when I see Jewish children being frightened away by rowdy Arab children in playgrounds. The truth is, when I am walking in Jerusalem, I most enjoy being in the non-mixed districts.

Sunday, April 30
25 *Nissan*

I saw Israel R. yesterday and sat with him for a while, although not for as long as he would have liked. He told me once again the same story he tells over and over again, the story of the destruction of his family. Yesterday he told me that his father had built a *shul* in the district of Czernovitz that was a long distance from the center of town and was impossible to walk to on Shabbat. He said that five hundred Jews lived in that area and that all were murdered except for him. Israel R. looked somewhat better sitting in the sun. He made it to *shul* for *yizkor* on the seventh day of Pesach, though he said that it was painful for him to walk. By listening to him, I feel that I am doing something to help him.

Yesterday in *shul*, I learned that Phil Chernofsky became a grandfather for the first time. I am very happy for him and his family. He is one of those people to whom I owe a debt of gratitude. His Torah teachings are delivered in such a clear and beautiful way. I would like to go to the *brit*, but do not expect to receive an invitation. He has a large family and a very large following, so that if all of his acquaintances were invited it would be a cast of thousands.

I am more troubled now by our negotiations with the Palestinians than by anything else. In a way, there is a question of *derech eretz* involved. At Oslo, we made a kind of agreement with them in which we assumed we would give them a demilitarized state in most of Judea and Samaria, while we would retain Jerusalem. It now appears that they are either breaking the agreement or have a completely different understanding of it. After receiving their end of the deal, it seems like they are reneging on the commitments they made. It is unquestionable folly on our part to have placed ourselves in such a vulnerable position, where we are now more threatened than ever. One could ask why it is that I do not have more sympathy for the Palestinians, who lost their homes and land in the war against us. The answer is that I do have sympathy for them, but I also know that a great number of Arabs, whether it be civilians, leaders or their military forces, were responsible for starting the wars. They killed and injured thousands of our people. They continue to engage in a war of attrition against us by fighting to steal and delegitimize our history in an attempt to defame us in the eyes of the world.

An old army friend, Moshe F., just called. *Baruch Dayan Emet*. His father died and he is sitting *shivah*. I told him that I would come right over, but he said that he would prefer it if I could come at a time when the two of us could talk at length, so I am going to visit him tomorrow at ten o' clock.

Monday, May 1
26 *Nissan*

I did not go to see Naomi yesterday. I also did not see Menahem in *shul* today. I will try to go to their home this afternoon, after my condolence visit to Moshe F.

Tonight is my mother's *yahrtzeit*. I miss her. She was a real giver and she certainly gave me all she could for most of my life. What can one do for those who are no longer with us in this world? We can say *kaddish* and remember them. But I know what my mother would say. My mother would say that it is what you do in life for others that counts. I know that my mother, whose main concern centered around her family, would want me to be considerate and caring to my own family. She would be happy if her children were happy. She would recommend that the way to do this is to be content with what one has and not try to chase big things. Unfortunately, not all of her children took her advice and instead followed our father's example, who was a more driven, rather than contented, person.

I spent four hours with my old army friend, Moshe F. He had a book of mine out on the table that I had given him many years before and wanted to discuss the points that I had raised in it. He is such a well-intentioned person. We talked on and on until we felt that we had covered the world. He did not want to talk politics but we ended up doing so anyway, and I heard his lament (much similar to mine) over the present government's inexplicable concessions. At the end of the visit, I met his wife, who has been in Israel for seven years. I politely refused their dinner invitation and was saved by a couple who came in just as I was about to leave. I was moved by my conversation with Moshe because we touched upon our mutual past and hopes when we were both young in the country. I only wish I had been able to give him more fertile ground for hope. When I left, he insisted on stuffing a package of papers into my pocket. He said that he always likes his guests to take something away with them. I feel a certain sadness when I think of his culture, his politeness, his love of books and the fact that he works on a delivery truck. It is strange. Tonight is *erev* Yom Hashoah. I remember an incident when, many years ago, we were at a museum with an army group on Yom Hashoah and some moron said something disrespectful. I still remember the way Moshe chided him, the way he expressed his love and appreciation for that lost world, for the Jews who suffered so much. He is a good person and I pray that he will know no future sorrow.

Tuesday, May 2
27 Nissan, Yom Hashoah
Ma's yahrtzeit

The subdued feeling that characterizes this day began last night at around seven o'clock. Hearing the stories of those who survived the worst atrocities, while most of their loved ones did not, is too painful.

Last night, Chaim W., a man I know, came over to me after the davvaning and told me to tie my shoelaces up because I might trip on them. Chaim W. lived in the woods for three years during the war, fighting as a partisan against the Nazis. He knew dangers and acts of evil (as well as courage) beyond any I will ever come close to seeing. He is a modest man who shouts when he talks because he is so hard of hearing. He, Shmuel G. (who lost his only daughter in the *Shoah*), Hanoch Mandelbaum (who was put on a train leaving Germany by his parents as a child, only to never see them again) and Moshe B. (who was in Auschwitz) are among those with whom I regularly pray. I always feel a special affection and respect when I am around these people, for they were *there*. They survived the worst nightmares and yet still managed to rebuild their lives in *Eretz Yisrael*.

I try to think of what I can do to honor this day of commemoration. Perhaps I will go to Yad Vashem, as I often do. Perhaps I should simply go out at ten o'clock, as I always do, and stand in silence when the siren for the two minutes of silent commemoration begins. I have been present at the shul's commemorations. Perhaps I will listen, read more accounts, learn more of the stories, more of the reality. But what is really gained by remembrance and why is it felt to be an almost religious duty?

One of the stories of one of the six people who lit the torches at the official remembrance ceremony at Yad Vashem particularly struck me. As a survivor himself, this man took it upon himself to collect the names and stories of what turns out to be four hundred and thirty-three individual survivors who were the only surviving members of their respective families and who fought and were killed in the Israeli War of Independence. He has not simply helped build a monument in stone for them, but has initiated a program in which their stories are taught in different schools across Israel. Since there was no one from these individuals' immediate families to help keep their memory alive, someone from their "extended family," from Israel, adopted this role. This moved me deeply, it is so noble and great.

There are certain lowlifes in Israel who are gambling in the casinos of Jericho today.

Remembering is a form of survival. It is a way of resisting the very act of annihilation, the murder itself. It is as if remembering is a way of canceling out and transcending the evil. But, of course, the human memory, like a human life, is limited. Which leads us back to the ultimate hope that God is the One who remembers.

Wednesday, May 3
28 Nissan

So far, I have spent most of today writing letters to two journalists, criticizing one for his anti-Israel bias and urging another to expand her valuable work to other outlets. I also wrote some "letters to the editor." *Hishtadlut* is required – even if the chances seem remote, we must still make our effort to improve the situation, to make the world a better place. *Derech eretz* is connected with *tikkun olam*, bettering the world in the way God demands of us.

What is interesting is that I can now see that all the core concepts that have informed my work for some years can be connected: the idea of being a co-partner with God in creation is connected with the idea of walking in the ways of God. Also, the idea of imitating the Creator is connected with the idea of serving God as the ultimate goal in life. Performing the will of God is to be His partner in improving and reshaping the world – *tikkun olam*. And *tikkun olam*, striving to make the world a better place, is certainly connected with *derech eretz*, treating others in a true and considerate way and walking in the ways of God as a result.

I feel a strange sense of self-sufficiency. I know that I must be careful to guard myself against pride and arrogance, especially when I seem to do less and less for others lately.

Thursday, May 4
29 Nissan

A major change has been instituted in Israeli society today: an effort to tax the capital markets in order to reduce the tax imposed on salaried workers for the first time. This would seem like a step in the right direction in that its aim is to reduce the growing financial inequality in our society. It seems to make sense, but I do not really understand the intricacies and implications of this measure.

The holy teacher's operation will be on Lag B'Omer. I pray for his full recovery. He called me yesterday and said that he could not make our private lesson, so I joined his Wednesday evening *shiur*. He was great during the class, but I saw him before it in Ramban synagogue and he appeared distracted and troubled. This is only natural considering what he is about to go through, although it contradicts the face with which he habitually greets the world. I think of how I can help him. I pray for him.

The world at large, and Israeli society in particular, seems to be moving so fast and in so many different directions and spheres that are alien to me, that I feel lost and confused about our future.

Friday, May 5
Rosh Chodesh Iyar

In this journal, I have not dwelt much on *derech eretz* as it relates to the world of business and financial dealings. One reason for this is that I try to think and deal with such matters only when necessary. I am not sure that this is a wise attitude, but it stems from a decision I made a long time ago that my real heart and interest must be in my writing. With regards to money, I pretty much follow the guidelines my parents set for me: I always pay on time. I never buy what I cannot afford. I try to never go into minus. I spend as little as possible on personal items for myself (the only exception being books, and here too I have my limits) and I rarely use my credit card. As I write this, I realize how removed I am from so many people in Israel who live on overdrafts, or who have lost their checking account privileges because they wrote too many uncovered checks, who suffer under kinds of limitations that I don't know about, and have never known.

I believe that these principles, those of my parents, are essentially in accord with Jewish teachings. There is a value of maintaining oneself free from dependence upon others. One might say that it is easy for me to adopt this approach to money because I am not short of means. But, of course, the answer is that there are many financially comfortable people who are tempted and squander their money away in many ways.

Every situation has its trials and challenges. I never claim to know the situation of other people, because I cannot speak from personal experience. I try to do the best I can with the situation I have been given, one that I am grateful for. Obviously, *derech eretz* is to give to those who do not have. But how, and in what way, and how much, depends on individual circumstances.

When I first came to Israel, my goal was to make my way as a writer and live from that income. I intended to live the life of a regular working Israeli. One of the great failures of my life is that I have not earned significant sums of money from my writing, certainly not enough to provide a livelihood. In this sense, and in this manifestation of *derech eretz*, I have been an almost complete failure.

Sunday, May 7
2 Iyar

There is a balance one must strike between telling the truth and protecting one's own children from the harmful effects of such disclosure. Today I choose to protect my children and so I will not discuss a problem that I am having now.

Throughout the period that I have been writing this journal, I have been able to take my own good health for granted. But recently, I have felt a deterioration in my health and I fear that I am coming to a stage where I will begin to dedicate most of my time and energy to self-preservation. Of course, one hears remarkable stories about those who run to help others even when they are going through the worst bouts of sickness, but I believe that the healthier we are, the stronger we can be in serving God. *Derech eretz* in preserving one's own health means, among other things, moderation in eating and abstinence from harmful habits like smoking and heavy drinking. Unfortunately, though, our health does not solely depend on these good habits alone. There are processes that work within us whether we want them to or not. I pray, as so many do, that when the time comes that I am not able to function independently, that I will not be a great burden on others. But I have seen cases where the most independent of beings, the greatest in mind and intelligence, are reduced to pathetic caricatures of themselves, sitting slumped in wheelchairs, unable to speak. I am aware of how the human soul can become so diminished even when the person, the physical body, still lives on. It is scary to think that this deterioration can occur suddenly, without warning and without apparent reason. Even though we must be careful to take proper care of ourselves, it does not guarantee good results.

I made up for a previous, brief visit to Anita with an overly long one. She is, thank God, doing much better. She moves around with the aid of a walker and is able to read slowly. She is such a good woman. There is now a little group of women who come almost every Shabbat to visit her. These include Ruth F., Judy B. and Judy G., all of whom I like very much. Of these four women, three are widows whose husbands were my good friends. All four women embody the traditional, hospitable, yet broad-minded female – the ideal wife.

When I see that there is a problem with my children, I tend to relegate other people around me to the side. Today I was caught up in my daughter's problem: her boyfriend has not returned to his military base. She called a short time ago from her base and told me that he is away with permission.

I worry about my friend Menahem and his wife, Naomi. I did not see Menahem in *shul* on Shabbat. I tried to call them this morning. I will try again now. I just got through – Naomi is in some pain, but the good news is that the biopsy that had been taken showed no signs of cancer.

Monday, May 8
3 Iyar

It is almost impossible to pay proper attention to all that is going on right now in Israel. As we prepare for our withdrawal from Lebanon, those villages close to the border become the front line and are very vulnerable. I know I pay much less attention to what is happening with them than I do to the situation in Jerusalem. It is not as if my paying more attention to one particular region is really going to help the situation anyway. But my thoughts do, in some way, constitute a prayer, perhaps indirect, to God for help. Why do I feel that I have to be aware of all the suffering in the world, wherever it may be, and try to help? Has my father's suffering in his childhood and my mother's perpetual effort at helping caused me to have this compulsion? Do I see this as a responsibility placed upon me by God that I must fulfill if I am not to be punished?

The government is, as I understand it, planning to do the cowardly thing: buy more time, give the Palestinians more territory, grant them a state and allow them to arm themselves. These moves are at best irresponsible and at worst, downright evil. For it entails creating greater problems for the future, instead of dealing with the real issues now. Placing the burden on future generations because one cannot handle the reality of the present seems to be a very great sin.

Demanding more of oneself than one demands of others has been my own rule of action. I sense, however, that the halachic teaching is not so. It is rather, not to demand of others that which one would not demand of oneself.

Tuesday, May 9
4 Iyar, Yom Hazikaron

On this day in Israel, our society becomes divided into those who have lost a loved one in the wars of Israel and those who have not. More than 19,000 soldiers have been killed over the years in Israel's struggle for its existence. I just heard Aryeh Bachrach, whose son was killed in a terrorist action while in the army, speak about the absurdity of not officially remembering victims of terror on Yom Hazikaron. He also said that all Jews who live in *Eretz Yisrael* are, in a sense, soldiers. I then heard another father of a soldier disagree with this view.

Wednesday, May 10
5 Iyar, Yom Ha'atzmaut

Today is the fifty-second Independence Day of the State of Israel. I reflect with gratitude on the years that God has given us and pray that He will help us improve in the future. I choose to do on this day what I most love to do, so I sit here reading and writing. I know that the custom is to go out into nature, to go on some kind of picnic or have a barbecue, to somehow connect with the land. But each person must celebrate in the way that is most meaningful to him. I will go to the Old City later, meet with my holy teacher and learn with him. Hopefully this will be a source of joy for us both.

I notice in myself a resentment and anger towards those Jews who are not willing to show any recognition or gratitude for the State of Israel and its accomplishments. I tell myself that such anger is not really justified and that each and every person has the right to their own approach and opinion. But when I think about how some of these people do not contribute to the defense of Israel and the Jewish people, I do feel resentment. Of course, I know all too well that my service in a civil defense unit was very far indeed from the kind of real army service that I so admire.

Gratitude, being thankful for the good that we have been given, is one of the most fundamental religious qualities. Therefore, to not show proper appreciation seems to me to be a sin.

Thursday, May 11
6 Iyar

Yesterday I went to the Old City to learn with the holy teacher but he was sleeping. I told his wife not to wake him. I returned after *Maariv*. His wife told me that he simply could not get up. Later in the evening, he called to apologize. We spoke a little Torah on the phone. At the *Kotel*, I prayed with all my heart for his total recovery. I pray for it all the time.

When I was in the Old City, I gave my last twenty shekels to an old acquaintance of mine, Akiva, who is a beggar. For years, we have been talking about his theory of physics, his search for the unified field theory, his relationship to Einstein and Israeli politics. Yesterday he asked me about Prime Minister Barak's dividing Jerusalem. I told him what I thought and knew. He expressed some of his fears and, as he did so, I was made to feel foolish in expressing some of my own fears that are based on a simplistic view of the situation. As I was talking to Akiva, a young man came by, saying that he needed money to help keep him out of prison. I was about to give him my last coins when he said that the reason he might go to prison is that the police had accused him of burning down a Church. At that point, I asked him if he was guilty. He said that he wasn't, but proceeded to argue about how necessary such action is against missionaries. I told him that such action is criminal and causes great harm to Israel. It is a *chilul Hashem*, a desecration of the name of God. After all, we are supposed to act in such a way so that those around us feel greater love and respect for God. We are not to act in a way that will bring shame and dishonor to Him.

I remember my surprise and dismay upon first encountering the lunatic fringes of the Israeli right-wing. I once made the error of believing these people to be harmless. They have already caused Israel great damage and must be opposed from within by those who love the Jewish people no less than them, but can think rationally and sanely of how to act to ensure its well-being.

As I was walking up the steps from the center in Ramat Eshkol, an elderly woman asked me if I could take her shopping cart to the top of the steps. I did, and when I learned that she had to walk all the way to Ma'alot Dafna, I said that I would take it there for her. She thanked me and told me that her back ached and that she had not known if she could make it. We walked and talked. I learned that she has been here for eight years, that she has a married son and daughter here, and many grandchildren and great-grandchildren. From her accent, my guess is that she came to America after the war. She told me that her husband is wheelchair-bound at home, attended to by a Philippino who refuses to do the shopping. She told me that her daughter, who had been an assistant head-nurse at a major hospital, had a stroke at the age of forty-nine and is now paralyzed. When we arrived at her front door, she thanked me and gave me her blessings.

Recently it seems to me that every other person in the street is suffering in some way. The elderly, the invalid, the lame, those who have facial injuries. I can imagine a stranger coming to the city from some calm, northern city and looking with dread at so many wounded people.

My own medical condition has deteriorated. At times, I feel so tired. I can no longer be as objective about people who are sick because I myself feel on the verge of becoming one of them. I will fight this, of course, but it may be that I will be able to do little or nothing about it. We are enjoined to guard our health and physical well-being very carefully.

A woman got on the bus with a heavy shopping bag. When a man in the front seat did not give her his seat, I asked him to. He pointed to his leg, and said, "What about me?" I looked to the parallel seat and saw a young girl sitting there who was blind. So I asked the woman if I could help and when she said I could, I picked the bag up and took it to the second row of seats. When she came to her stop, I picked the bag up for her and brought it down to the sidewalk. She thanked me. What I found strange was that no one else thought to offer her assistance. Then again, there seemed to be no one else on the bus who was young and healthy enough to pick up the bag for her.

Sunday, May 14
9 Iyar

On Shabbat, I thought of skipping my visit to Anita, but then I decided that I must make the effort. It was the right decision – no one else had come. We spoke for about an hour and had a really good talk. This time I feel that I helped.

Last night, I went to hear Rabbi Lopes Cardozo speak on his new book, *Judaism on Trial*. He is a mensch and quite courageous in countering insular, xenophobic attitudes within the religious world. I looked at his book and he seems to have thanked just about everyone he knows. I think that there is something very kind and good in mentioning many people whose names would otherwise probably never be seen in print.

Derech eretz is clearly connected with the effort to sanctify God's name in the world, to be *kadosh*. As Phil Chernofsky points out in one of his Torah Tidbits sheets, each individual Jew represents, in a sense, the Jewish people as a whole when we interact with non-Jews. And so, each one of us has a special obligation to act in a way that will help bring them to respect and honor God.

I am constantly distressed by manifestations of pagan behavior in Israel. The tattoos, nose-rings and general desecration of the body is the external aspect. The mimicking of the worst kinds of rudeness and ugliness in cultural activity and scorning of any Jewish inner content is the spiritual aspect.

How should we react when members of our own people seek to debase us? How can we possibly contend with or change this reality? Should we simply overcome our own anger and shame? We have on one extreme an ultra-religious world that is insular, parochial and contemptuous of others. On the other extreme, we have a secular world that is ignorant, impressionable and devoid of any inner sense of Jewishness. These two extremes have become increasingly dominant in our society. The center has diminished and with it, our humanity. What I would like to suggest is the strengthening of the centrist approach in an attempt to diminish this polarization and bring the worlds that are so far apart closer together. As I understand it, there are many people who identify with this problem. It is people like Rabbi Shlomo Riskin, Rabbi David Hartman, Rabbi Lopes Cardozo, Rabbi Daniel Tropper, Rabbi Berel Wein, Rav Yoni Berlin, Rav Motti Elon, David Herzberg, Professor Shalom Rosenberg, Phil Chernofsky and Yaakov Fogelman who work to promote the kind of humane Judaism that I believe typifies *derech eretz* and serves to sanctify God's name in the world.

Monday, May 15
10 *Iyar*

In his book, Rabbi Lopes Cardozo brings our attention to the lack of *derech eretz* of those religious passengers who choose to form *minyanim* at the back of airplanes on flights to and from Israel. These *minyanim* block the aisle and prevent the flight attendants access, as well as other travelers who want to go to the bathroom. He says it is better for people to pray privately in their seats rather than inconvenience others. I have been of this opinion for years but it is the first time that I have seen it in print.

I had a special prayer said for the holy teacher, whose operation is next week. While doing so, I learned that an elderly man with whom I pray each morning was operated on yesterday. I wonder if a visit from me, who he knows, but not that well, would be of any help.

I hear that Prime Minister Barak is pushing the proposal to transfer Abu Dis and Al Azariya to Palestinian military control forward. This will give them even broader access to the Temple Mount.

Today, Palestinian police shot an Israeli soldier. The word is that Barak is going through with the transfer because having been stalled on the Syrian and socio-economic fronts, he needs some "achievement." I do not know if this is the case, but I do know that Abu Dis was supposed to be the last concession we were to make in a final agreement over Jerusalem. Now it is not even a concession as part of an agreement. I am outraged and frustrated and, of course, do not know what to do. Yesterday I wrote letters of protest. Tonight there is a demonstration that I will go to.

I met somebody while I was walking and I began to talk about how the Barak government is conceding land to the same Palestinian Authority that has told its soldiers to shoot at ours. I cursed. Cursing is ugly and something I usually manage to completely avoid. I was wrong to do so. Of course, I know that the provocation was great, but there was no excuse.

Today is the *bar mitzvah* party that my good friend Dov is making for his grandson. I have to go. I will try to leave early, though, so that I can make it to the demonstration in Kikar Tzion, even though I usually dislike crowds and noisy demonstrations.

Tuesday, May 16
11 *Iyar*

I went to both the *bar mitzvah* celebration and the demonstration. To be among so many young people at the demonstration gave me hope. I also spoke with a number of people who share my views on government action. It is a kind of minor consolation to have others share one's misgivings.

Yesterday morning, I saw Israel R. sitting in distress. I learned that he was troubled because he did not have the strength to get up and get his newspaper. I did this for him. Later today, I will go over and make sure that he has a copy of today's newspaper.

The holy teacher called. I will go to his house tomorrow night at 8:30 and if he is up to teaching, I will be his student.

I just heard a radio program with Dana Harari, a broadcaster, and Nitza Ayal, a psychologist. They spoke of ways to counter despair and how to remain optimistic. One way mentioned is to set small, achievable goals for oneself. The central insight here is that despair comes when a person has nothing to look forward to. I now wonder not only about using this insight more with myself, but of somehow communicating it to my most pessimistic of friends who is always in despair, especially with regard to what is happening here.

This insight is confirmed by my own experience. I can be sitting at home, thinking of the deepest, most problematic question and feel despair. I can then go out and run an errand, such as paying a bill or mailing a letter, and will then feel tremendously better. So it is clear that a tactic to counter despair is to carry on performing mundane chores. Ayal also recommended any type of physical activity, especially walking, as a goal-oriented task.

I feel that this journal rambles on and on, without any apparent goal. Perhaps it would be more considerate to provide step-by-step guidelines and topical chapters so that the reader can feel that this work has more practical direction.

Wednesday, May 17
12 *Iyar*

While reading Rabbi Lopes Cardozo's *Judaism on Trial*, I was reminded of a concept that I was taught by my *cheder* teacher, Mr. Friend. The concept is that God watches our every deed and is with us all the time. The implications of this on our lives are enormous: it means that our actions are under constant scrutiny and so should be deliberated on before their execution. It means that we are always being tested. It means that we should be walking in God's ways even in our thoughts. I think of how my thoughts often deviate and are impure. I need to put more effort into changing this in order to become closer with God.

I feel a righteous sense of indignation when I think of how the Arabs portray a completely false message to the world. They, the initiators of violence, make themselves out to be the innocent victims, the underdogs. They win the support of the world with their lies of victimization, when we retaliate simply out of self-defense. I am even more outraged when we do nothing to curb this violence and ignore it, as we seem to be doing with regard to the transfer of Abu Dis.

I feel like I have become more isolated of late. I visit people less. This morning, Mrs. B. called and I gave her the help she needed by referring her to the relevant person to post her notice in the newspaper. She is one of the few people who calls me. The truth is that I somehow prefer it this way. So often, my desire to help stems from a feeling of obligation and is not a spontaneous act of goodness.

After seven years of struggling, it appears that my nephews are about to lose the family business, which they took over when my brother died. I have been of no help to them, which is a source of guilt to me. I attempted to help them in various ways but am distant, both geographically and mentally, from the business. I now may be required to help them in other ways. I hope that they will be all right and that I can do something to help them. One thing is clear – now is not the time to run away and hide, shirking my responsibility. I must try to help.

Thursday, May 18
13 Iyar

I went to the holy teacher's house after davvaning at the *Kotel* last night. He looks very thin and frail. We began the class and then a number of people came in, including a young woman who had just published a book on the *parashot hashavuah*. The holy teacher looked like he was in discomfort, tried too hard to make jokes and had difficulty in delivering his lesson. The participants behaved properly and were patient. When the lesson was over, I went up to him to give him *tzedakah* money to distribute. I asked him if he needed any help. He said that his operation had been paid for. How does one deal with the frustration and feelings of impotence that are associated with wanting to help, but being unable to? Such situations lead us to pray to God and also, hopefully, builds humility. But it is nonetheless still frustrating and painful.

Perhaps I did help the holy teacher yesterday – I initiated the lesson, which others later joined. On the other hand, when I observed the holy teacher's discomfort, I do not know if I did the right thing by not stopping it. Perhaps the class was more of a hindrance than anything else.

I had planned to go to the hospital on the day of the holy teacher's operation. I probably still will, but his family will be with him. He has other close friends. There is, as far as I know, nothing practical that needs to be done. I already spoke with his wife and asked if I could help in any way. The situation is beyond mere practical help and so I pray all the time for his full recovery, *refuah shlemah min hashamayim*.

I called my nephew again and he did not return my call.

I was in a hurry yesterday when I saw Mr. H. sitting on a bench with his Philippino caretaker. As I had not spoken with him for a long time, I went over and asked him how he was. He told me that he is the same. I think of what an active man he once was and how he is now reduced to this state.

I just learned that the eighteen-year-old son of a woman I know died from a drug overdose a few days ago. I called a close friend of hers to ask when the funeral is. The family does not want an autopsy, so there is a question of when it will be. It may be this afternoon.

How can you help a person when the worst thing in the world has happened to them? I have a feeling of inadequacy because of my failure to help others. For example, I received a call from someone and I was very curt and businesslike. Later on, I realized that she had wanted sympathy and to talk about her family. True *derech eretz* requires intuition and sensitivity. I also did not manage to get through to my brother's family.

Friday, May 19
14 *Iyar*

I went to the young man's funeral last night. It was very painful. He was a young person who apparently had many friends and was greatly involved in trying to help them. It is difficult to imagine anything more heart-rending than a parent saying *kaddish* for a child. May God have mercy on the family.

I spoke with my holy teacher this morning. His operation has been postponed for a week. I am praying for him all the time.

I went as usual to give the former dentist his weekly *tzedakah* money. He then asked me if I pass through town sometimes because he would like to speak with me. At that moment, I was distracted, thinking about how I had to call the holy teacher when I got home, so I answered him very abruptly. I must make an effort next week to meet him early and hear what he has to say. One problem, though, is that he does not really speak Hebrew and I do not really understand Yiddish.

The constant pressure from the Palestinians to assert their cause makes our lives miserable. Their shooting at us with guns we gave them is certainly not a wonderful sign. Nor are the riots and violence. What does this have to do with *derech eretz*? I think it is connected with the challenge of maintaining a calm, friendly and positive face with which to greet the world. The problem is how does one maintain one's composure when one is constantly subject to such attacks? How do we act towards those who tirelessly oppose and slander us, and who seek to undermine our security? Also, how do we deal with fellow Jews who we believe are causing great harm to the Jewish people? On one level it is obvious that we should speak out against them and oppose them when we can. However, they are more numerous and powerful a group, and they have greater access to the media than we do. I do not know the answer. I increasingly sense my own powerlessness. Even the one outlet I had, my letters that were printed in The Jerusalem Post, has come to an end. Perhaps I should be more actively involved with those people and organizations who are writing in service of the Jewish people and the State of Israel. Perhaps I should focus more on connecting with allies, rather than criticizing opponents who do not pay attention to the criticism anyway.

Sunday, May 21
15 *Iyar*

I visited Anita yesterday. I see how much my visits mean to her and will try to make it every week. I also spoke with Israel R., who I now believe sits on the bench in front of my house and waits for me. He told me again about how the Nazis destroyed his whole family. I could not say to him, "You know I have heard this story many times from you and it is Shabbat – it's not pleasant." Instead, I listened in silence and pain, with a sense of helplessness.

I heard on the news this morning that a two-year-old baby was severely burned by a Molotov cocktail that was thrown by a Palestinian in Jericho. This is just one incident of many where countless bullets and stones have been aimed at Jews. Apparently, this is a culture that does not believe in dialogue and compromise, but rather one that uses force to get things done. We cannot help others if they are unwilling to help themselves. One also does not help others by giving in to their every whim and, in so doing, creating a feeling in them that they have the right to demand more and more.

I changed my routine yesterday. I gave up my favorite Shabbat davvaning and my lesson with Rav Yoni Berlin. Instead, I prayed at the local *shul* because it is Dr. Veschler's *yahrtzeit* this week and one of his good friends asked me to come. I could not refuse because I truly wanted to honor the memory of this good man. I met his widow on the way home. She seems much better now than when it first happened. Apparently, a year has healed the pain somewhat. I asked her about her daughter because I knew that she would be happy to speak about her career success as a correspondent for an army journal.

Monday, May 22
17 *Iyar*

I went to donate blood yesterday, but my medical condition did not permit it, which made me feel badly. When one wants to give but cannot, he acutely feels his own uselessness.

I went to the *shivah* of the young man who died when I did not want to go. I helped complete the *minyan* for *Minchah* and I helped move chairs, but I said nothing. I said nothing because I did not know what to say. There were others there who knew the boy, who were closer to his mother. I was just present. It was very difficult for me.

I was shocked and disheartened by the report that came out last week on "white slavery" in Israel. I knew that there was prostitution, but I had no idea that there is the buying and selling of human beings. This type of crime represents the exact opposite of what we are supposed to be. It is something that we should fight against with all our being. I tremble for our nation when I realize that there are Jews who could be involved in such things. This is the kind of evil that must be dealt with as quickly and efficiently as possible.

Tuesday, May 23
18 *Iyar, Lag B'Omer*

Our withdrawal from Lebanon took a humiliating turn yesterday. People who had collaborated with us were imprisoned by the Hezbollah after our forces left. Apparently, we are letting our friends down. As with Oslo, this is another governmental betrayal of people who have provided valuable information for the good of our security. I don't think that this demonstrates proper *derech eretz*. It certainly doesn't seem to add to our image of "a light unto the nations." It also undermines our future security in a serious way.

It is difficult for me to think and write about my own situation in life when the situation in Israel is so dire. I pray. I write letters. But I really have no power. I do not have the capability or knowledge to have power. I am just a small person and am not part of the world of those who make the decisions. And yet it pains me so much to see what is happening here. It pains me to see us retreating, falling back and giving up. I understand the tactic behind the withdrawal from Lebanon, but I cannot comprehend how we can contemplate conceding parts of the land of Israel.

Wednesday, May 24
19 *Iyar*

I did not demonstrate proper *derech eretz* at the reading last night. When called upon to read, I showed a lack of consideration for the audience by not using the microphone. I read difficult material without people having copies at hand with which to follow along. Judging by the reaction of the audience, my reading was not enjoyable, although the previous four readers were also met with the same iciness. My lack of consideration was probably a response to the impatience of the audience, who had already heard so many other readers. The truth is that I was hesitant to read and would have happily sat there if not for the fact that I was spotted and asked to read.

There are people who I want to help but cannot. They know this, they do not even seek my help. They may even avoid me. My feelings of guilt are irrelevant. I think in particular of my nephews and an old friend in America.

We abandoned our Lebanese friends and now many of them are becoming refugees in Israel. This is painful to see. We withdrew in the hope of putting an end to the attacks from Lebanon. I am not sure that this is what we have done. We may have made the situation worse.

Thursday, May 25
20 *Iyar*

This morning Dov fell after *shul*. I ran outside and found him being supported by two people. His face was smeared with blood. One of the *gabbaim* went and brought his car and the two of us took him to the emergency room at Hadassah. After his wounds were dressed, I went with him to get an x-ray. Here began a process that had to be done three times instead of once. Moving him was difficult and caused him pain. It would have been easier if the people who gave him his x-ray were more sensitive to this.

I waited with Dov while the *gabbai* went to bring his wife. She herself looked pale and troubled. After he came out of the x-ray, Dov told us that there was no point in our staying. Their grandson's *brit milah* is tomorrow in Beit El.

I went back to Hadassah in the evening. Dov's son was with him, feeding him. I believe that his brother was also there. He was still in the emergency ward. He will be discharged soon. He thanked me. There was nothing broken, although he did have to have stitches.

Friday, May 26
21 *Iyar*

I went downtown this morning especially so that the former dentist would not miss his weekly *tzedakah* money from me. I then went to Rabbi Eisen's class, where I did not pay attention as well as I might have.

It may be that my strong sense of independence makes me ill-equipped to demonstrate what proper *derech eretz* is to others because it means that I am not used to including others in the good acts that I perform.

Sunday, May 28
23 Iyar

I was greatly helped yesterday by a long conversation I had with my friend Larry B. I really appreciated his ability to listen to me, especially when I sense how tired he was. The truth is that I needed to talk to him much more than he needed to talk to me. He is in constant dialogue with many people from his own academic and intellectual world, yet I have very few people to whom I can talk in this way. He is an extremely learned person from whom I can learn a lot. He always gives me his honest opinion.

Yesterday, a man who has attended the *shul* before came to *seudah shlishit*. I always considered him to be a sourpuss, but somehow this time he was part of the conversation. Later I saw how his whole manner had changed. This proves what I have felt myself so many times – when one feels included, one's attitude positively changes. The human craving to participate, to belong, is a very real one. To be marginalized and left out can create feelings of resentment and anger.

I think that Israel R. now waits for me every Shabbat morning. This past Shabbat morning, he was standing at the front of his house, shuffling his feet. I came out to talk to him. He told me that he wanted to go back to his own house, as he felt pains in his back. I walked with him and tried to shade him from the sun. He thanked me profusely, as he always does. I am reminded of the famous story of a humble Jew who, when asked what it is he most wishes for, replied that he only asks to be given a crust of bread each day.

Monday, May 29
24 Iyar

Yesterday, I left the house early to go to a *brit milah*. I arrived early. I know both the father and the grandfather of the baby and stayed for the *seudah*. Before the *brit*, I went to the house of the holy teacher. He had just gone out. When I came back, I asked his stepson if he was well enough for a visit. The holy teacher then came into the room, looking thinner and wearier than I had ever seen him. He told me that he had been speaking with his daughter. I just wished him well and left. I felt that my interruption had been a disturbance. I had come to help, yet I probably achieved the opposite result. After this incident, I went down to the *Kotel* to pray for the holy teacher's complete recovery.

There are so many people I know who are on the edge. I saw Menahem this morning after the davvaning. His wife was in hospital at the end of the week and he himself is frail and sick. He looks troubled and frightened. I now realize that instead of simply wishing him well, I should have offered him my help. On the other hand, he knows that I will help him and his wife in any way I can. The problem is that I cannot help them in any real way.

Leiberman is in Sha'arei Tsedek hospital. I do not know whether or not to visit as he is such a shy person. I have also not spoken with Dov. Another of the morning regulars, Zamir, who is also a veteran of the War of Independence, has not fully recovered from an ear operation. So many people in the *shul* are sick that the prayers begin without *kaddish d'rabbanan* (which requires a *minyan*).

Last night I heard one of the most interesting talks that I have ever heard. It was given by Leon Kass on the subject of the indefinite extension of life (something he predicts medical advances may soon enable), and why he believes it to be undesirable. I was patient and waited until everyone else had made their remarks and then interjected by raising the question of the possibility of individual lives being extended indefinitely, while the species yields predominance to a humanly constructed successor species. We spoke briefly about the literature on this subject. I asked for a copy of his remarks and he said that he would send them to me. I thanked him and we exchanged a warm farewell. The great and special pleasure of this for me was derived from listening and learning from someone who has given the subject deep thought and addressed questions that have troubled me for years. This lecture also made me realize how I long for "real" learning and how deeply appreciative I am when I receive it. It is not a problem for me to acknowledge that someone else knows more than I do or is on a higher intellectual level than me if I can learn from that person. In fact, I realize more and more that this is precisely what I am searching for – those who know what I do not and who can really be my teachers.

In this journal, I have dedicated much attention to everyday life in Israel, without dealing with more global issues such as worldwide violence, malnutrition, mass poverty, exploitation of labor, drug abuse, crime and the environment. It is true, though, that in some ways Israel provides a microcosm of the suffering that exists in the world at large. Yet the scope and dimensions of problems on a worldwide scale are so much greater.

Mankind's inhumanity to mankind, mankind's lack of consideration and caring for the other, and mankind's poor stewardship of the earth is apparent everywhere. Moreover, it is senseless to expect that even if we, as Israel, were perfect within ourselves, we could somehow be impervious to the world as a whole. When there are problems in the world, it means that there are problems within us. I am not dismissing Israel's efforts to help, as it did this year in bringing aid to Turkey during its earthquakes. I see that as part of our responsibility, bringing light to other nations.

The challenges and threats that confront humanity by technological advances are great. Innovation and creation can benefit humanity in so many ways, but they also have far-reaching implications that extend beyond their immediate good. And it seems that there is no one to supervise all this, to consider the situation of mankind as a whole. Kass referred to this problem as "a runaway train without a conductor." The mentality of those who have *derech eretz* is that they consider the totality of the situation, the broader picture, when they look at new phenomenon.

Tuesday, May 30
25 *Iyar*

I went to Sha'arei Tsedek Hospital yesterday to visit Leiberman, but they told me that he had been discharged the day before. I had debated over whether or not to visit him since he is a shy and private person. I was happy to see him return to *shul* today.

The holy teacher called. The operation has been postponed again, this time until Sunday. He sounds well. He is going to rest. I asked him if there was any *sefer* he wanted. He responded by saying that there were many, but that he did not want to trouble me.

Wednesday, May 31
26 *Iyar*

I chose to go to the political presentation on the future of Israel rather than to my weekly *shiur*. I did this more for myself than out of the sense that I would be of great service to Israel at the presentation. I did, however, ask my questions and also defended an elderly woman whose opinion the panel scorned. She spoke about her children and the stonings in Chevron. They attacked her when they found out that she does not live in Israel. I defended her by raising questions about the ideological divide in Israel, the post-Zionist movement and the Palestinization of the Israeli Arabs.

Thursday, June 1
27 *Iyar*

A typical Jerusalem scene: a woman with a baby is at a street corner. A taxi stops to pick her up. The cars behind the taxi see all of this clearly, yet they nonetheless begin to honk their horns ferociously because they cannot wait a minute for her to get into the car. I shout at them futilely to be quiet, but they do not hear me.

The holy teacher told me not to bother about the walkman he asked for. He had asked for it when I offered to bring him something. We both understood that the gift was more for the giver than for the receiver, my feeling of being able to do something. He had asked me if I could bring it to him on Monday after the operation.

I have not contacted Dov for over a week. I also did not call Menahem, even though I did not see him today. Tomorrow I hope to try and see what is going on with them. I heard that Dov has to be at home for at least two weeks. I will offer to meet him each morning and walk with him to *shul*. I hope that this will help.

Friday, June 2
28 Iyar, Yom Yerushalayim

I spoke to Dov a few minutes ago. He is in pain. His wife also sounds ill. I pray that God will help them recover.

The former dentist asked me if I had a moment to speak with him when I was rushing to my *shiur*. I waited and listened. He showed me his identification card, which indicated that he is a doctor. He also showed me his certificate of graduation from a Shiatsu course. He is looking for work as a massage therapist. When I asked him if he had been to the various health institutes, he told me that he is looking to work with only one or two people a day. The help that he wants is clients. I told him that I would try to think of appropriate people and I will, but I honestly doubt that I will be able to help him.

I heard two presentations on the meaning of Yom Yerushalayim, one from Rav Yoni Berlin and the other from Rabbi Eisen. Both spoke of how much we have to be grateful for the return to and the building of the city, and how far we are from the ultimate redemption. I also heard Phil Chernofsky speak about the feelings of freedom, of coming out of Exodus, yet not quite being content where we are in Israel. There was no mention of the current negotiations or the struggle for the city.

Many believe that one way to be pure in *derech eretz* is to stay away from politics. The problem is that it is doubtful that *derech eretz* can be found in abandoning one's responsibility to one's community.

Sunday, June 4
Rosh Chodesh Sivan

The holy teacher is to be operated on today. I am one of many who are praying for his complete recovery. I had hoped to finish with this journal this week but I will not. I will call the publisher and speak to him briefly about it and will also suggest that he reconsider his decision to publish it, as it seems to me that it will be no different from my other books and will not sell very well. It is one thing for me to lose money, but I do not want others to lose money on account of me.

If I needed to learn humility, I had yet another opportunity on Shabbat. The *gabbai* was looking for a prayer leader for the Shabbat morning service. He kept asking a young man near me who had come in late and who declined because he had not yet davvaned the preliminaries. Finally the *gabbai* turned to me. I said no at first, but when repeated efforts to rally others failed, I said yes in order to help. I knew that I would regret this. My davvaning was poor. I messed *kedushah* up. I sang alone in places where we were meant to sing together. I really felt that I did not do the prayers justice. I saw how poor a prayer leader I am when it comes to anything beyond daily prayer. This raises the question of someone trying to help when they are not really competent or qualified to do so. One needs the wisdom to know when to say no.

Perhaps the most effective help I give to others is by trying to make people feel a little better about themselves and the world. I think of how other people I know, those with a better sense of humor than me, do a much better job of this than I do.

Monday, June 5
2 *Sivan*

I have been praying with all my strength for the holy teacher's recovery. He was still in the recovery room last night at around 8:30. This morning, we said a *misheberach* for him in *shul*. I bought the walkman he requested, and some tapes. I do not know whether or not to go there today. Why do I have the illusion that my presence can help when it may simply disturb those who are really caring for him, his wife and daughters? I often have no other means besides prayer to help people and I am fully aware of this limitation.

It is a relief to put on the radio and not wait with dread for news of the next possible casualty from Lebanon. I perhaps should apologize, even if only in my own mind, for the harsh thoughts I fostered against the government during the days of the humiliation and abandonment of our allies, the Southern Lebanese Army. They are receiving humanitarian aid in Israel, as well as citizenship. It can be argued that our sacrifice of their cause was a necessary act of realpolitik. The hope and prayer is, of course, that the present quiet will continue and that the withdrawal will not lead to some greater disaster later.

Tuesday, June 6
3 *Sivan*

Thank God. I saw the holy teacher yesterday and he seems to be recovering nicely from the operation. I stayed only for a minute and spoke briefly with his wife and his brother. I also brought him the walkman and cassettes.

I heard another important piece of good news today: Dov is feeling much better.

A strange incident occurred yesterday at Hadassah hospital. I went to the bus-stop after my visit. There was some confusion there: a Russian woman could not make herself understood. I tried to help. I thought that she wanted to go to the hospital. I took her heavy bundle and carried it with her to the entrance. There it became clear that she was not looking for the hospital. Finally, one of the guards tried to understand her Russian. It seems that she was looking for a convent of Russian nuns. I tried to explain to her the bus route. A heavy woman in a strange country, exhausted from carrying things to the wrong place. I suggested a taxi, went over to speak with the driver and paid him to take her to the convent in Ein Kerem. I was not sure it was the right one but I guessed that any convent would help her find the one she was looking for. The woman kissed my hand in gratitude. I then left. I later realized I should have stayed and supervised, as the taxi-driver might simply have taken the money and not taken her in the end.

I spoke to the holy teacher's wife about the possibility of her or someone from the family staying over at the hospital for the holiday. She said that she wasn't sure that she could do it because of the children. She suggested her daughters or me. I would prefer not to but will, if called upon.

I didn't feel well after the hospital visit yesterday. I got off the bus at the Old Central Bus Station and walked down Jaffa Street to the *shul* opposite the shuk. I then walked downtown, in the direction of Meah Shearim, but chose my route carefully so that I was always on a quieter street that was not crowded with people. I enjoyed this walk and felt revived by it. As I was coming toward Yirmiyahu Street on Tsephaniah Street, I saw a little *charedi* girl carrying a basket. There was such innocence and brightness in her face. Young children give me hope. What does this have to do with *derech eretz*? I think that part of the problem of focusing on people's problems, illnesses and suffering as I do, is that one can easily forget the brightness and hope that is represented by the sweet innocence of youth. An essential part of *derech eretz* is appreciating the goodness in God's world.

Wednesday, June 7
4 *Sivan*

Sacrificing one's own pleasure to perform a good deed is a fundamental principle of *derech eretz*. Yesterday I used time that I had allocated for work to go to the ceremony in memory of the late Dr. Veschler and visit the holy teacher. Today I will give up my planned pre-Shavuot bookstore searches to go and visit the holy teacher again.

Yesterday, I was sitting in Rabbi Isaacs' *shiur*, which was very crowded, when I saw an old regular, Rav Aryeh, enter. I gave up my seat for him and went to sit at the back table. Later, Rav Mordechai, my friend the *gabbai*, complimented me for doing so. I wanted to tell him that I had wanted to do it and that the act of helping someone meant much more to me than having the seat.

I had always thought of one of the *gabbaim* as being the weakest person possible. I had judged him unfavorably based on my own preconceptions. This is a fundamental error in *derech eretz*. Yesterday I heard him relate some of his stories about the War of Independence. Without intending to, he revealed how he had risked his life to help create the Jewish state. This degree of risk, sacrifice and dedication is something beyond my own personal experience, something I will never know.

Yesterday, after Rabbi Isaacs' *shiur*, I approached Shlomo A., who had given me his war memoirs to read a few days earlier. I thanked him and spoke with him about it. Part of his story included his four years in hiding from the Nazis during the war in Holland. He is yet another person who has endured tests in life of the kind I hope to never know. I know so many small, unsung heroes in Israel – modest people who have gone through great trials and sufferings, yet have nonetheless contributed to the building of the Jewish people and State. Only those close to them know their names and even those people probably do not know their full stories.

Despite all the medical advances that we have witnessed in this age, so much sickness has riddled this generation of quiet heroes.

Tuesday, June 8
5 Sivan, Erev Shavuot

Yesterday I went to visit the holy teacher, only unlike the day before, I came at the wrong time. His wife had just finished her break and was with a friend who had been visiting, so she did not need me to cover for her. An important element of *derech eretz* in visiting the sick is to show consideration for those doing the caretaking. Sensing that I was disturbing, I decided to make my visit brief, but the holy teacher was awake and motioned for me to move over to his side. I was just happy and relieved to see him look so well and strong that he was even able to give me some Torah teachings. As he was telling me a *dvar Torah* on the differences between Ruth and Orpah (a lesson that he had heard from a friend of his in America), a couple came in with their baby. A minute later, two more friends came in with a *megillah* that they had had especially written for him for Shavuot. A moment later, one of the medical staff came in and requested that all the visitors leave. The holy teacher asked for a minute more to complete his *dvar Torah* and when he finished, I said good-bye and left. My presence was not needed and, in fact, was a hindrance. The holy teacher inferred that we would speak on the phone before Shavuot, hinting that another visit would not be necessary.

My daughter will be at her army base for Shavuot. My son will be celebrating the holiday in Dharamasala with Chabad.

I think of my effect in influencing people to greater *derech eretz* through my everyday actions and my writing. I feel as though I have very little effect, but as I do not really know what the effects are that I am having upon people, it is futile for me to be so negative. One of my great teachers, Rabbi Chaim Pearl, may his soul rest in peace, taught me that each lesson is like a drop of water which is absorbed over time, without apparent influence, but may help something real and important to grow one day. Look at how Hadassah Hospital has recently banned smoking. I wonder if the letter I wrote some months ago, which appeared in a local Jerusalem paper, condemning the hospital management for tolerating smoking had some influence. I also know that there are many people whose lives I may not have saved, but who I helped in making their lives slightly more pleasurable, even if only for a short moment. I have lent a sympathetic ear to many; I have also given *tzedakah* that served as some assistance to those in need.

I have no yardstick by which I can judge Israel as a society in comparison to where it was a year ago. At a time when those at the center of political life seem more and more concerned with their own narrow party interests rather than the general good of society, it appears that there has been a decline in political *derech eretz*. The electoral reform that enabled the split ballot and led to an increase in the power of small factions has weakened general *derech eretz* in political life. Having said that, there seems to be a greater degree of accountability, which will make future politicians more wary of certain kinds of questionable practices. There also seems to be an increased awareness of the importance of preserving the environment. Where there is polluted air and water, mankind is showing disrespect for the natural world, for God's world.

Derech eretz involves a willingness to recognize past errors and make a *tikkun*, a fundamental correction. In religious terms, this process might be thought of as *teshuvah*, an effort to restore and return to some kind of more ideal world of relationships, in which *Am Yisrael* is closer to doing the will of God. I understand that for staunch secular Israelis, such a definition is threatening and exclusive. This brings to mind another important and painful subject regarding Israeli society, the poor relations between religious and non-religious Jews.

It seems to me that I am about to conclude when I have come to no definitive conclusions. The tests of my own life have not been clearly resolved and go on as they have before and I do not know what the effects are, and what will be the effects, of my words and actions. I pray to God that I have done some good and will be given the strength to continue on this path.

Sunday, June 11
8 Sivan

I seem unable to finish writing. On Shavuot, I went to the second late *minyan* of the old-timers. Dov returned for the first time since his fall. He is shaky, but thank God, he was there. Israel R. was also there, as was Menahem. They are still plodding on – these three people who I have regularly visited in the past year. Three old friends. I visited Anita. She had been in the hospital during the week when her blood pressure rose alarmingly high. She was subdued.

On Shabbat, I walked back from the davvaning I enjoy in Ramat Eshkol. I saw Israel R. sitting on the bench not far from my house. He told me that he had been waiting for me. I sat and listened to his painful story again. He lamented over his poor Hebrew. This is the *derech eretz* of devoting time and attention to a person who most needs it.

I began this journal by relating a meeting with Israel R., and perhaps it would be fitting for me to conclude the same way. One year later, he is in more pain and his fundamental situation is unchanged. Perhaps I have become slightly more patient over the year. I sit with him a little longer than I used to. But, of course, I do not stay long enough for his liking.

So the struggle goes on, doing a little more here and a little more there. And rarely, if ever, achieving perfection or full satisfaction in truly helping others. I help a little. But not enough.

Derech Eretz in Israel: A Few Thoughts on Improving the Situation

There remains much to be done to improve the general level of public display of *derech eretz* in Israel. Israel is a nation that has been, and still is being, formed from a diverse mixture of people from many different countries with varying mentalities and customs. Rudeness often results from simple misunderstandings, for what is polite in one world can be rude in another. Those from Arab countries, for example, value being physically close to the person they speak to, however those from the West perceive this proximity to be an offensive intrusion into their personal space. While Anglo-Saxon immigrants consider environmental protection to be a major value, those from much poorer regions of the world would place greater emphasis on increasing their total material wealth despite the environmental implications.

Unfortunately, one clear conclusion that can be drawn from my encounters with representatives of various communities across the public forum is that a deep ignorance of the values of other communities exists. Various cultures tend to be very kind and generous within their own immediate circles, without showing any real thought or consideration for others at the periphery or for *Klal Yisrael* as a whole.

This is, of course, most apparent in one of the great divides in Israel, the fragmentation between the secular and the religious. Each camp has its own stereotypes and misconceptions of the other, its own form of intolerance, and each feels threatened by what it sees as the intrusive behavior of the other, the imposition of a foreign outlook on its own way of life.

Thus, it may be argued that true *derech eretz* lies in a greater and more pervasive tolerance and respect for one another. This, no doubt, has to be an important guiding principle in most areas and situations. However, *derech eretz* within a Jewish state – which seeks to continue as a Jewish state – has to have within it a certain capacity for resistance and self-defense. In my opinion, one of the greatest desecrations in Israel, which is a clear violation of *derech eretz*, is the non-conscription of a large proportion of the population, who do not contribute to the defense of the country as a result. After centuries of persecution, the Jewish people finally have their own sovereign power – a requisite willingness to contribute to the struggle against one's enemies is therefore required. There can be no true *derech eretz* in Israel without this dimension of personal contribution, or at least organized social voluntary work intended to assist the welfare and safety of the country, which inevitably involves personal risk and sacrifice.

An even greater violation of *derech eretz* is the attack against, and undermining of, those government institutions and leaders responsible for our safety and the safety of our families. In Israel, this kind of abysmal ingratitude is often displayed by a good share of its intellectual and cultural elite. People who are endowed with great talent and opportunity exploit their gifts and privileges to the peril of those members of society who facilitate their continued well-being. Surely such ingratitude stands out starkly as one of the worst forms of violations of *derech eretz* in Israel. My hope is that a new intellectual power that will be more steeped in Jewish values will prevail here.

The difficulty of implementing this new value system is apparent when one considers the many periods of violence and war that Israel has endured throughout its existence, and from which it continues to suffer. Surely the continued acts of aggression and violence, the terrorism that has been directed against the Jewish people in Israel, have doubly threatened to endanger the Jewish state. They have not only endangered us physically, but have also caused damage to our moral and spiritual fiber. One is tempted to retaliate, without restraint, against an enemy that uses all and any means to bring about our destruction. The Israeli army, and Israeli society in general, have displayed a remarkable amount of restraint and ethical persistence. Perhaps more than any other army in the world, the Israeli army, in contradiction to the libels its enemies have fomented against it, has demonstrated exceptional consideration for the citizens of the peoples attacking it. The challenge of retaining one's humanity in the face of attack, in the midst of a fight for survival, is one that Israel has constantly faced throughout its history, and will most likely continue to face in the years ahead.

True *derech eretz* involves acting with respect towards others and entails having a great degree of modesty, of walking humbly with God. The opposite of this ideal is a know-it-all arrogance. It has been noted that there are people who, when asked for directions on a street in Israel, would rather give questionable or even wrong directions than admit that they do not know the right way. Frequent criticism leveled against Israeli leaders is that they never admit it when they are wrong. They do not concede when they have erred, nor do they ask for forgiveness. There are leaders who have maintained their careers for many decades, yet have made so many grave errors that any other democracy would have long forced them to retire. However they simply ignore whatever evidence stands against them and continue on in the same way. Stiff-necked stubbornness and arrogance is, of course, nothing new to the people of Israel.

Likewise, conceitedness and impatience are displayed in many other areas of life. One conspicuous example, which has catastrophic consequences, is the behavior of Israeli drivers on the road. The accident rate in Israel is relatively high and appears to be a direct consequence of a lack of consideration for others. It derives from a selfish desire to arrive at one's destination, without caring about the consequences to others on the road.

The same can be said for many other forms of public amenities where employees show carelessness and indifference, with no real thought for the effects on those concerned. This is especially true for those who are employees of state-owned enterprises and have received tenure in their work. They demonstrate a disturbing complacency and do not give a passing thought to the welfare of the public.

The *tikkun* towards greater *derech eretz* involves a prior step of acknowledging the wrongfulness of carelessness and indifference towards others and requires acts of consciousness and recognition. It requires a re-education of society towards a greater degree of attentiveness in work and caring in service. It means teaching the ideal of doing something not simply with the aim of getting it over and done with, but doing it in the best way possible.

This is an especially crucial lesson for today's youth when they are often educated in the values of a self-indulgent consumer society. Here it is appropriate to talk about the influence of Western culture on contemporary youth in encouraging violence and instant gratification. It is also possible to establish a correlation between social disorder and violence and youthful rebelliousness and aggression. It is possible to think of Israel as being just another satellite state of America, an imitator of its Hollywood culture and values.

One recurrent scene comes to mind, of loud and rude youths shouting insults at older passengers on a bus. The question is raised as to what kind of example are these children being given in their homes and what kind of education are they receiving in their schools? Additionally, surveys indicate that a significant number of Israeli youths are ignorant of traditional Jewish learning.

Derech eretz in this sense is not something that comes natural, but rather is something that must be taught. Identifying this need, a number of teachers in Israel, including Rabbi Chaim Eisen and Rabbi Nathan Lopes Cardozo, believe it necessary to devise a new kind of curriculum, in this case in religious schools, in order to transmit basic Jewish values.

One implication of all this is that *derech eretz* means more than simply showing consideration towards other individuals. True *derech eretz* involves being able to think broadly – absorbing the whole picture – not only about what is beneficial for oneself, one's family and friends, but what is most helpful for society as a whole. It involves consideration, not only of how our actions may affect others in face-to-face encounters, but also of the broader implications of our actions. True *derech eretz* means acting with great consideration for one's society, one's people as a whole, and for mankind. When one thinks and acts with this in mind, one should have a heightened awareness of one's own smallness and humility, but must also realize that this does not free one of the obligation to do what he can for the greater good of all.

As mentioned, this effort towards *tikkun olam*, towards making Israel a better society in the area of *derech eretz*, must be based on a re-education of society. It must be based on traditional Jewish values, combined with a special awareness of the challenges brought by our modern technological society. The principles of loving our neighbor as we do ourselves, walking humbly with God, emulating His traits of kindness and compassion, demonstrating *gemilut chassadim* in caring for the widow, the orphan, the poor and those who suffer, are the basis for our renewal and require application into all areas of life.

Can we achieve this? Can we become a better people in the area of *derech eretz*? Can we advance closer to our goal of being a kingdom of priests, a holy nation which serves as a light unto the nations?

The answer must be provided in the coming years by each and every one of us, by showing greater consideration towards others, thus bringing blessing upon ourselves and the entire world. In religious Zionist terms, an essential part of the whole process of *tikkun*, of repairing ourselves and the world, parallels the very process of redemption itself.

In returning to the land of Israel, ingathering the exiles and building a modern state of great strength and competence in many aspects, the Jewish people have made great strides forward in this process. But there is still a great deal to be achieved if we are to bring about that higher quality of society with compassion, where mercy and justice prevail and where all walk humbly with God.

A Year Later: The Changes in the Situations of, and my Relationships with, the Central Characters in this Work

Israel R. I see him much less than I used to. At one time, I thought he might be so ill as to be on the verge of leaving this world. But, in truth, it is difficult to see any real change in him in the year that has passed. Just a few days ago, I stopped and spoke with him. He tipped his hat to me as usual.

There has been one small surprising development in his life. When he sits outside now, a small, very wrinkled Russian woman who looks at least his age sits next to him. She speaks with him in Yiddish. Whether this means that his sense of loneliness has abated, I do not know. But he does seem somehow more glad to be alive.

Ruth F. After spending this summer in Canada with her children, she recently returned to Jerusalem. The overwhelming fact of her life is still the absence of her husband, Mel. She is friendly and warm, but at the same time carries around with her a prevailing sense of loneliness and loss. I see her less than I did before.

The Russian former dentist. He is still at his regular spot at the corner of King George Street. After all the help I tried to give him in securing him employment, the former dentist remains where he is. He did not take advantage of the opportunities provided to him to better his life. He looks more troubled now than he did a few years ago.

I debate in my mind whether to simply go over one time and give him the same *tzedakah* I used to give him every week. He seems older, more ragged, more tired, and smiles less.

Yigal. For a long time, I regretted my having questioned his honesty by offering him a check and not cash for his rent. Many months went by and I was sure that he had died. Then, on Yom Yerushalayim, a few weeks ago, I walked by the old bench on Strauss Street from which he had begged, and there he was. Only instead of having the yellow jaundiced look of the dying kidney and liver patient he claimed to be, he looked healthy and contented with himself.

I was relieved and happy to see him, but I did not go over to say hello. I do not ever want to be involved in his world of half-truths again.

Dov E. I pray for his *refuah shlemah*. He is very weak and has been unable to leave his house for the past few weeks. He has also become very, very thin. The last time I saw him was a week ago on Shabbat, when I helped take him home from *shul*. He could not stay more than a minute. My sense is that he needs more intense medical help than he has been receiving.

This past year, he has also had a number of family tragedies. A member of a family that one of his children married into was murdered by Palestinian gunmen. Another relative, his wife's brother, who was living in the Jerusalem suburb of Gilo, had his eye shot out by a terrorist sniper. Recently, Dov's mother died at the age of ninety-six.

Menahem and Naomi K. They both had pacemakers put in this year. They are constantly struggling to maintain their health, but they carry on as a couple who consider and help one another.

The Holy Teacher, David Herzberg. Thank God, he has overcome his illness. He still teaches in the Old City a few nights a week. He is still bringing *simchah* into the lives of so many people. We no longer learn privately together as we once did, but I try to attend his *shiurim* once a week.

Anita P. She has made a great recovery from her two strokes. She has decided to let go of her Philippino nurse, who had been taking over her house. I am now no longer able to see her every week, but enjoy visiting her on those Shabbatot that I am in her neighborhood.

What Most Bothers You in the Area of *Derech Eretz*?

During the course of writing this work, I would pose the following question to whoever I would happen to meet: "Which aspects of the '*derech eretz* problem' most disturb you in your daily life in Israel?" I did not record their remarks word for word, but simply paraphrased their comments. A sample of their answers follows:

David Dvor: *Noise really disturbs me. People speak loudly, and they drive loudly. They do not seem to have any awareness that they may be disturbing you by doing so.*

Harvey Goldberg: *On the roads, people seem to be so focused on reaching their destinations that they do not notice what is going on around them. They seem to concentrate solely on what is immediately before them, and do not see the whole field. This means that they run the risk of not being as safe as drivers as they might be.*

Sarah (Zooey) Besserman: *Verbal sexual harassment is something that I think every young woman has to contend with here. It happens all the time.*

Cantor George Wald: *I think it's rudeness that bothers me the most. People do not seem to know how to say the simplest things without somehow being rude*

Frank Mozer: *After over fifty years of living here, I am used to everything except for what goes on on the roads. The cutting in and out, the speeding and the lack of consideration makes driving a very difficult task. It may take many years until a culture of safe driving develops. After all, most of the people in Israel do not come from North America or England where such a culture has long been in place. It will take time, but eventually people here will also learn how to do it right.*

Hanoch Zeitlin: *I pick up the litter around the Beit Knesset each day and the next morning I have to start all over again. People do not seem to have a sense of the importance of the cleanliness of their surroundings.*

Israel Edelson: *People do not know how to form a proper line. There is always disorder, with people pushing in from all sides.*

HaChazan Y. M.: *It is not right to ask the question as if one were looking to find things wrong with Eretz Yisrael. That is the approach of the spies who spoke evil of the land and caused their generation never to enter it. One must first look at the positive sides of Eretz Yisrael. Then one can ask if there are ways of improving the society.*

I believe that in the area of customer service, Israel could learn much from the United States. It is not right to look at customers as if they are only going to make a one-time purchase. It is important to consider how to service them and meet their needs so that they will continue to patronize the particular establishment in question. Answering politely and listening to others' needs are important elements in the kind of service that should be provided in all business matters.

Lewis Rosen: *There is a lot of derech eretz that we do not see, a lot under the surface. Israelis are, for instance, much closer to each other, even within their families, than people are in America. There are, of course, different degrees of caring for those who we have a relationship with. But there is a lot that goes in Israel that demonstrates that people do show a great deal of caring and consideration towards one another. Perhaps this doesn't always appear to be the case.*

There is the story of the person throwing litter on the street and someone saying to him, "Would you do that in your own home?" The answer was, "Of course not, but the street is not my home." I am not justifying this attitude, but I do think that Israelis have a sense of caring when it comes to those who are close to them.

Graphic Designer Yael Aisenthal: *I dislike the way people interrupt your conversations, interfere in your business and give you advice when no one asked them for it.*

Steve of Steve's Backpacks: *The lack of attention to detail in work. The problem is not that people act manipulatively – they are not even that sophisticated. They simply act impulsively and rudely without showing any real thought.*

Zeev Samuels: *People are often especially kind and polite to those within their own small group, but once they must deal with other groups, they can turn cruel and indifferent.*

Margalit: *The lack of discipline, order and respect in schools, and in the educational system in general. Children do what they want without any regard for their teachers.*

Also, the idea that no one can tell us what to do here, that we are in our own land, has led to great damage. For people do not know how to listen and to properly respond to the suggestions of others.

Rifkah Goldberg: *In work situations, people often promise that they will call back and do not. They often suggest that they will send work and do not. They promise freely and simply do not keep their word.*

Also, people expect you to argue and fight for what is rightfully coming to you.

Ruth Barneis (of blessed memory): *People bump into you in the street. They act as if you are not there. They do not apologize. This happens all the time. And when I tell someone that they have bumped into me they often say that they did not notice I was there.*

People are so preoccupied with their own matters and worlds that they do not pay proper attention to anyone else. Lack of derech eretz in this sense means a total inconsideration for the worlds and realities of others.

Nellie Zylber: *There is no sense of kavod or respect for people in positions of authority. An exaggerated sense of equality means the floor sweeper shouts at the president of the company with impunity. This is also reflected in the way that people talk so freely about things that they know nothing about. Everyone believes that they have a right to an opinion and are qualified to pass judgment on all issues.*

Allyn Rothman: *It is the tax system that especially makes people feel that they are "fryers" or "suckers" for simply doing the right thing. The system does not provide the services that taxpayers are rightfully entitled to. The lack of response from the government concerning the needs of the people causes certain individuals to want to disregard the government whenever they can.*

Carol Clapsaddle: *People expect to be taken care of without taking responsibility for themselves. To me this is a lack of derech eretz.*

There is a familiar scene in which children come into a store and cry to get something. The parents say "no" at first and then the children cry louder and louder until the parents give in. This kind of spoiling creates a people who believe that they can get anything they want by complaining.

Moshe Fushman: *I am bothered by the indifference and apathy that people display towards others. The general neglect of others is an important aspect of the lack of derech eretz here.*

Felice Kahn-Ziskin: *There is a great deal of kindness and good deeds in Israeli society which are done out of the public eye. I think that it is especially in emergency situations that people reveal this sort of special kindness towards others. I think that this degree of caring for others is special. Today I had a fall in Meah Shearim and a schoolgirl came over and helped me. I believe it is unfortunate that it takes emergencies and crises to bring out this caring for one another.*

My Personal Development in the Area of *Derech Eretz*

What have I myself learned on a personal level from this one-year experiment in which I have concentrated my efforts on living a life of *derech eretz*?

I believe the first, and in a way the most important, lesson that I have learned is something I already knew and which I experienced time and again in my daily encounters with others: how great the gap is between one's aspirations to help and one's actual ability to do so. I learned how limited I am in my power to help others. If I were to ever need greater evidence of my humble state, then this year supplied it.

This was manifest not only in how little of a change was affected in people to whom I devoted much time and attention, but also in my being foolish enough to let myself be deceived by certain people who I was trying to help. I learned that there is a kind of wisdom in discerning between those who can and cannot be helped; those who one should strive to be involved with and those who one should avoid.

On a more positive note, though, one thing that I understood throughout the experience, and was tested and reaffirmed time and time again, was that by helping others we can truly give meaning to our own lives. I discovered that giving time and attention to those who the world seems to have abandoned can greatly enrich one's own life. I found that in some profound way, "goodness pays" and that the one who helps is often ultimately the one who is most helped. I think of those moments when I visited and listened to elderly friends who suffered from isolation and loneliness in their lives. The time I would spend with them enriched my life time and again. I could also feel, during my visits, that these people were being restored of their sense of dignity and identity through the caring and attention of another.

The pages of this journal are filled with all kinds of decisions I made in my mundane everyday encounters. Often, upon rereading the journal, I identify within myself someone who is overly concerned and particular, and, in effect, conscience-ridden, in my attempts to conduct each trivial matter in the correct way. I am clearly unable to overcome my childhood legacy of exaggeration in striving not to cause hurt and suffering to others.

I thus raise the possibility that in being too focused on acting with *derech eretz*, I lose all proportion and balance. It seems that my concern to act in the proper manner comes at the expense of my good sense and the result of this is that I have become involved in areas where I should not be involved, thus leaving myself to be made a fool of by others. This is especially true in the domain of my giving *tzedakah*.

Yet, I believe that my intense concentration on the minor encounters of everyday life does point a way for the improvement of *derech eretz*. Each of us has many small encounters in the course of a day in which we can choose to be rude, impatient, greedy, or just the opposite. Each one of us has the ability to display a degree of generosity and kindness which will, in turn, inspire others to greater generosity and goodness. It is not a rule set in stone, but I have seen time and again that when we are polite and considerate to others, they too become more polite and considerate to us.

But again, I must distinguish here between small, and perhaps momentary, acts of kindness, and persistent fundamental efforts to help people change their lives for the good. I know that despite all my efforts in the past year, I have not helped people in any significant way. The sick were not healed; the lonely did not find their mates; those who were unemployed and dependent on welfare were not provided with means for earning their own incomes. Yet in the same way that I do not wish to praise myself too excessively, likewise I do not wish to be overly critical of my efforts. The ideal stated in *Pirkei Avot*, to strive to be a human being when no one else dares to do so, is for me a central element of *derech eretz*. There is a connection between our survival and existence in Israel and our steadfastness in courage, which enables us to be distinct in our righteousness, even when we are mocked and condemned for our approach. At times, then, it would seem that our intense efforts in trying to help others are justified, regardless of the outcome.

It thus appears that even with regard to my own feelings of guilt and remorse for my inability to help others, I should learn humility, for the world is filled with idiosyncratic, difficult and even impossible characters who may request help while at the same time do not want or know how to respond to it. I have learned that there is much for which I am simply not responsible, no matter how hard I try. This work thus affirms a central precept of Judaism, of the essential correlation between humility and correct actions, between walking humbly in the world and performing the will of God.

Derech eretz means having true consideration for others, which thus requires a wisdom in self-knowledge, a humility with regard to one's own place and power in the world. It means being free of the arrogance and impatience which causes so much pain to others.

Perhaps it is because I was not a young man when I wrote this work that the journal includes meetings with so many people who have long since passed their physical peak, and is thus marked by a tone of comprehension of fundamental human limitation.

I am aware of how distant I am, and will always be, from my aspirations. Yet I also know that all of us are commanded to follow the injunction of *Pirkei Avot* which tells us that, "It is not for me to finish this work, nor am I free to desist from undertaking it." It is in this spirit that I have written this small work, with the prayer that it will make some contribution to our living in the way that God demands of us.

Works That Can Help One Achieve Greater Levels of *Derech Eretz*

The Book of Jewish Values, Joseph Telushkin (Bell Press, NY: 2000)

Guide to Derech Eretz, Rabbi S. Wagschall (Targum, Jerusalem: 1993)

It's Not as Tough As You Think: How to Smooth Out Life's Bumps, Rabbi Abraham Twerski (Shaar Press, NY: 1999)

Jewish Spiritual Practices, Yitzhak Buxbaum, (Jason Aronson, NJ: 1990)

Judaism on Trial: An Unconventional Discussion about Jews, Judaism and the State of Israel, Rabbi Nathan Lopes Cardozo (Urim Publications, Jerusalem: 2000)

Kavvanah: Directing the Jewish Heart in Prayer, Seth Kaddish (Jason Aronson, N.J: 1997)

Kindness, Zelig Pliskin (Shaar Press, NY: 2000)

Living with Difficult People (Including Yourself), Miriam Adahan (Feldheim, Jerusalem: 1991)

A Tzaddik in Our Time: The Life of Rabbi Aryeh Levin, Simcha Raz (Feldheim, Jerusalem: 1989)

Collective *Derech Eretz* – Two Years Later

This work was, by and large, completed by Shavuot of the year 5760, May 2000. It is now being published about three years later. During these years, much has taken place in Israel, most notably the outbreak of violence that began on Rosh Hashanah 5760 in late September 2000 and which continues to this day.

It seems to me that there have been certain significant changes during this time with regard to *derech eretz* in Israel. It seems to me – and this is an impression I have confirmed through conversations with many others – that people have become more considerate towards each other in the public arena. One clear reason for this is that when there is a threat from the outside, it is natural to bond together internally. When people feel threatened, they are less likely to be arrogant about going it alone and much more likely to seek help in receiving support from others.

There is also an understanding that when, God forbid, family, friends and neighbors are endangered, when people one knows are being killed and injured, it makes little sense to fight over small things. There is an awareness of the pettiness involved in so much rudeness.

Beyond this, I know that there are many in Israel who feel real pain from witnessing the suffering of others, the losses others have endured. They experience anger and sympathy for the victims and are eager to help. Such sympathy translates into greater compassion in ordinary life encounters.

In the last few years, there has been a tremendous amount of dedication, effort, self-sacrifice and courage displayed on the part of Israeli citizens. It is as if the challenge of this violence has led many of us to bring out the best in ourselves. This is not only true in the stories of remarkable rescue attempts which involved soldiers and civilians risking their lives – and sometimes ultimately sacrificing them – to save others. It is also reflected in many quiet unrecorded acts of assistance. It is as if we are, in many ways, a better people than we thought we were, or knew ourselves to be.

This kind of goodness that extends the call of duty, of helping others in a time of great threat and violence, reveals the true strength of Israeli society. One of the great consequences of so many individuals acting in a worthy, and often heroic, manner is that our faith in society as a whole is reaffirmed. Therefore, *derech eretz* strengthens both our society and people.

There is, however, another dimension to all of this. The tension and stress caused by these threats of violence, the painful physical injuries and the losses, have increased the general level of pain and suffering in the society to a large degree. Most importantly, one should consider the survivors of the violence and their immediate relatives. Many people are hurting much more than they did before, and when people hurt they are less inclined to be arrogant and inconsiderate. In this sense, it is possible to speculate that the violence meted against us has, in some way, mellowed us, making us kinder, while at the same time increasing our sense of determination not to surrender to such violence.

Israel is now going through a very harrowing and difficult time. Pressures have increased tremendously. Worries about safety are far greater. Economic pressures are also taking their toll. Perhaps this has helped many people understand once more what is really important in life in that it has hopefully increased our value of and caring for others.

GLOSSARY

Alav Hashalom– may his soul rest in peace
Aliyah– being called up to read the Torah
Amidah– the Eighteen Blessings, the principal prayer of Jewish services
Amud– page
Arbah Minim– the four species of vegetation used in ritual observance during the holiday of *Sukkot*
Avodat Hashem– service of God
Azkarah– memorial service
Bar mitzvah– the celebration when a thirteen-year-old boy reaches the age of taking upon himself the duties of Torah observance
Beit hesped– funeral home
Beit Knesset– Synagogue
Berachot– blessings
Bikkur cholim– the commandment of visiting the sick
Birkhat kohanim– priestly blessing
Bituach leumi– Israeli national insurance institute
Brit Milah– circumcision of an eight-day-old infant
Challah– traditional bread eaten on Shabbat
Chametz– leavened bread, which is forbidden on Passover
Charedi– ultra-Orthodox
Chassidut– a mystical approach to Judaism first developed in the 18th century
Cheder– kindergarten
Chesed– kindness
Chilul Hashem– a descecration of God's name
Chol Hamoed– minor festival days that take place during Sukkot and Passover
Davvan– pray
Emet– truth
Eshet Chayil– a woman of valor
Gabbai– Synagogue beadle
Gemilut chassadim– specific acts of kindness mandated by the tradition, such as visiting the sick, participating in a wedding ceremony or in a funeral.
Hachnasat Orchim– welcoming guests into one's home
Hakafot– traditional Sukkot ceremony
Hakarat hatov– showing gratitude
Halachah– Jewish Law
Hallel– special prayer said on holdays
Hashem yirachem– may God be merciful
Hasid– someone who emphasizes the emotional aspects of religious expression; often a devoted adherent of a particular Jewish sect and rabbi
Havdalah– ceremony to mark the end of Shabbat
Hishtadlut– making as much as an effort as humanly possible
Ilui neshamah– may the soul be elevated
Kaddish– mourning prayer
Kadosh– holy
Kashrut– Jewish dietary laws
Kavvanah– with the right spirit/intention
Kedushah– holiness
Kibbud– refreshments provided for ritual occasions
Kiddush levanah– the blessing on the new moon
Kippah– head covering generally worn by religious Jews
Kohen– priest
Kotel– the Western Wall
Kuppat cholim– Israeli health service center
Lashon harah– speaking slanderously
Lifnim meshurat hadin– going above and beyond what we are commanded to do
Likkutei Moharan– the seminal work of Reb Nachman of Bratslav
Maariv– evening prayer service

Makolet– corner grocery store
Masechet Ta'anit– a tractate of the Talmud containing a section on minor fast days
Matanot l'evyonim– the *mitzvah* of giving gifts to the poor on Purim
Matzah– unleavened bread, eaten on Passover
Mazal tov– expression of congratulation
Mesorati– traditional
Middah– trait
Midrashim– biblical interpretations that go beyond the literal meaning of the text
Minchah– afternoon prayer service
Minyan– quorum of ten men
Misheberach– special prayer for the specific requests
Mishloach manot– the *mitzvah* of sending food packages to others on Purim
Mitzvah– divine commandment
Mussaf– the additional prayer service recited on holidays
Mussar– spiritual advice
Nusach– a style of Jewish prayer
Parashat hashavuah– the weekly Torah portion
Parnasah– livelihood
Refuah Shlemah– have a full recovery
Ribbono Shel Olam– God Almighty
Rova– The Jewish quarter of the Old City of Jerusalem
Schnor– beg
Seder– the traditional ceremony and meal on Passover
Sefer– book
Sefer Torah– Torah scrolls
Seudah shlishit– third meal on Shabbat
Sever panim yafot– greeting someone with a positive countenance
Shacharit– morning prayer service
Shaliach tsibbur– leader of a prayer group
Shanah tovah– have a good year
Shemurah matzah– specially supervised *matzah*
Shidduch– an arranged meeting between prospective marriage partners
Shiur– lecture
Shivah– 7-day period of mourning
Shloshim– 30-day mourning period
Shmoneh esreh– the main prayer of each prayer service
Shoah– Holocaust
Shuk– market
Shul– Synagogue
Siddur– prayerbook
Simchah– happiness; festivities
Siyyum– feast/party celebrating the end of a chapter or section of learning
Tefillin– phylacteries
Teshuvah– to return; repentance process
Tikkun olam– rectification of the world through one's good deeds
Tzaddik– righteous person
Tzedakah– charity
Ulpan– course of study to learn Hebrew
Va'ad habayit– the board in charge of maintenance of an apartment building
Yahrtzeit– yearly memorial
Yashar koach– an expression of commendation made by one congregant to another after performance of a part in the prayer service
Yeshiva–Talmudic college
Yetzer harah– evil inclination
Yishtabach– a prayer of praise in the morning prayer service
Yizkor– the special prayer said for loved ones who have passed away
Yom iyyun– designated day of learning
Zechut– honor; merit
Zemirot– songs sung during the Shabbat meal

ABOUT THE AUTHOR

Shalom Freedman moved to Israel in 1974 in the wake of the Yom Kippur War. He studied Hebrew in the *ulpan* at Beit Ha'Am before serving in the Civil Defense Unit of the Israeli Army over a period of twelve years. He has worked in Israel as a writer, regularly contributing to many Jewish publications. He has also devoted much time to traditional Jewish learning in houses of study in the Holy City of Jerusalem.

Mr. Freedman was born in Troy, New York and received his Ph.D. in English and American Literature from Cornell University. He is the father of two children, Yitzhak and Dina, and is married to the Jerusalem painter and poet, Rifkah Goldberg.

His publishing credits include an autobiographical work, *Seven Years in Israel: A Zionist Storybook*, and a book of poems entitled, *Mourning For My Father*. He co-authored two works of interviews with teachers of Torah, *In the Service of God* and *Learning in Jerusalem*, and a book on the life and thought of Rabbi Irving (Yitz) Greenberg entitled, *Living in the Image of God*. He has also written a work of Jewish thought entitled, *Life as Creation: A Jewish Way of Thinking of the World*.